How to Plan for a Secure Retirement

HOW TO PLAN FOR A
S·E·C·U·R·E
RETIREMENT

BARRY DICKMAN
TRUDY LIEBERMAN
ELIAS ZUCKERMAN

AND THE EDITORS OF
CONSUMER REPORTS

Zuckerman, Elias.
    How to Plan for a Secure Retirement / Elias Zuckerman, Trudy Lieberman,
Barry Dickman, and the editors of Consumer Reports.
Includes index.
ISBN: 0-89043-889-7
1. Retirement—United States—Planning. 2. Retirement income—United States—
Planning. I. Lieberman, Trudy. II. Consumer Reports. III. Title.

Certain portions of the tax information contained in this book have been drawn from
    Consumer Reports Books Guide to Income Tax Preparation by Warren H. Esanu,
        Barry Dickman, Elias H. Zuckerman, Michael N. Pollet, and the Editors of
Consumer Reports Books, who with the law firm of Esanu, Katsky, Korins & Siger,
            Inc., have given their permission to use this material.

Third printing, December 1999
Manufactured in the United States of America
This book is printed on recycled paper ♻
Design by Susi Oberhelman

Published by Consumers Union of United States, Inc., Yonkers, New York 10703.

How to Plan for a Secure Retirement is published by CONSUMER REPORTS, the monthly
magazine best known for test reports, product Ratings, and buying guidance. We are
also a comprehensive source of unbiased advice about services, personal finance, health
and nutrition, and other consumer concerns. Since 1936, our mission has been to test
products, inform the public, and protect consumers. Our income is derived solely from
the sale of CONSUMER REPORTS magazine and our other publications and services, and
from nonrestrictive, noncommercial contributions, grants, and fees. We buy all the
products we test, just as you do. We accept no ads from companies, nor do we let any
company use our reports or Ratings for commercial purposes.

To my parents, Belle and Abe Lieberman, with love
—Trudy Lieberman

To my wife, Caren, without whose support I could not have undertaken this project.
—Elias Zuckerman

C·O·N·T·E·N·T·S

ACKNOWLEDGMENTS

Thanks to Beth Peppe for her tremendous support and wise counsel on so many matters big and little; to Marge Frohne of CONSUMER REPORTS for updating and checking some of the tables for this book and her moral support during the book's revision; to Bonnie Burns of the California Health Insurance Counseling and Advocacy Program for reading the chapters on Medicare and all her help through the years in understanding the complexities of Medicare; to Peggy Sparr and her colleagues at the Health Care Financing Administration for their assistance in making sense of the new Medicare + Choice options; to Katie Sloan of the American Association of Retired Persons for helping to update the housing chapters; to Trish Nemore of the National Senior Citizens Law Center for her tutelage in the fine points of the Medicaid program; and to Deborah Cloud of the American Association of Homes and Services for the Aging for her suggestions in making the chapter on continuing-care retirement communities and assisted living more current.

—Trudy Lieberman

Special thanks to my colleagues at Esanu Katsky Korins & Siger, LLP, including Louise E. Lipman, who provided invaluable assistance in the revision of the chapters on estate planning as well as the revision of other chapters discussing topics of elder care law. Also, thanks to Bonnie Schwenke Carmicino and Jennifer Amengual, who reviewed materials on Social Security; Barbara Josefowicz of the accounting firm of Grant Thornton, LLP, who assisted with the revision of the pension chapter; and Ken Scholen of the AARP Foundation Home Equity Information Center, who reviewed the chapter on home equity conversion plans.

I am also most appreciative of the painstaking effort of our diligent word-processing crew, Christine Becknel, Christine Corr, and Mary Moylan, in keeping up with the seemingly endless changes in the manuscript.

I also wish to thank our editors, Andrea Scott and Linda Coyner, and all our friends at CONSUMER REPORTS, for their helpful guidance.

Finally, I would like to express my gratitude to my wife Caren, who waited patiently while I tried to shed light on some of the tax aspects of retirement.

—Elias Zuckerman

INTRODUCTION

TO THE

REVISED EDITION

RETIREMENT: NEW OPTIONS, SAME LIFE

ASK FIVE PEOPLE WHAT'S THE FIRST THING that comes to mind when you say "retirement," and you'll be surprised at the variety of answers you get.

Some will conjure up images of rest, relaxation, and a home in Arizona. Freedom to travel. New frontiers to explore. More time to spend with the grandchildren and family. Others will see a new career, a chance at long last to finally do the work they really want to do—whether it's opening a bed-and-breakfast, consulting, or making "a-better-world" commitments to their community.

"Retirement" can also evoke darker visions: A struggle to make ends meet and fear that resources will run out too soon. Boredom from having *too much* free time. Loneliness. Not enough money to cope with failing health.

Your retirement can be any or all of these things. The choice is yours—more than you may realize—and this book is designed to help you sort out those choices and better manage some of the legal and financial aspects and decision-making processes of retirement. But it's important to recognize that as much as your life will be significantly different in retirement, it will also be quite surprisingly the same. Most important, your financial life as you've known it will not suddenly end when you reach retirement age. Yes, you'll have to learn a number of new and sometimes complex financial rules as you settle into your senior years—and that is the subject of this book. But most of the other facts of financial life are the same on *that* side of retirement age as they are on *this* side.

ARE YOU READY FOR THE *NEW* REALITIES OF RETIREMENT?

Not too many years ago, retirement was viewed as the well-deserved reward for a lifetime of hard work—time to relax and retreat to a life with no bosses, no commuting hassles, no pressures. Consequently, a lot of the advice about retirement planning revolves around the conventional wisdom of winding down, hoarding for life's long winter, and getting one's affairs in order. But a funny thing happened on the way to the reading of the will. Sometime during the last two decades, while Baby Boomers were rewriting the political, professional, cultural, and sexual rules, their parents were changing a few rules themselves.

• Seniors today enjoy far greater income and affluence than ever before. This affluence, of course, has not gone unnoticed by banks, stockbrokers, retailers, manufacturers, the travel industry, and others intent on tapping the huge amount of dollars held by the over-65 market. The omnipresent senior discount is the most obvious marketing device designed to attract middle-income and well-to-do seniors.

• The ever-upward postwar U.S. economy converted home ownership from a dream into a significantly appreciating reality. As a result, previously little-used financial tools, such as the reverse mortgage, have become potent symbols of a new way of thinking about retirement. With a regular mortgage, you borrow a large lump sum and repay it in small installments of principal and interest over time. A reverse mortgage is, well, just the reverse: A senior draws down the equity in his or her home in small monthly installments, ultimately selling the property to the holder of the reverse mortgage and moving to a smaller, more manageable home or dying. This financing innovation represents a significant shift in thinking about retirement, because it recognizes that your credit life does not end with your income-producing work life. Reverse mortgages have some important drawbacks, to be sure, but they allow seniors to tap the assets they've built up without a one-transaction sale and without a major change in the manner or quality of their living. (Reverse mortgages are discussed in detail in Chapter 15.)

• Retirees are living longer, and often are healthier, thanks to advances in medicine. While the life expectancy at birth is about 75 for men and 79 for women, people who have already made it to 65 have a good chance of living another 20 years. That longevity is changing the conventional advice given to seniors, who have been typically advised to shift assets out of stocks into less risky investments that provide more reliable returns.

To get that extra security, you'll have to trade away the juicy returns of equities—which historically average about 10 to 12 percent per year over the long term—for the paltry returns you can get from securities like Treasury bills, corporate bonds, and bank certificates of deposit, which have historically averaged just 3 to 5 percent per year. To get that 10 to 12 percent annual return from the stock market, you have to invest long-term—buying and holding for at least 5 to 10 years. Conventional thinking held that a 65-year-old had no time for a long-term investment strategy. But a 65-year-old in good health has plenty of time for a strategy that includes keeping a portion of his or her assets in the stock market—if one's tolerance for risk allows.

How you decide to apportion your investments must be based on your tolerance for investment risk, your personal health, and your family longevity and risk factors. Ironically, many Americans are ill-equipped to confidently make that decision. They often have little or no investment-management experience, because company pension-fund managers have handled their investments; limited 401(k) plan investment menus have kept them on a short leash; and prepro-grammed investing concepts, such as bank Individual Retirement Accounts, have channeled their money without the need for much decision making.

So by the time many Americans reach their 50s, they have a sub-stantial amount of money spread out over a variety of investment vehi-cles and may not be sure exactly what to do with it to maximize returns and preserve the assets. Inheritances, early-retirement buyouts, and life-insurance proceeds only add to the complexity.

That's a high-class problem to have, to be sure. Here's a quick brush-up course on how to best deal with it.

THE IMPORTANCE OF GOOD
MONEY MANAGEMENT

You can't know where to go with your finances and investments unless you know where you stand. To determine this, you don't need a financial planner, who will charge you several hundred dollars in fees or commisions earned from selling you investment products. Instead, use the standard financial-planning tools that anyone can use.

These tools bring order to the chaos of your paychecks, bills, assets, debts, financial-account statements, and what you plan to accomplish—your goals. They can be mastered with paper, pencil, and a calculator. (The worksheets at the back of this book can help.) Or, for less than a hundred dollars, personal-finance computer software, such as Quicken or Microsoft Money, can simplify this process by walking you through easy-to-understand worksheets, investment-return calculations, and income-and-expense projections. Alternatively, many mutual-fund companies will give you retirement-planning software for free, in hopes that you will bring your investable assets to them.

The most important thing to remember about financial planning is to keep it simple. Too much record keeping, too many details, too much complexity will quickly derail your plans because you'll hate doing all that work. Taken together, these money tools give you an up-to-the-minute snapshot of your financial position:

Cash-flow statement. The first step in financial planning, a cash-flow statement will show you how your revenue is spent throughout the month. By learning where the bulk of your money goes, you identify your good and bad spending habits.

There's nothing complex about a cash-flow statement. Get a sheet of paper, write "Income" at the top, and jot down your monthly household pretax income. Get this information from your pay stubs (or from Social Security, pension, and other benefit receipts after retirement) and other income receipts or checks, and total up all the income.

Under that, write "Expenses," and jot down all of those for the month—mortgage or rent, income and any payroll taxes, food, gasoline, utilities, credit-card payments, and so forth. Find that information in your checkbook register, pay stub, bill pile, and pocket expense diary.

A cash-flow analysis is useful in ferreting out wasteful spending habits, particularly small out-of-pocket expenses that add up to a lot over time. Here is where you'll discover you spend $35 a week on $3 cups of cappuccino, a persuasive statistic that could get you to switch back to the 80-cent cups of regular Joe.

While you're focused on creating a cash-flow statement, you'll already have gotten started on more advanced financial planning, because the cash-flow statement forms the basis of your budget.

The budget. You may think you don't have a budget because you don't keep track of every expenditure on neatly lined pages in a set of ledger books. But everybody lives on a budget, whether they know it or not. A budget is simply the maximum income you have and how you spend it over a given period of time. If you're a truck driver earning $30,000 a year, you have a $30,000 budget; if you're a cardiologist earning $300,000 a year, you have a $300,000 budget. You can stretch the budget with smart shopping techniques, you can temporarily— and artificially—increase the budget with debt, and you can expand the budget truly by getting a higher-paying job. One way or another, your budget is the ceiling of your expenditures.

What you may lack is a formal budget *system*. A budget system need not be very complex. Some people keep track of their budget on paper. Today, budgeting software allows you to keep track of your money electronically on your home computer and adds a little high-tech excitement to the otherwise dull chore. There is no one right system. Whatever method you're comfortable with and which does the job, that's the one you should use.

A budget is used to order your priorities. By mapping out your expenditures and income, you can more carefully and more reasonably separate "needs" from "wants." That helps you fund your needs first, followed by your most important wants.

To get into the budgeting habit, write down your short- and long-term goals at the top of every budget period. That way, you'll have something to shoot for. If you write down these goals here, your budget will do double duty as a financial plan. For anyone earning income, the goal should be to determine how much of your monthly income is available for saving and investing and how to free up more of it for that objective. The budget can help you keep track of your progress. Don't just invest what's left over after expenses. Earmark a regular portion of your income for saving and try to have that money deducted automatically from your paycheck or checking account and deposited into a separate investment account.

A budget is also used to control spending and squeeze more value out of the same amount of money. Whether they make $20,000 a year or $120,000, too many people spend most or all of their income, and when they get a pay raise, they increase their lifestyle and spending to match the new, higher income. A budget can help you allocate the increase to investments instead. Later, you can always review carefully whether you want to reallocate part of that money from investment to other expenditures.

Net-worth statement. A net-worth statement is derived by totaling up the value of all the things you own (your assets) and subtracting what you owe (your liabilities). Hopefully, the bottom line is positive.

A net-worth statement tells where you stand financially right now so that you know where it's possible for you to go. By creating a net-worth statement, you'll likely come to appreciate how much you have, and you may be shocked to see how deeply in debt you are.

Be sure to categorize your assets by type. Different assets have different characteristics. Liquid assets, for example, include cash or near-cash equivalents like certificates of deposits (CDs). Real-estate and mutual-fund investments are not so easily available to be compared to cash that can be spent. A large percentage of your assets may be liquid, but you may not need so much ready cash, and your assets would more likely earn a higher return if they're kept in less liquid form.

On one sheet of paper, list all your assets by five types: liquid assets (such as cash on hand, check, and savings balances, money-market funds, income-producing contracts, and the cash value of your life insurance); personal property (furniture, cars, antiques); real estate (your home and other real estate); your investments (mutual funds, 401(k) plan, pension, stocks, and bonds); and other assets, such as that $600 your brother borrowed a year ago and says he's going to repay really soon. On a second page, list your liabilities, divided into four types: your current bills; the outstanding balance on your loans, including mortgages and car loans; taxes due; and other liabilities (for example, leases and legal obligations such as alimony and child support).

Chapter 1 explains how to use a cash-flow statement, budget, and net-worth statement to create a retirement plan. You may also find the worksheets in the back of the book helpful.

A QUICK COURSE IN INVESTING

Once you've established your financial bearings, you can turn your attention to the business of investing. Investing has nothing to do with what everybody else—your brother-in-law or some cable-TV money guru—is doing. It's about just two goals involving you: (1) preserving your assets, and (2) squeezing as much growth as possible out of those assets, given your tolerance for the risks associated with every investment. Your challenge is to balance those two competing objectives. The more you stubbornly hew to the preservation side of the scale with super-secure investment vehicles, the lower your growth rate. Likewise, if you go with high-risk, high-return investments, you could end up losing most or all of your nest egg. Happily, there are ways to accommodate both goals.

Investment vehicles line up on a spectrum running from extremely safe to very high risk. At the safe and secure end are such things as:

• U.S. Treasury securities (bills, notes, and bonds, in order of increasing term), which are backed by the full faith and credit of the U.S. Treasury.

• Bank certificates of deposit and savings accounts, which are protected up to certain limits by federal deposit insurance.

• A-rated government and corporate bonds and insurance company fixed- and variable-rate annuities backed by the creditworthiness and financial strength of the issuers.

• Money-market mutual funds that invest in T-bills, bank repurchase agreements, and other short-term debt instruments called commercial paper, issued by corporations.

In return for safety, return is on the low side—anywhere from 2 to 9 percent, depending on economic conditions.

At the other end of the spectrum are such things as:

• Commodities futures—contracts for the purchase of large quantities of raw materials like lumber, grains, metals, and oil—whose prices are volatile and unpredictable.

• So-called penny stocks—the shares of tiny, little-known start-up companies in everything from oil and minerals to windmills and ostrich farms—which are big on hope and short on capital, management expertise, and a proven track record you can reasonably assess.

• Real-estate such as condominium time-shares, and undeveloped land located in remote locations that promise to become the next Orlando, Florida.

• Real-estate investment trusts (REITs).

• Precious metals, whose prices can be volatile.

• Junk bonds, issued by companies with questionable credit-worthiness.

In the broad middle of the risk/reward spectrum are stocks—percentage ownership shares of companies whose fortunes ride up or down based on a wide variety of factors, including the state of the economy, the competitive dynamics of a fast-changing marketplace, and the quality of their management.

The first step in investing is determining how much risk you can afford to take by weighing the following factors:

Your health. Based on your family medical history and your own current health and fitness, are you likely to have a relatively trouble-free old age with few medical complications to slow you down? Does longevity in your bloodline give you a good chance of sitting down to a birthday cake with 80 or more candles to blow out—like your parents and their parents before them? If so, you can probably shoulder more risk than someone whose health is not so robust. (Indeed, adopting a healthy lifestyle may be the most important retirement-planning step you can take—right now.)

Your current finances. The better your financial condition, the more risk you can take. If you have already built up assets in your home, 401(k) plan, pension, or other investments, you have more choices about what to do with your money. You cannot afford to commit to stock-market investments money you'll need to meet living expenses over the next three years. For stock investments to realize their potential, you have to be able to ride out the market's short-term fluctuation.

Your income-earning capacity. Your ability to generate income is the foundation of your financial life before age 65, and it may well remain so after age 65. Chances are good you'll work in retirement—whether it's part-time, as a self-employed entrepreneur, or even full-time—thanks to increased longevity and improved health, which is already separating the elderly into "junior seniors" (who are still fit and vigorous through their 70s) and "senior seniors" (who are 80 and older before showing significant effects of aging). There's another good reason to work in retirement: Every dollar of employment income you bring in to meet living expenses is one less dollar you have to take from assets. When you're in your 50s, you can lay the groundwork for your post-65 work life by developing self-employment income from consulting work or by turning hobbies and other skills into part-time businesses. Take classes. Keep your work skills up to date.

Once you've determined whether you're in physical and financial shape to take an investment risk, you need to understand the four major kinds of investment risk you face:

Market risk. Investments that grow through appreciation are generally tied to the health of the U.S. and international economy. When the economy is expanding and business is booming, for example, ever-upward corporate sales and earnings generally cause stock prices to appreciate. The reverse is true when the economy is in a period of contraction or recession. A rising or falling economy also affects the value of real-estate investments. How other investors perceive the effect of shifting economic conditions on their investments by bidding their value up or down is the market risk you face.

Inflation risk. Fixed-income investments, whose gains come from the payment of interest, are less prone to market risk, providing a cushion against your more volatile equity holdings. But they can suffer from the corrosive effects of inflation. For example, if you're earning 7 percent on Treasury bonds and inflation is running at 4 or 5 percent, your money is achieving real net annual growth of only 2 or 3 percent before taxes. If inflation rises to 10 percent, however, your super-secure investment is losing a net 3 percent per year.

Capital risk. This type of risk comes from the possibility that the individual company whose stocks, bonds, or annuities you own suffers from serious business problems, inept management, or out-and-out fraud. These or any of a wide variety of other problems can result in stagnant growth in the price of the company's shares, an inability to pay the agreed-upon rates on its bonds or annuities, operating losses, or bankruptcy.

Liquidity risk. Sometimes it will be difficult or excessively costly to convert assets like shares of stock, REIT certificates, CDs, or bonds into cash. At times, as was the case with REITs in the 1980s, there may be no buyers willing to pay you the full value of what you've invested, making the investment illiquid. At other times, there may be buyers, but only at a price that forces you to take less out than you put into the investment, as happens when you want to sell off bonds paying 6 percent a year when new bond issues are paying 9 percent.

Risk, of course, is only one half of the investment equation. How much reward do you want or need? If you've developed your budget properly, you know how much you need to live on currently.

To determine what your expenditures will be as you get older, you need to factor in the effects of inflation. How can you possibly know the inflation rate over the next 20 or 30 years? While it's true that the economy can run into periods of high inflation, as it did in the late 1970s, or deflation, as occurred during the Great Depression of the 1930s, historically the inflation rate has averaged about 4 percent per year.

Using a computer spreadsheet, a calculator, or old-fashioned paper and pencil, calculate your future expenses by starting with your present annual expenses and multiplying them by 104 percent for each of the next 30 successive years. Thus, if your expenses are $40,000 this year, next year's expenses will be $40,000 x 1.04, or $41,600; the year after that, your expenses would equal $41,600 x 1.04, or $43,264; and so on.

One benefit of doing this calculation is that it tempers the overoptimism created by long-term investment-return projections. Investment advisers dazzle inexperienced investors by showing how investing a small weekly amount over 20 years can result in a seemingly huge $150,000 when you retire. That looks like a lot until you realize that annual expenses of $40,000 will top $80,000 a year in 20 years, with inflation at 4 percent.

Your assets will grow sufficiently if you get a return significantly higher than the rate of inflation. From 1926 to 1997, fixed-income securities such as T-bills and long-term government bonds have only produced compound annual returns just 0.5 to 2 percentage points above the rate of inflation, according to Ibbotson Associates, a Chicago investment-research firm. After taxes, rates like that will barely keep your assets treading water. On the other hand, a pure investment over the same period in large-cap stocks (stock for companies with a market value of $5 billion or more) produced a compound annual return 7.6 percentage points above inflation, while the returns on small-cap stocks (for companies with a market capitalization of less than $1 billion) were 9.5 points ahead.

Don't avoid fixed-income investments and put everything into stocks. You can invest in a blend of each and get a return somewhere between the two extremes. For example, $1 invested totally in the stock market in 1925 would have grown to $3,284 by 1997, while the same dollar invested in bonds would have grown to only $37. A 50/50 stock/bond mix, however, would have grown to $604, while a 70/30 mix would have increased to $1,355.

The process of determining the mix is called asset allocation. Based on your tolerance for risk and your desire for the highest possible return, you allocate your investment assets to a certain proportion of equities and fixed-income securities. You can also determine the mix of stocks, allocating assets among those that pay high dividends, offer high-growth possibilities, or represent ownership in solid-value blue-chip companies. In this fashion, you can reduce your market risks and boost your returns.

What is the best asset allocation for you? As mentioned earlier, old-school advisers who expect retirees to stop working at age 65 recommend that 20 percent of your assets be allocated to stocks by the time you're retired. Some experts who see the new realities of longevity and working retirement suggest you keep much more in stocks—as much as 80 percent. You have to make your own call, based on your financial and health situation and your tolerance for risk.

For example, when the stock market is rising, it's easy to love stocks, but when the market takes a nosedive everyone second-guesses their investment wisdom. You need to have sufficient faith in the long-term upward trend of the stock market to get through the down periods.

Stocks are less risky than they once were because of *stock mutual funds,* investments that pool the money of many investors to buy shares of dozens to hundreds of companies. The rise of these funds in the 1980s and 1990s greatly reduced the risk of investing in stocks. They offer a number of important advantages:

• **Diversification.** By spreading your investment dollars over the shares of many companies, the mutual fund reduces capital risk. If one stock performs poorly, total returns may be buoyed by the good performance of the other stocks in the funds portfolio.

• **Lower commissions.** If you buy and sell stocks as an individual and can only afford to invest, say, a $100 a month, you'll have to pay relatively high sales commissions on each transaction, even if you use an inexpensive discount broker or online brokerage service. Big investors, such as pension funds, banks, and mutual funds, typically pay lower commissions because they deal in large-volume purchases and sales. Mutual funds pass this saving right on to individual fund investors. These lower costs make mutual funds particularly suited for a popular investing technique called "dollar-cost averaging," which involves investing a fixed amount at regular intervals. By so doing, you make investing a disciplined habit.

• **Professional management.** Few people have the time or inclination to master the world of stock tables, price-earnings ratios, and the like. The professional managers of a stock mutual fund do this job for you and provide a somewhat higher level of protection for investors by keeping in close touch with the markets on a continuous basis, adjusting their portfolios as market conditions change.

Because mutual funds have evolved over the last two decades, they also provide the ability to target your investing on certain types of companies (large, small, and midsized) or investment characteristics (long-term growth potential, solid value, or income from high-dividend stocks). So-called sector funds focus on companies in only one industry (such as oil, technology, pharmaceuticals, or financial services) or on foreign companies worldwide or confined to specific geographic regions (such as Europe, Asia, or Japan). Sectoring, however, tends to undercut the diversification advantage that mutual funds are supposed to provide, as occurred during the Asian financial crisis in the late 1990s.

Yet another type of fund is the *balanced fund*, which invests in both stocks and bonds. You can also invest in *bond funds,* which invest only in corporate and/or government bonds and government-agency securities. Unlike a single bond that pays a fixed rate of interest, bond-fund returns can rise and fall in relation to interest rates and the resulting value of the bonds in their portfolio. In general, the potential gains and losses from a bond fund are smaller than those of a stock fund.

Most stock funds are actively managed, which means investing professionals attempt to select stocks that will provide returns that are better than the average return provided by the stock market as a whole, as expressed by market indexes like the Standard & Poor's 500, Russel 2000, or Wilshire 5000. But there is no evidence that an actively managed fund can consistently beat the market average over the long haul. *Index funds* were created in the mid-1980s on the principle of "If you can't beat the market, copy it." Index-fund managers don't try to pick stocks or shift their holdings in anticipation of where they think the market may be headed. Indeed, by the rules that govern these funds, they are prohibited from even trying. Apart from a small buffer of cash reserves, index-fund managers must invest nearly all the money you send them in a portfolio that exactly mirrors the stock-market index it tracks. Thus, their performance is nearly identical to that of the target market in general, minus a fraction of a percentage point that pays for the small cost of operating the fund.

The mechanics of investing in a mutual fund are relatively simple and involve getting the offering prospectuses and annual reports of the funds you're considering, opening an account with anywhere from a few hundred to a few thousand dollars, and adding to your investments by checks sent via mail or automatic transfers from your checking account.

Mutual-fund families—investment companies that operate a large number of funds with different objectives—usually allow you to apportion and reapportion your invested assets according to your changing goals. CONSUMER REPORTS has long advised against attempting to "time" the stock market by shifting your fund holdings in light of changing short-term conditions. (A better strategy: Buy stocks and hold them for the long term, through the short-term ups and downs that have accompanied the overall upward trend in stock prices over many years and decades.)

Because of their investing options, a fund family may be a good place to simplify your money management and consolidate all your various investments—your IRAs and CDs from four different banks, pension assets managed by a previous employer, the 401(k) plan with your current employer. You could also consolidate your investments with a bank or stock brokerage, but highly efficient and consumer-friendly mutual funds tend to charge less for their services.

The hardest part of investing in mutual funds is picking one or two to put your money into from the more than 8,000 equity and bond funds available. In general, CONSUMER REPORTS has long recommended funds that don't charge sales commissions (so called no-load funds, in industry parlance) or 12b-1 fees (which pay for advertising and other marketing expenses). There is no evidence to suggest that these charges do anything to increase your returns and may actually reduce them. A fund should also operate efficiently and have a low expense ratio—shoot for one less than 1.5 percent of assets.

We recommend you use a large-cap index fund as the core of your equities portfolio and add one or more managed funds if you can bear a slightly higher rate of risk. Unfortunately, there is no proven method of picking future top performers from among today's managed funds. A fund's track record—whether for one, three, or five years—is no guarantee that its future performance will be any better than other funds or the market in general. The dignified name for this theory is "the efficient market hypothesis." In plain language: Any success a mutual-fund manager scores in the stock market is due to (1) overall market movement and (2) luck. Although some funds provide much better than market returns for short periods—one to a few years—mutual-fund returns rarely if ever beat the market over the long term. That's why the U.S. Securities and Exchange Commission, which regulates funds, requires that they disclose the warning that past returns are no guarantee of future performance.

Properly planning for retirement should not provoke fear. By learning what you need to know and facing the new realities of retirement in the coming century, you'll be able to take control of the situation and take appropriate action. The detailed and specific information that follows in this book will give you the additional tools you'll need to give true luster to your golden years.

—Jeff Blyskal
Associate Editor
CONSUMER REPORTS

PART ONE

INCOME

GETTING READY TO
R·E·T·I·R·E

WILL YOU HAVE ENOUGH MONEY?

THE OVERRIDING QUESTION FACING YOU as you prepare to retire is whether you will have enough money to live comfortably. Ideally, you should begin planning for retirement the day you take your first job, and saving for your future should continue throughout your entire working life. But in practice, putting aside money for a far-off retirement is not always possible—taking vacations, paying school tuitions, and balancing credit-card payments often get in the way of building up an adequate retirement fund. Often, families come up short on the eve of retirement; many people must continue working, whether or not they want to, because their living costs are greater than their income.

HOW MUCH YOU NEED Conventional wisdom says that you need less income in retirement than during your working years. How much less depends on your situation and your expectations. The rule of thumb is that you need between 70 and 80 percent of your pretax preretirement monthly income to maintain a comparable standard of living in retirement, but some people need more and some less. Many pension plans are designed so that you receive, when combined with Social Security benefits, a certain percentage of preretirement income, usually 50 to 80 percent.

The amount of retirement income you need also depends on whether your spouse continues to work. If he or she remains in the work force for several more years after you retire, your immediate need for income may be less important. In that case, keep your nest egg invested as long as possible. Housing costs are another consideration. If your home is already paid for, you need less income than if you have a hefty mortgage or pay rent each month.

When you retire, some of your monthly expenditures will go down. For example, you won't be paying Medicare taxes, union dues, or even Social Security taxes (unless you continue to work part-time). You may also spend less for commuting and clothing, and your income taxes will probably decrease. However, other costs will increase.

One of the biggest increases you are likely to face in your retirement expenditures is health-insurance premiums. This is certainly the case if your employer pays for your health coverage and you currently have no significant out-of-pocket medical expenses. If you retire at age 65, you will have to pay for Medicare Part B premiums, which are $526 for 1998 and sure to increase. In addition, a good Medicare-supplement policy costs between $1,000 and $2,000 a year, and good long-term-care coverage adds another $1,500 to $2,000. If your spouse also needs coverage, double those amounts. What all this means is your postretirement health-insurance bill can easily total $6,000 to $8,000 a year unless your spouse continues to work and you can obtain coverage under his or her policy.

Automobile insurance premiums are likely to remain the same, although many companies give discounts to retirees, whom they consider to be better risks than younger drivers. Inquire about these discounts from your current insurer. Expenditures for life insurance should also go down unless you have a specific need to continue your policy. Most older people don't.

You may find yourself spending more money on leisure activities and hobbies. If you spend more time at home, utility bills may increase, too. If you decide to begin a new business, you'll face start-up expenses.

If your housing costs are substantial and you're worried about paying for maintenance and repairs later on, you may want to move to smaller, less expensive, and easier-to-maintain quarters. Check out the benefits of any tax breaks from the sale of your home (see Chapter 16).

ADDING UP YOUR ASSETS AND EXPENSES At least 10 years before you retire, you should have a good idea of what your monthly and yearly expenses are and what you need in the way of income to sustain your current lifestyle. Complete Worksheet 1, "Assessing income and expenses before retirement." By listing your monthly income and monthly expenses, you will get a sense of your cash flow and how it supports your current standard of living. For example, if you are taking money out of savings or using credit-card debt to pay bills each month, then your expenses exceed your income. If you are adding to savings every month, then your income is sufficient to cover your bills. Obviously, in the years prior to retirement, add as much as you can to your savings. If expenses regularly exceed your income, reexamine your spending and try to increase your savings cushion as you approach your retirement years.

Worksheet 2, "Savings, investments and pensions," helps you categorize your savings and tells you at a glance where your money is accumulating. The worksheet also helps you decide whether it's wiser to invest your money in other types of instruments or investments that may net a larger return.

As your retirement date draws closer, complete *Worksheet 3*, "Estimate expenses after retirement," in the back of the book. Unless your spouse is still working or you plan to work part-time, your income will come mainly from Social Security, employer pensions, IRA and Keogh plans, 401(k) plans, profit-sharing plans, and any savings or investments that you can draw on. If you have worked for several employers and have earned a pension from each, contact the benefits administrator of each employer and ask for an estimate of what your pension will be worth both in the form of monthly payments or as a lump-sum payment, if you have that option. (Use total pension income in completing the worksheet. If you opt for a lump-sum payment, add that to the savings and investments from which you can expect to draw income.)

Once you have completed the preretirement and postretirement worksheets, you can fill in *Worksheet 4*, "Scenarios for retirement." (We recommend that you complete this worksheet every few years to find out whether your projected income will match projected expenses.) If your expenses exceed income and other resources, you have to make some changes. For example, you may have to postpone your retirement date, change plans about selling your home and buying a new one, work part-time to supplement your income, or increase your savings.

Note: All items in the worksheets are measured in present dollars.

Items not expected to grow at the rate of inflation are adjusted for the difference between their rate of growth and the assumed 3-percent rate of inflation. Investments are assumed to earn 4 percent more than inflation. If the worksheets show that your projected resources will meet your needs measured in present dollars, then you can expect the growth in your resources to keep up with inflation *if* you follow some of our guidelines in this chapter.

Make several copies of the worksheets so that you can reuse them as your circumstances change.

STRATEGIES FOR MATCHING INCOME AND EXPENSES

Three or four years before retirement—ideally, much earlier—consider your options for getting the most retirement income possible in your situation. Carefully weigh the various annuity payouts versus lump-sum payments, and ways that your money can continue to grow after you leave the work force. Too often, people fail to look beyond the first couple of years of retirement. You should look at least 10 to 20 years into the future and make sure your income will be sufficient to match increasing expenses resulting from inflation in later years.

Let's look at the facts. At an inflation rate of 3 percent a year, prices will double in approximately 23.5 years; at an inflation rate of 5 percent a year, prices will double in approximately 14 years and quadruple in approximately 28 years. For this reason, you should continue to invest a portion of your retirement savings for steady growth. Even if you choose an annuity option that provides a fixed monthly payment, keep some of your cash free and prudently invested so that your money will grow and help cover higher expenses in your later years. But be careful—don't go overboard, especially with stocks. If you decide to invest all your spare cash for growth, you could take a loss if you are forced to sell an investment when the stock market is down. Be sure you are comfortable with this risk before investing.

INVESTING FOR THE FUTURE

No one knows what may happen to change the current financial scene, but your money has the best chance of growing if you put part of it into a diversified portfolio of stocks or stock mutual funds. Over the

72-year period from 1926 to 1997, the average annual return on common stocks was 11 percent, compared to 3.8 percent for U.S. Treasury bills, 5.2 percent for long-term government bonds, and 5.7 percent for long-term corporate bonds. Small-company stocks returned an average of 12.7 percent. In general, stocks of small companies returned more than those of larger companies, although they involved more risk.

If you can't sleep at night worrying about the ups and downs of the stock market, then choose more predictable and conservative investments, such as municipal bonds or bank CDs. But remember, over a long period, these investments probably won't keep pace with inflation. And make investments for the long term, not because you expect the market to rise (or fall) over the next year or so. Market values of stocks always rise and fall over time, so don't panic and sell when the value initially falls.

It's also wiser to choose investment vehicles for their return rather than for tax considerations. Differences in investment results generally outweigh any tax savings. Furthermore, tax laws change, and you don't know what the law will be when you decide to cash in your investments. But if two investments appear equal, then tax considerations might tip the balance.

It's important to keep your acquisition expenses as low as possible, and you can do that by buying no-load, that is, without-a-sales-charge, mutual funds. Select funds that have no loads, no redemption charges, and low expense charges. Unless you are an expert who can spend 40 hours a week studying investments, don't try to decide which individual stocks to buy. Stock mutual funds allow you to invest in a diversified portfolio of many stocks, under the management of investment professionals. Be cautious in dealing with stockbrokers and others who get a commission on the investments they sell. They can provide helpful information, but don't expect them to be completely objective about the investments they recommend or too concerned about possible losses.

OTHER SAVINGS STRATEGIES

Before you head into retirement, begin to repay any outstanding debts. After you retire, you don't want to be struggling to pay off loans that you took out years before, especially home-equity loans. (However, in your later retirement years, you may have to tap the equity in your home to help meet your monthly expenses.)

Also repay any outstanding loans on your life-insurance policies. This is especially important if you are counting on insurance to provide income for a spouse after your death. Policy loans and the nondeductible interest on them decrease the value of the death benefit as well as the amount of cash value you'll receive if you cash in the policy. If you forget about an old life-insurance loan and die suddenly, your spouse or your children will be left with less than you had intended. If you cash in the policy (as most older people should) and haven't paid off the old loan, you'll receive less to invest elsewhere.

CONVERTING SAVINGS TO RETIREMENT INCOME

When you retire, you have to convert your savings into a monthly income stream. None of the options for doing that is perfect. Each strategy has its advantages and disadvantages.

PURCHASE A FIXED ANNUITY FROM A LIFE-INSURANCE COMPANY An annuity provides an income for you and your spouse for as long as you live. In other words, you can't outlive your income. However, your monthly payment is fixed and won't increase over time. If you live for 20 or more years after buying the annuity, your monthly payment is bound to shrink in value. Moreover, after you (and your spouse) die, nothing is left for your heirs. In 1998, a 65-year-old could buy a monthly payment of between $8 and $9 for each $1,000 put into the annuity. Converting $100,000 of savings yields a monthly payment of about $740 (see Chapter 4).

BUY A VARIABLE ANNUITY FROM A LIFE-INSURANCE COMPANY Over several years, the income keeps pace with inflation, but the income fluctuates each month. For most people, living with this kind of uncertainty is difficult—erratic income levels don't always get the bills paid.

USE YOUR SAVINGS OVER YOUR LIFE EXPECTANCY Few people, however, can predict how long they will live. If you outlive your life expectancy, you could run out of money.

LIVE OFF THE INCOME FROM YOUR CURRENT INVESTMENTS If your investments grow with inflation, this strategy may work. But if you have mostly bonds and CDs that produce high income now, they are unlikely to grow much more. On the other hand, if you select only investments for growth, you may have little current income.

This strategy requires a careful mix of your investments.

INVEST FOR LONG-TERM TOTAL GROWTH, AND USE A PORTION OF YOUR INVESTMENTS FOR MONTHLY EXPENSES This is the "4-percent strategy." One pension consultant recommends investing with the expectation that your return will average about 4 percent more than inflation. For example, if inflation is running about 5 percent, try to earn an average of 9 percent; if at 3 percent, try for 7 percent, and so forth.

The adviser also suggests using $\frac{1}{12}$ of 4 percent of your investments each month for current expenses after you retire. Each year, recalculate the market value of your investments. If the value has risen, increase your monthly withdrawal to $\frac{1}{12}$ of the new amount. If the value has not increased or has decreased, continue to use the amount you started with for another year. If your investments earn 4 percent more than inflation, your monthly retirement income will rise 4 percent each year (this probably won't happen every year). Your actual return will vary substantially from year to year, exceeding the expectation of earning 4 percent in some years and becoming negative in other years. For example, the return on stocks was –26 percent in 1974 and +37 percent in 1975. This strategy gives you less money initially, but if you live a long time after retiring, it is your best chance of maintaining an adequate income for the rest of your life.

Example: Your retirement nest egg amounts to $300,000. During the first year of retirement, you withdraw 4 percent—$12,000 annually or $1,000 monthly. If your $300,000 earns 9 percent or $27,000 ($300,000 x .09 = $27,000), at the end of the year, you would have $315,000 ($300,000 + $27,000 - $12,000). At the beginning of the second year, you recalculate the amount of your monthly withdrawal. In this case, $\frac{1}{12}$ of 4 percent of $315,000 is $1,050. This is 5 percent more than you withdrew the first year, enabling you to keep up with a 5-percent increase in the cost of living. In the third year, you do a similar calculation, and so on.

This is a basic example of a technique that you can adapt to your own situation. Your particular investment goal may vary widely (within prudent limits), depending on your need for income, your tolerance for risk, and your available funds. You can tailor your own plan, investing as money is available and selling part of your investments whenever income is insufficient.

Investing in stocks that produce this kind of growth can entail more risk than you are comfortable with—your investments are not perfectly safe from the standpoint of preserving your capital. Other "safer" investments are also risky, though, because they are unlikely to keep pace with inflation.

WHICH INVESTMENTS TO SPEND FIRST

You need to decide early which investments to tap first for living expenses. It's probably best to:

Use investments that are not tax-deferred, if you can afford to do so. Do not, for example, take money out of traditional IRAs and Keogh and 401(k) plans unless you are at least 70½ years old. (At that point, you ordinarily must begin withdrawing the money.) Try to avoid ever taking money out of a Roth IRA. (You are never required to withdraw funds from this type of IRA during your lifetime.)

Finally, use other assets if necessary.

TAKING EARLY RETIREMENT

Your employer may offer what appear to be attractive incentives to encourage you to leave early. At first blush, they may appear attractive, but they almost always require careful consideration.

The incentives usually include a higher pension benefit than is normally available to people your age. For example, your employer may also add three to five years of service when figuring your benefit. However, these additions usually don't increase your pension to the amount you would ordinarily receive if you had worked up to your employer's normal retirement age.

Your employer may also offer a severance payment of $20,000 or $30,000 or a supplemental payment if you're under 62 and too young to qualify for Social Security benefits. In addition, some health insurance may be added to the package, enabling you to stay on your employer's plan for a longer period. If your employer is very generous, you may be able to retain medical coverage until you're eligible for Medicare or for the rest of your life (though such arrangements are rare).

The decision to leave the work force early depends on whether you really want to retire, your other options for employment or leisure activities, your age, your savings cushion, and what kind of retirement package your employer offers.

If your employer asks you to take early retirement, first consider whether you really want to and whether you have a choice. If you don't want to leave, find out if the retirement package is available to a large number of employees or just to employees over a certain age or in a particular division. If it's offered to only a few people, that could mean the company is planning to eliminate your division or transfer employees elsewhere. If you can't accept a transfer or if you fear you will eventually be laid off, you may have little choice. If you gamble and stay, you could lose your job and end up without the incentives. If you have marketable skills and can easily find another job, that, too, will influence your decision.

Your age also determines how seriously you should consider early retirement. If you're in your mid-50s, early retirement could be a financial disaster. You are too young for Social Security benefits, too young for Medicare, too young to withdraw money from IRA, Keogh, and 401(k) accounts without penalty, and you will lose several years of service that contribute to a larger pension from your employer as well as sacrifice a larger benefit from Social Security. All of this means you must have significant savings or a spouse with a secure income to tide you over until you qualify for various benefits. Even if your employer offers an extra year's salary as an inducement to retire, that sum may be paltry when you consider how many years you will have to live on it. Once you've spent that year's pay, what will you live on for the next three, five, 10, or 20 years?

If you have relied on term life insurance from your employer for the bulk of your protection, you could lose it unless your employer agrees to continue the coverage for an indefinite period. This may be important if you are relying on that coverage to support a spouse or other dependent who will have no other income after your death.

Health insurance is a major consideration. You will be able to continue coverage under your employer's plan for only 18 months (unless your employer makes a better offer or provides coverage after retirement). After that, you have to find your own policy or take a conversion option that lets you convert to an individual policy—but usually at a very high price. The first option may be impossible if you have health problems. The second is very costly. Your employer's offer to increase your pension by adding three or five years of service may not outweigh the higher costs for health coverage if you retire early. Having to pay for your own health insurance may well be the deciding factor in whether to take early retirement.

On the other hand, suppose you are 62 or 63 when your employer offers a ticket out of the work force. At this point, you can qualify for Social Security early-retirement benefits, although you shouldn't take them unless it's a necessity (see Chapter 2). You may also be able to remain on your employer's health-insurance plan until you're eligible for Medicare. You will be able to draw on money in IRA, Keogh, and 401(k) plans, and your savings may be large enough to tide you over until you qualify for full Social Security benefits. If your spouse continues to work and your family can live for a few years on one salary, then you might be able to leave your job early. Remember, though, retiring early means that contributions to your 401(k) plan or other company savings plan will stop and you will be losing the benefit of several years of compounded growth.

In any case, if you are offered such a package, consider it very carefully. You may be given only 30 to 90 days to make your decision, but if you need more time, ask for it. This could be one of the most important decisions you ever make, and it will have financial ramifications for the rest of your life. If you don't like some part of your employer's package, try negotiating for a better deal. For example, if your company says you can stay on its health plan for three years and you have five years until you're eligible for Medicare, negotiate to see if they can continue your coverage until then.

Then again, you might decide to take early retirement but defer your retirement compensation until normal retirement age. Use *Worksheet 4,* "Scenarios for retirement," in the back of the book and work through all the scenarios: early retirement with the benefit enhancements; early retirement while deferring your compensation until later; waiting until normal retirement age. If delaying your payout nets you more later and you have enough savings to live on in the meantime, or you can get by on a spouse's income or you have other ideas for earning income, then choose that option. However, that course is more realistic if you are only a few years away from normal retirement.

STAYING ON THE JOB

You may want to continue working after you turn 65. If your employer allows that, by all means do so. Besides job satisfaction, you are enhancing your future financial position.

One big advantage is a larger Social Security benefit—you receive "delayed-retirement credits" if you don't take your Social Security benefits at age 65. In addition, your pension will probably increase. Most people retire from a company with only about 15 years of service. Obviously, staying a few more years increases the pension benefit. If you've been with your employer a long time, however, check to see whether additional years of service no longer count after some point. Some plans limit the number of years of service that count toward your pension. If, for example, you've already worked for 30 years at your company and you want to continue working past age 65, the additional years of service may not increase your benefit.

If you continue to work and receive raises, your higher salary will go into calculating your pension benefit. Many companies use a "final average salary" plan—the higher your final average salary, the higher your benefit.

In addition, in calculating your pension benefits, some companies will give you additional credits if you continue to work past normal retirement age. In certain respects, these credits are analogous to the "delayed-retirement credits" you receive from Social Security if you don't take your benefits at age 65 (see Chapter 2). In both cases, the credits partly compensate you for the benefits you have given up by postponing your retirement.

Delaying retirement also means that contributions to 401(k) and other company savings plans continue to grow, as do investments you may have in IRAs and Keogh accounts. By April 1 following the year you turn 70½, you generally have to begin withdrawing money from these accounts. (But as a result of a change in the tax law made in 1996, if you are not a 5-percent owner of your employer, you may delay distribution of money from a qualified plan—other than a traditional IRA—until April 1 of the year following the year you retire from the employer maintaining the plan.) Once you are required to begin withdrawals, whether at age 70½ or later, your retirement planning needs to focus on the best option for withdrawing your money.

Remaining on your employer's health-insurance plan is another plus. If you don't have to pay for health insurance, you might consider using that money to buy a good long-term-care policy whose benefits increase with inflation (see Chapter 12). If you continue to work, postpone your Social Security benefits, and remain on your employer's health plan, check the rules for enrolling in Medicare. If you do not sign up when you are first eligible for coverage, that is, at age 65, you have to pay a higher premium for Part B coverage (see Chapter 8).

Planning for your spouse's welfare

If your spouse will have no means of support after your death, any preparation for retirement necessarily involves providing for him or her. Make a rough estimate of your spouse's income needs. Will he or she remain in the family home? Will travel expenses (to visit family members) increase? What expenses are likely to decrease? Obviously, food bills and car expenses (if you have more than one car) will decline. (*Worksheet 3*, "Estimate expenses after retirement," on page 304, can help you calculate expenses and income for your spouse.)

For many families, survivors' benefits from Social Security are a spouse's main source of income. Table 4 in Chapter 2 shows you how large a benefit to expect. But for most people, this benefit does not cover expected expenses. You must make up the shortfall from your pension, savings, or life insurance. If your spouse will have no other income, we strongly recommend that you choose a 100-percent joint-and-survivor option (see Chapter 3). Most people, however, shouldn't keep life insurance in retirement. The money spent on premiums or the cash value tied up in a policy usually can be better spent or invested elsewhere, even though life-insurance salespeople try to convince you otherwise (see Chapter 5).

If you have substantial assets, you may also find it advantageous to set up a trust for your spouse (see Chapter 19).

Remarriage

Remarriage can cause some of the thorniest problems in retirement planning. If you remarry, give careful consideration to whom will get your assets when you die. You may want to provide for children from your first marriage, so prenuptial agreements are one way to specify exactly what your new spouse is entitled to. Chapters 18 and 19 provide help in setting up trusts for children from a first marriage. To avoid problems later on, it's best to make these decisions before remarrying.

S·O·C·I·A·L
SECURITY

THE BACKBONE OF RETIREMENT INCOME

RETIREMENT INCOME IS OFTEN COMPARED to a stool with three legs—Social Security is one, pensions from employers the second, and private savings the third. The legs of the stool, however, are not equal. For most people, Social Security provides the bulk of their retirement income.

During the Depression, savings set aside by many of the elderly for retirement were wiped out, and younger people, often without jobs, could not afford to care for aged parents. It was under the stress of such conditions that in 1935 President Franklin D. Roosevelt and Congress created the Social Security system.

Social Security is financed by a payroll tax paid equally by employees and employers. Throughout their working years, current workers pay the tax to support current retirees. Thus, the money is not an annuity invested at interest to pay for each employee's own future benefits. And contrary to what many think, there is no bank account in Baltimore (where the Social Security Administration is located) that has your contributions earmarked for your retirement. Instead, when you reach retirement age, SSA computers determine your benefit by plugging the number of years you have paid payroll taxes and your yearly earnings into complex formulas to determine the amount you receive each month. It then sends payments from the funds the system has on hand.

Over the years, Congress has expanded both the benefits and the categories of workers eligible for them, so the system is now practically universal. Four types of benefits are available: retirement, survivors', disability, and Medicare. (Medicare is discussed in Chapter 8.)

RETIREMENT BENEFITS

To qualify for retirement benefits under the Social Security system, you must be "fully insured," that is, you must have accumulated at least 40 "quarters of coverage" under Social Security. In other words, you must have worked for about 10 years in employment covered by the Social Security program. Social Security now bases covered quarters on each worker's annual earnings. In 1998, one quarter of coverage is credited for every $700 of earnings during the year, but only four quarters of coverage can be earned in any one year. If you were born after 1928, you need 40 quarters to qualify for retirement benefits. Workers born in 1928 need 39 quarters; in 1927, 38 quarters; in 1926, 37 quarters; in 1925, 36 quarters; and so on.

Figuring your benefit is complicated, and you probably won't want to do it yourself (see the following pages for other ways to get the information). However, you should know how the benefit is calculated and understand why you receive the amount you do each month. The benefits you receive are based on a magic number called your *primary insurance amount,* or PIA. Here's how a PIA is figured for most new retirees:

SSA uses a wage-index factor to adjust your earnings for each year until you reach age 60. The adjustment increases your earlier earnings to approximately their current equivalent value. Only earnings up to the "wage base"—the maximum amount of earnings each year on which you must pay Social Security taxes—are counted. (If you earned more than the wage base in any year, those earnings are not counted.) Earnings after you reach age 60 are not indexed; actual earnings are used instead.

Once your earnings are indexed, SSA determines the number of years needed to calculate the average of your indexed earnings. To arrive at the number of years, subtract 5 from the number of quarters of coverage you must have to be "fully insured." If you need 40 quarters of coverage, you use 35 years in your average. Everyone first eligible to retire in 1991 or later uses 35 years in his or her average.

Next, SSA picks your highest earning years for the number of years you need, averages your earnings for those years, and divides by 12 to arrive at your *average indexed monthly earnings,* or AIME.

A benefit formula is then applied to the AIME to arrive at your primary insurance amount, or PIA. For someone first eligible to retire in 1998, the PIA is figured by adding 90 percent of the first $477 of average indexed monthly earnings, 32 percent of the next $2,398, and 15 percent of the AIME that exceeds $2,875. These dollar amounts, known as *bend points,* change each year.

The weighting in the benefit formula gives workers who earned low wages a greater percentage of their preretirement income than high-wage earners. If your earnings have equaled the U.S. average wage and you retire at the normal retirement age (currently 65, but scheduled to increase beginning in 2003), your Social Security check will replace about 42 percent of your pay. If your earnings have always equaled or exceeded the maximum amount of wages on which Social Security taxes are levied, your individual benefit will equal about 25 percent of the current wage base. (In each case, your spouse may be eligible to receive additional benefits.)

The PIA is then adjusted for changes in the cost of living. Changes in the Consumer Price Index (CPI) are applied for each year, beginning in the year a person turns 62. A worker who retires in 1998 at age 65 will have his or her final PIA determined by increasing the amount of the preliminary PIA by 2.6 percent, 2.9 percent, and 2.1 percent. These are the CPI increases for the three preceding years. The result is the final PIA, which becomes the basis for all benefits paid to you and your dependents. Once you begin to receive retirement benefits, they are increased each January by the percentage increase in the CPI through the third quarter of the immediately preceding year.

There are several ways to estimate your benefits. *Table 1* gives you a rough idea if you have been steadily employed and have had average wage increases throughout your career (increases at about the same rate as all workers in the country). *Example:* You have turned 65 and are about to retire. Your current salary is $40,000. Your spouse is also 65 and qualifies for a benefit based on your earnings. According to Social Security rules, your combined monthly benefit currently totals $1,795. But if you haven't earned the same percentage of the U.S. average wage for most of your working years or have been employed only intermittently, these estimates are not very accurate.

You can get a more accurate estimate from the SSA and check the information in your records at the same time. SSA will send you a statement (your "Personal Earnings and Benefit Estimate Statement") of your earnings record and estimates of retirement, disability, and survivors' benefits. The estimate for retirement benefits will be approximate because it depends on an assumption of your future earnings. Estimates for survivors' and disability benefits will be more accurate, since they are calculated as if you died or became disabled on the day you requested the estimate. (Call 800 772-1213 to request your Personal Earnings and Benefit Estimate Statement.)

When you receive your statement, check it for errors. If you find any, contact your local SSA office. The law requires SSA to go back only about three years to correct mistakes. The agency can try to correct

TABLE 1 · ESTIMATED MONTHLY RETIREMENT BENEFITS

▶ *For a worker who retires at full retirement age and had steady lifetime earnings*

		Retired worker's earnings in 1997				
Worker's age in 1998	Worker's family	$20,000	$30,000	$40,000	$50,000	Maximum
45	RETIRED WORKER ONLY	$809	$1,076	$1,265	$1,390	$1,592
	WORKER AND SPOUSE	1,213	1,614	1,897	2,085	2,388
55	RETIRED WORKER ONLY	809	1,076	1,265	1,377	1,525
	WORKER AND SPOUSE	1,213	1,614	1,897	2,065	2,287
65	RETIRED WORKER ONLY	784	1,043	1,197	1,269	1,342
	WORKER AND SPOUSE	1,176	1,564	1,795	1,903	2,013

Maximum assumes earnings equal to or greater than Social Security wage base from age 22 through 1997. For 1997, the wage base was $65,400. In each case, the spouse is assumed to be the same age as the worker. Spouse may qualify for a higher retirement benefit based on his or her own work record.

Source: Social Security Administration

older errors, but it may be unable to do so. To catch errors in time for corrections, request a statement of your earnings every three years or so.

Check to see that you have not paid more than the maximum Social Security tax each year. If you have held more than one job in a particular year and have earned more than the maximum earnings for Social Security taxes, you have paid more. In that case, you're entitled to a credit on your Form 1040 against your federal income tax.

You can also figure out your benefit with a computer program sold by the Social Security Administration. The software calculates your benefits in a number of different situations. If you have an IBM-compatible personal computer, the program could be a handy tool for retirement planning. To obtain the program, write to Sales, National Technical Information Service, 5285 Port Royal Rd., Springfield, VA 22161, or call 703 605-6000. Ask for the Social Security Benefit Estimate Program for personal computers, product number PB97-503478 (for a 3-inch disk). The cost is approximately $50.

NORMAL RETIREMENT BENEFITS The *normal retirement age* is the age when you qualify for a full (unreduced) benefit. This age varies, depending on the year in which you were born. If you were born before 1938, the normal retirement age is 65. It gradually increases after that. *Table 2* shows how the normal retirement age goes up over the next several years.

If you retire at the normal retirement age, your benefit will equal the primary insurance amount discussed previously.

GETTING LESS WHEN YOU RETIRE EARLY You can still receive Social Security benefits if you retire after you turn 62 but before your normal retirement age. The benefit is reduced, however, and the reduction is permanent—that is, your primary insurance amount does not increase when you reach the normal retirement age. This happens because early-retirement benefits are "actuarially" reduced to offset the longer time you will be receiving checks. And you also won't have the advantage of three extra years of earnings (probably high earnings, at that) to go into your average.

How much your benefit is reduced depends on when you retire. The reduction is ⅚ of 1 percent for each month (up to 36 months) that you receive benefits before the normal retirement age, plus another 5⁄12 of 1 percent for any additional month(s) prior to normal retirement age. For example, if your normal retirement age is 65 and you retire at 62, your benefit is 80 percent of your primary insurance amount—a reduction of 20 percent, or ⅓ of 1 percent for each of the 36 months before you're 65. If your PIA is $1,000, your monthly benefit is $800. But if you wait until 64 to retire, you receive 93⅓ percent of your primary insurance amount. On the same PIA of $1,000, your benefit is $933. If your normal retirement age is 67, the benefit payable at 62 is 70 percent of the PIA (a reduction of ⅝ of 1 percent for 36 months and a reduction of ⁵⁄₁₂ of 1 percent for 24 months). On the same PIA of $1,000, your benefit is $700.

From the standpoint of maximizing your income, it pays to wait until your normal retirement age or later to apply for Social Security benefits, if possible, even if you retire earlier. We recommend taking a reduced benefit only if you have other income sources. If you are in poor health, you may have to leave the work force early. Even so, delay taking your benefit as long as possible.

GETTING MORE IF YOU RETIRE LATE If you work beyond the normal retirement age, you will receive a larger benefit when you do leave

TABLE 2 · 'NORMAL' RETIREMENT AGE

▶ *What the Social Security Administration considers retirement age*

Year of birth	Age that qualifies for full Social Security
1937 OR EARLIER	65
1938	65 AND 2 MONTHS
1939	65 AND 4 MONTHS
1940	65 AND 6 MONTHS
1941	65 AND 8 MONTHS
1942	65 AND 10 MONTHS
1943-1954	66
1955	66 AND 2 MONTHS
1956	66 AND 4 MONTHS
1957	66 AND 6 MONTHS
1958	66 AND 8 MONTHS
1959	66 AND 10 MONTHS
1960 AND LATER	67

the work force. Your primary insurance amount is figured the usual way and then increased by a certain percentage for each month you delay retirement. For those born between 1917 and 1924, the increase was ¼ of 1 percent per month, or 3 percent per year for each month payment of benefits was delayed. For those born after 1924, the percentage by which benefits increase gradually rises, reaching ⅔ of 1 percent per month, or 8 percent per year for people born after 1942. If you turned 65 in January 1998, the annual increase factor is 5½ percent. If you wait until 68 to retire, your benefit increases by a total of 16½ percent. *Table 3* shows your benefit if you delay retirement.

As you can see, delaying retirement significantly increases monthly benefits. Besides the percentage increase SSA allows, your earnings after age 65 may go up, increasing your AIME and, therefore, your benefits. Spousal and other family benefits are also increased to reflect the higher average earnings, but they do not include the increase resulting from the delayed-retirement credit. If your spouse outlives

TABLE 3 • ADDITIONAL SOCIAL SECURITY
BENEFITS IF YOU DELAY RETIREMENT

Year of birth	Percentage added to benefit for each year of retirement delayed after normal retirement age
BEFORE 1917	1%
1917-1924	3
1925-1926	3½
1927-1928	4
1929-1930	4¼
1931-1932	5
1933-1934	5½
1935-1936	6
1937-1938	6½
1939-1940	7
1941-1942	7½
1943 AND LATER	8

you, survivors' benefits based on your earnings are increased by any delayed-retirement increment for which you qualify.

On the other hand, the percentage increase in your delayed-retirement benefit is currently too low to compensate fully for the benefits you have forgone by retiring after the normal retirement age. Yes, delayed retirement increases your monthly benefit, but it also reduces the lifetime value of all your benefits. However, once the annual increase percentage rises to 8 percent, this inequity disappears, and the expected lifetime value of your benefits is approximately the same regardless of when you begin to receive payments.

To see what the delayed-retirement credit means in dollars and cents, let's look at your benefits with the assumption that you've always paid maximum Social Security taxes. If you turned 65 and retired in January 1996, your monthly benefit would have been $1,250. But if you had retired in 1993 at age 62, the benefit would have been $901 when you retired and about $975 in 1996. On the other hand, if you worked until January 1998 when you turned 67, your benefit would have been about $1,478 (including interim cost-of-living increases). If you continue to work until age 70, the monthly benefit jumps to $1,742 before future cost-of-living adjustments.

BENEFITS FOR SPOUSES Once you begin to receive monthly retirement checks, your spouse, if he or she is 62 or older, is also eligible for benefits. If your spouse has reached normal retirement age, currently 65, the benefit equals one-half of your PIA unless your spouse receives a benefit based on his or her own earnings. If your PIA is $700, your spouse's benefit is $350. (As we noted, the benefit increases with cost-of-living adjustments each January.) If your spouse is between 62 and his or her normal retirement age when you retire, he or she can take an early-retirement benefit, although it is reduced by $25/36$ of 1 percent for each of the first 36 months and $\frac{5}{12}$ of 1 percent for any additional months before your spouse's normal retirement age. If your PIA is $700, the benefit for your 62-year-old spouse (whose normal retirement age is 65) is $350 reduced by 25 percent, or $263. A spouse younger than 62 is not eligible for a retirement benefit unless he or she is caring for an eligible child under age 16.

Even if you retire at 62 and your spouse is 62, it's best if he or she waits until normal retirement age to receive benefits. By waiting until the normal retirement age, your spouse maximizes the family income.

However, there is no advantage for a spouse to delay taking a benefit after reaching this age. Spousal benefits that commence after normal retirement age don't increase the way your benefits do if you stay in the work force longer.

If you are divorced, you may also be eligible for benefits based on a former spouse's PIA. You may receive benefits after turning 62 so long as you were married for at least 10 years and have not remarried. Your ex-spouse on whose PIA the spousal benefits are based must be at least 62, though not necessarily retired or receiving Social Security disability benefits. If you remarry, monthly checks stop unless your new spouse is already receiving benefits.

Once you begin collecting Social Security benefits, even if your spouse is under age 62, he or she may also be eligible to collect benefits equal to 50 percent of your PIA if he or she is caring for your child who is under age 16 (or disabled and receiving benefits). Your spouse must have been married to you for at least one year or be the parent of the child in order to receive this benefit. If your spouse is eligible, there is no reduction in his or her benefit because you retired early.

As we've noted, if a spouse has his or her own earnings record, based on his or her own work experience, SSA calculates benefits using that record. The spouse then receives the benefit based on his or her earnings record or one based on the spouse's PIA, whichever is larger. As more women enter and remain in the work force, their benefits will be based on their earnings records.

CHILDREN'S BENEFITS When you retire, your unmarried children under age 18 (under age 19 if still in high school) and those who become disabled before age 22 are also eligible for benefits based on your PIA. Their benefit ordinarily equals one-half of your PIA.

MAXIMUM FAMILY BENEFITS SSA places a cap on the benefit your family gets when you retire. The maximum amount payable depends on the level of your PIA—it varies from 150 to 188 percent of the PIA.

If your family is eligible for benefits, SSA figures the sum of the individual benefits based on your earnings record as well as the maximum family benefit. If the sum of the individual benefits is larger than the maximum benefit, the benefits for each family member (though not yours) are reduced proportionately so the total family benefit does not exceed the maximum.

WORKING AFTER RETIREMENT

Social Security is meant to replace a portion of your earnings that are lost because of retirement, death, or disability. Nevertheless, you can still collect Social Security benefits and continue working, but if your earnings exceed a specified amount, your benefits are reduced. For 1998, if you're at least 65 but have not reached your 70th birthday and continue to work, your benefit is reduced by $1 for every $3 earned above $14,500. (The earnings limitation also applies to those under 65 who receive benefits. For them, the 1998 reduction is $1 for every $2 in earnings over $9,120.) Any earnings that exceed the allowable amounts affect not only your benefit but also those of your family members. The earnings test also applies to working spouses and children of retired workers. After you reach age 70, the earnings limitation does not apply.

Let's see how the earnings test works. Suppose your monthly benefit is $1,000 in 1998, but you also earn $16,300 a year doing small jobs for your former employer. If you're at least 65 but have not reached your 70th birthday, your excess earnings are $1,800 ($16,300 - $14,500). After the earnings test is applied, your benefits for the year are reduced by $600 ($1,800 ÷ 3 = $600). In effect, you lose 60 percent of one month's benefits. Sometimes continuing to work wipes out your entire benefit. However, you still receive full Medicare benefits if you otherwise qualify for them.

Self-employed people must also comply with the earnings test. If you own a business, subtract your business deductions from your business income to determine your earnings for the year. If that figure exceeds the earnings limitation, your benefits are reduced. If you work for others and also have your own business on the side, SSA adds your wages and salary plus any net income from the side business to determine whether your total income exceeds the earnings limitation.

Note, however, that during the year you retire, you can continue to work and receive full benefits for the rest of that year regardless of your total annual earnings, so long as you do not perform substantial work as a self-employed person and your wages do not exceed a certain exempt amount each month after you retire. In 1998, the monthly exempt amount is $1,209 for people ages 65 through 69 and $720 for those under 65. Therefore, if you earned $50,000 during the first six months of the year, you could still retire and receive benefits during the last six months, so long as your earnings in each month were less than the monthly exempt amount.

WHAT COUNTS AS INCOME? In general, only wages and earnings from self-employment count toward the earnings test for Social Security benefits. Income from the following doesn't count: pensions, annuity payments, IRA and 401(k) distributions, dividends and interest, capital gains, rental income (unless you are in the real-estate business), tips of less than $20 a month, sick pay received more than six months after leaving work, workers' compensation, unemployment benefits, court settlements, gifts, life-insurance proceeds, inheritance proceeds, and contest or lottery winnings.

SPECIAL RULE FOR GOVERNMENT WORKERS If you worked for federal, state, or local government, were not covered by Social Security when you retired, and are eligible for a Social Security benefit as a spouse, widow, or widower, that benefit is generally reduced by up to two-thirds of the amount of your government pension. The net result: Some government workers don't get Social Security benefits. There are exceptions to this rule, however, and you should check with your local Social Security office to see if they apply to you. If you qualify for Social Security through other nongovernmental employment and you are also eligible for a pension as a government worker, your Social Security benefit may also be reduced. Your local Social Security office can tell you what that reduction will be.

TAXING YOUR BENEFITS If you have substantial total retirement income, you may have to include part of your Social Security benefits in your taxable income when you fill out Form 1040. To see if your benefits are taxable, add together your regular adjusted gross income from Form 1040 (this number includes all taxable investment income but for this purpose excludes any taxable Social Security benefits), any interest earned on tax-exempt bonds (which is ordinarily not taxable), any interest earned on Series EE educational bonds (which is excluded from tax), and 50 percent of your Social Security benefits. If the sum exceeds $25,000 for a single person (or head of household) or $32,000 for married couples filing jointly, then you owe some tax.

If the sum does not exceed $34,000 if you are single (or head of household) or exceed $44,000 if you are married filing jointly, then no more than 50 percent of your benefits will be taxed. To calculate the amount of the tax in either of these cases, determine the excess by which your adjusted gross income, nontaxable bond interest, and half of your benefits exceed either $25,000 or $32,000, whichever applies. Then take 50 percent of that amount but not more than 50 percent of your Social Security benefits and add it to your adjusted gross income. (The IRS instructions can guide you through this calculation.)

Suppose, for example, you and your spouse receive $10,000 in Social Security benefits and file a joint return. You also have $16,000 of taxable income from your company pension, $5,000 of taxable interest, and $5,000 of taxable dividends. Your adjusted gross income is $26,000 ($16,000 + $5,000 + $5,000). Your adjusted gross income ($26,000) plus half of your Social Security benefit ($5,000) equals $31,000, which is less than the $32,000 threshold for retirees filing joint returns, so your Social Security benefits are not taxable. But if you also had another $2,000 of tax-exempt interest from municipal bonds, your adjusted gross income plus tax-exempt interest plus half of your Social Security benefits would rise to $33,000, which is $1,000 over the threshold. You would then include one-half of the $1,000 excess amount (or $500) in your taxable income.

If the sum of your adjusted gross income plus your nontaxable interest plus 50 percent of your benefits does exceed $34,000 if you are single (or head of household) or $44,000 if you are married filing jointly, up to 85 percent of your benefits will be taxed. In either of these cases, the taxable portion of your benefits is equal to the lesser of (1) 85 percent of your benefits, or (2) the sum of (a) 85 percent of the amount by which your adjusted gross income plus your nontaxable interest plus 50 percent of your benefits exceeds $34,000 ($44,000 if you are married filing jointly), plus (b) the lesser of (i) the amount determined by applying the formula for calculating the taxable portion of your benefits if only 50 percent of your benefits were subject to tax, or (ii) $4,500 ($6,000 for married taxpayers filing jointly).

Suppose, for example, you and your spouse receive $12,000 of Social Security benefits. You also receive $15,000 of interest, $10,000 of dividends, and $19,000 of pension benefits (fully taxable). You and your spouse file a joint return. Your adjusted gross income (excluding any taxable Social Security benefits) is $44,000 ($15,000 plus $10,000 plus $19,000). This sum plus one-half of your Social Security benefits ($6,000) equals $50,000. You must include in your income $10,200 of your Social Security benefits. This amount represents the lesser of (1) 85 percent of your benefits (0.85 x $12,000 = $10,200), or (2) (a) 85 percent of the difference between your adjusted gross income ($50,000) and $44,000 plus, (b) $6,000.

Some states also tax Social Security benefits. Your local Social Security office can tell you if your state is one of them.

BENEFITS FOR SURVIVORS

The eligibility requirements for survivors' benefits differ from those for retirement benefits. SSA determines the required number of quarters for you to be fully insured by counting the number of years after 1950, or after the year you become age 21, if later, up through the year before death or through the year you turn age 61, whichever occurs earlier. For example, if you were born in 1925 and die in 1998, you need 36 quarters of coverage. Someone born in 1965 who died in 1998 would need only 11. To be currently insured for survivors' benefits, you must have earned at least 6 quarters of coverage during the previous 13 calendar quarters, ending with the quarter in which you die.

What survivors' benefits your family members are eligible to collect depend on your insured status at the time of your death. If you're fully insured, all types of survivors' benefits are available. If you are currently insured, only some benefits are.

For fully insured workers, benefits are available to the following family members:

Surviving spouses who have reached their 60th birthday. Your spouse must have been married to you for at least nine months before your death, be the parent of your child, or meet other eligibility requirements. If you die in an accident, this time limit doesn't apply. If your spouse is 65 or older, he or she generally receives 100 percent of your PIA. For younger spouses, the benefit is reduced. A spouse age 62 receives 82.9 percent of your PIA (assuming your spouse's normal retirement age is 65); the benefits for a spouse age 60 equal 71.5 percent of your PIA (regardless of your spouse's normal retirement age).

If you retire before age 65 (or before the normal retirement age if you were born after 1937) and then die, your surviving spouse also receives the reduced benefit you were receiving unless it is less than 82.5 percent of your PIA. In that case, his or her benefit equals 82.5 percent of your PIA. For example, suppose you retire at age 64 and your PIA is $700. Your benefit is then $653. Your surviving spouse also receives $653. But if you retire at age 62, your benefit is only $560. Since that's less than 82.5 percent of your PIA, your spouse gets

$577. If you retire after age 65, your spouse's survivors' benefit increases by the same delayed retirement credit that you received. As noted in Chapter 1, it's important to consider survivors' benefits when you begin planning for retirement.

If your spouse has established his or her own earnings record and is also eligible for retirement benefits, he or she gets only *one* benefit, normally the larger one. An attractive option for widowed spouses under the normal retirement age is to take a reduced benefit based on the deceased partner's earnings record and delay benefits based on his or her own earnings record until he or she reaches normal retirement age. A spouse who takes a survivors' benefit can later switch to his or her own retirement benefit if it is larger. The opposite can also occur. Your spouse can take a retirement benefit at normal retirement age based on his or her own earnings record and later convert to a survivors' benefit based on your work record if the benefit is larger. (A spouse who remarries also continues to receive survivors' benefits.)

Divorced spouses. If your ex-spouse is age 60 or older and was married to you for at least 10 years, he or she receives the same benefits as he or she would have if you had remained married.

Disabled surviving spouses. If your spouse is at least 50 years old, he or she is eligible for survivors' benefits if he or she is severely mentally or physically impaired and the disability has lasted five months. In this case, the benefit equals 71.5 percent of your primary insurance amount. As with benefits payable to surviving spouses who are not disabled, benefits continue even if the disabled spouse remarries.

Surviving spouses caring for children. Regardless of your spouse's age, if your youngest child is under 16 or you have a child who was disabled before reaching his or her 22nd birthday, your spouse is eligible for benefits equaling 75 percent of your PIA. This benefit stops when the youngest child turns 16 (unless a disabled child is in the home) or if the spouse remarries.

Eligible children. Unmarried children meeting certain requirements also receive benefits equal to 75 percent of your PIA. The eligibility rules are the same as for children qualifying under a retired worker's benefit. If both parents are dead, the children can qualify for benefits based on the earnings record of either parent, whichever is larger. In such cases, the law also provides for a limited pooling of the family maximum amounts for the two parents.

Maximum family benefit rules and the earnings test also apply to survivors' benefits. *Example:* A 60-year-old widow is eligible for an $800 monthly benefit in 1998, but she continues to work. Her annual benefit is then reduced by $1 for every $2 of earnings in excess of $9,120. If she earns $12,000, a total of $1,440 will be withheld for the year. Thus, she loses almost two months of benefits ($12,000 - $9,120 = $2,880 ÷ 2 = $1,440). When she is eligible for her own retirement benefit, that benefit is also subject to the earnings test.

If you die and are only currently insured, Social Security benefits are payable to your so-called young survivors. In other words, the program pays benefits to a surviving or divorced spouse who is caring for either a child under age 16 or a child who was disabled before age 22. Unmarried children under age 18 (under age 19 if the child is still in high school) and disabled children are also eligible for their own benefits. Those eligible for survivors' benefits receive the same percentage of the worker's PIA that survivors of fully insured workers receive.

Table 4 will help you estimate your survivors' benefits if you should die in 1998. The table gives you a good estimate only if you have worked steadily and earned the same percentage of the U.S. average wage for most of your working years. If you haven't worked steadily or want to know what benefits your survivors can expect based on your PIA, contact the Social Security Administration at 800 772-1213 for your Personal Earnings and Benefit Statement.

LUMP-SUM DEATH BENEFIT When you die, a payment of $255 is made to a spouse who is still living with you. Your spouse is eligible for this benefit whether you are retired or still working. If no spouse lives with you, the SSA pays the benefit to any spouse or children who are eligible for monthly benefits based on your earnings record. If you have no eligible survivors, SSA pays no benefit.

DISABILITY BENEFITS

To receive Social Security disability benefits, you must comply with strict rules, and those rules tend to be rigidly enforced.

QUALIFYING FOR BENEFITS To be eligible for benefits, you must have suffered severe mental or physical impairment. You must be unable to perform any *substantial* gainful work (considering your age, education, and work experience), and your impairment must be expected to continue at least 12 months or result in death. Whether your illness or disability renders you "severely" impaired and unable to perform "substantial" work is occasionally subjective and open to interpretation.

Your state's Disability Determination Service decides whether your disability fits the SSA's definition of a disability. In cases that don't neatly meet the standard criteria, officials tend to deny benefits. As a result, over two-thirds of those applying for disability benefits are initially denied. Approximately 50 percent of them appeal the deci-

TABLE 4 · ESTIMATED MONTHLY SURVIVORS' BENEFITS

▶ *For a worker who had steady earnings and died in 1998*

Worker's age	Worker's family	Deceased worker's earnings in 1997			
		$30,000	$40,000	$50,000	Maximum
35	SPOUSE AND ONE CHILD	$1,614	$1,897	$2,085	$2,348
	SPOUSE AND TWO CHILDREN	1,914	2,215	2,434	2,741
	ONE CHILD ONLY	807	948	1,042	1,174
	SPOUSE AT AGE 60	769	904	994	1,119
45	SPOUSE AND ONE CHILD	1,614	1,897	2,085	2,302
	SPOUSE AND TWO CHILDREN	1,914	2,215	2,434	2,687
	ONE CHILD ONLY	807	948	1,042	1,151
	SPOUSE AT AGE 60	767	904	994	1,097
55	SPOUSE AND ONE CHILD	1,614	1,886	2,023	2,164
	SPOUSE AND TWO CHILDREN	1,914	2,201	2,361	2,526
	ONE CHILD ONLY	807	943	1,011	1,082
	SPOUSE AT AGE 60	769	899	964	1,031

Maximum assumes earnings equal to or greater than Social Security wage base from age 22 through 1997. For 1997, the wage base was $65,400. Amounts for spouse and one child also equal the benefits paid to two children if no parent survives or surviving parent has substantial earnings. Amounts for spouse and two children equal the maximum family benefit. Amounts for spouse at age 60 are payable in 1998. Spouse turning 60 in the future would receive higher benefits.

Source: Social Security Administration

sions. On reconsideration, approximately 10 percent of the claims are allowed. About 80 percent of the claims denied are appealed to administrative-law judges who work for the Social Security Administration. They reverse those initial decisions about 60 percent of the time. If you are severely disabled but Social Security has turned you down, pursue all available appeals and seek guidance from a lawyer, if necessary, to gain your benefits.

To qualify for disability benefits, you must be fully insured and have *disability-insured status.* Disability-insured status means you must have earned at least 20 quarters of coverage in the 40-quarter period ending with the quarter in which you were disabled. (Less stringent rules apply for people under age 31.) *Table 5* shows how many quarters of coverage you need, based on your age, to be fully insured. The requirements are a bit different for workers born before 1929.

PAYMENT OF BENEFITS Social Security disability benefits, like those from private insurance carriers, are paid only after a waiting

TABLE 5 • WHAT YOU NEED TO QUALIFY FOR DISABILITY BENEFITS

▶ *Quarters of coverage required for persons disabled in 1989 or later*

Age at onset of disability	Quarters needed to be fully insured	Quarters needed for disability insured status
25	6	8 IN 16-QUARTER PERIOD
30	8	18 IN 36-QUARTER PERIOD
35	13	20 IN 40-QUARTER PERIOD
40	18	20 IN 40-QUARTER PERIOD
45	23	20 IN 40-QUARTER PERIOD
50	28	20 IN 40-QUARTER PERIOD
55	33	20 IN 40-QUARTER PERIOD
60	38	20 IN 40-QUARTER PERIOD

Both fully insured status and disability-insured status requirements must be met to qualify for benefits. Worker is assumed to reach the age shown in the same calendar quarter in which he or she becomes disabled. Number of quarters of coverage required can vary by one or two if this assumption is not met. Special provisions apply to blind persons and persons who were previously disabled.

Source: Social Security Administration

period. You must be disabled for five full calendar months before any benefits are paid, but you won't have to satisfy a second waiting period if you have already received disability benefits that ended less than five years before your current disability began. *Example:* You were injured on the job four years ago and received Social Security disability benefits for one year. You then returned to work. The work proved too arduous, and after eight months, you had to stop working. You are again eligible for disability benefits and do not have to satisfy another waiting period.

TABLE 6 · ESTIMATED MONTHLY DISABILITY BENEFITS

▶ *For a worker who became disabled in 1998 and had steady earnings*

Worker's age	Worker's family	Disabled worker's earnings in 1997			
		$30,000	$40,000	$50,000	Maximum
25	DISABLED WORKER ONLY	$1,076	$1,265	$1,390	$1,566
	DISABLED WORKER, SPOUSE, AND CHILD	1,614	1,897	2,085	2,349
35	DISABLED WORKER ONLY	1,076	1,265	1,390	1,559
	DISABLED WORKER, SPOUSE, AND CHILD	1,614	1,897	2,085	2,338
45	DISABLED WORKER ONLY	1,076	1,265	1,390	1,528
	DISABLED WORKER, SPOUSE, AND CHILD	1,614	1,897	2,085	2,293
55	DISABLED WORKER ONLY	1,076	1,257	1,348	1,442
	DISABLED WORKER, SPOUSE, AND CHILD	1,614	1,886	2,023	2,164
65	DISABLED WORKER ONLY	1,041	1,195	1,266	1,340
	DISABLED WORKER, SPOUSE, AND CHILD	1,562	1,793	1,900	2,010

Maximum assumes earnings equal to or greater than the Social Security wage base from age 22 through 1997. Wage base for 1997 was $65,400. Amounts for disabled worker, spouse, and child equals the maximum family benefit.

Source: Social Security Administration

After you have received benefits for nine months, your local Social Security office reviews your case and decides whether your benefits should continue. If they determine that you can work again, the benefits stop. If you return to work and your earnings subsequently drop below the "substantial gainful activity" level, Social Security reinstates benefits without a new application as long as three years have not passed in the interim.

FIGURING THE BENEFIT Your disability benefit equals your PIA on the day you become disabled and is adjusted according to the Consumer Price Index, the same as normal retirement benefits. Other than cost-of-living increases, the benefit does not increase as you get older. When you reach normal retirement age, your disability benefit becomes a retirement benefit, but the monthly check remains the same.

Table 6 shows your disability benefits if you become disabled in 1998. *Example:* You are 55 years old and earn $40,000 a year. You suddenly become disabled and cannot support your spouse and young child. Social Security will pay your family a disability benefit of $1,886 a month. Again, the table assumes you have earned the same percentage of the U.S. average wage and have worked steadily throughout your career.

FAMILY BENEFITS If you're disabled, your family members are also eligible for benefits based on your PIA. A spouse at normal retirement age receives 50 percent of your primary insurance amount; a spouse age 62, 37 percent, if the normal retirement age is 65. Regardless of his or her age, if your spouse is caring for children who are disabled or who are under age 16, he or she receives 50 percent of your PIA. Those of your children who meet the eligibility requirements also receive 50 percent of your PIA. The maximum family benefit, however, is lower than the maximum paid for retirement or survivors' benefits.

Example: You become disabled at age 59. Your spouse is 53 and you have a 13-year-old child. If your PIA and thus your benefit is $900, your spouse is eligible for a benefit of $450, because he or she is caring for a child who's eligible for benefits. The child is also eligible to receive $450. Your family's benefit, however, is not $1,800, because the maximum-benefit provision applies. Total benefits cannot exceed 85 percent of your AIME or 150 percent of your PIA, whichever is lower. In this example, total family benefits come to $1,350. Your spouse and child receive a total of $450 each month in addition to your benefit of $900, which is not subject to a reduction.

The earnings test also applies to benefits paid to other family members. If your spouse works, his or her benefit is reduced by $1 for every $2 he or she earns in excess of $9,120. (In this instance, however, the child's benefit increases as the spouse's benefit decreases, and the family benefit stays the same.)

COORDINATING DISABILITY BENEFITS Disability benefits may be reduced if you receive workers' compensation or other disability benefits from another federal program or a state or local government insurance program. The total benefits from all government sources cannot exceed 80 percent of your earnings before you were disabled. Disability benefits from a private insurance carrier or a company pension don't count for this test.

DISABLED SPOUSES As we've noted, disabled widows and widowers between ages 50 and 59 are also eligible for benefits based on your PIA. The benefit equals 71.5 percent of the PIA you would have had at normal retirement age and does not increase except for cost-of-living increases.

To be eligible, a widow or widower must have been disabled within seven years after a spouse's death or seven years after your last child reaches age 16 (or is no longer disabled). The definition of disability is the same as we described previously.

DISABLED BENEFICIARIES AND MEDICARE A disabled person receiving Social Security benefits for at least 24 months is also entitled to Medicare benefits. This includes disabled workers, disabled widows and widowers, and disabled children over 18 whose disability occurred before age 22. Medicare may well be the only source of health insurance for disabled persons (see Chapter 8).

HOW TO APPLY FOR SOCIAL SECURITY BENEFITS

As soon as you decide when you want your benefits to begin, contact your local Social Security office. Although you can make an appointment to apply in person, you can usually complete the application over the phone. If you plan to retire before you turn 65, be sure to apply for benefits no later than the last day of the month you want benefits to begin. Benefits payable for the months before you turn 65 usually can begin no earlier than the month in which you first apply.

If you apply for benefits after you turn 65, the Social Security

Administration may make back payments to you for up to six months before the month in which you apply. We recommend, therefore, that you apply up to three months *before* the month in which you want benefits to begin. It takes about eight weeks for the application to be processed. Keep this in mind as you begin to plan for your income in retirement.

When you apply for benefits, you need your Social Security number, birth certificates for yourself and your children (or other proof of age, such as a passport), and a record of your recent earnings, such as last year's W-2 form or last year's self-employment tax return. If you're applying for benefits based on a spouse's earnings, bring a marriage certificate as well as your birth certificate. If your family is applying for survivors' benefits, they must bring a death certificate.

If you want Social Security checks deposited directly in your checking or savings account, bring the numbers of those accounts. Direct deposit is safer and more convenient for most people. But if you want your checks sent in the mail, Social Security will do that, too.

If you're applying for disability benefits, the application process can be lengthy. Apply as soon as you become disabled.

YOUR
P·E·N·S·I·O·N

PENSION-PLAN ASSETS CONSTITUTE THE largest single source of capital in the United States. U.S. Department of Labor figures indicate that in 1997 there were over 700,000 pension plans covering more than 85 million participants and beneficiaries with $3.5 trillion in assets.

Pension benefits come from employer plans that defer income or provide payments after retirement. Such plans include 401(k), Keogh, profit-sharing, and employee stock-ownership plans (ESOPs) as well as traditional pension plans. IRA accounts—individual pensions funded with your own money over the years and with funds you have rolled over from your employer's plans—also provide retirement funds.

Your employer pension is most likely a *qualified* plan. That means contributions escape taxation, and you have to pay taxes on the money when you receive it—either at the time you retire or sometime thereafter. You may also have a nonqualified pension plan or other deferred-compensation plan. In a nonqualified plan, the money, if any, set aside by your employer is ordinarily not placed in a separate trust and, in any event, remains subject to the claims of the employer's creditors. If you are to receive benefits from any of these, your employer or a tax adviser can help you with any tax consequences. Obviously, taxes figure prominently into how much you can expect to get from your pension, but besides taxes, the actual dollars you receive depend on the type of plan your employer has established, your years of service with the employer, your age, the specific benefit formulas built into the plan, your compensation, and the amount of contributions made by you and your employer. To understand how all these factors interact, it's important to review some pension basics.

HOW PENSIONS WORK

TYPES OF PLANS Your pension plan is either a defined-benefit plan or a defined-contribution plan. Sometimes you may have both. A *defined-benefit* plan is one in which your employer determines in advance what monthly benefit (or lump-sum payment) you eventually receive, usually depending on age, years of service, and compensation. Specific formulas, established when the plan was set up, are used to figure your retirement benefits. During your working years, your employer funds the plan so that it can meet this predetermined level of benefits.

This type of plan may use one of the following three formulas. The first is not based on the amount of an employee's pay; the others are.

• Dollars per year of service. Under this formula, an employee receives a specified number of dollars per month multiplied by the number of years of service. Therefore, if a plan gives $60 per month per year of service and an employee works for 20 years, the pension would be $900 per month or $10,800 a year.

• Career-average salary plan. This type of plan credits a percentage of salary for each year of service. For example, your plan might credit a pension of 1 percent of your salary for each year. The annual credits are added to determine your total pension. Employers using this method sometimes adjust the early years' salaries to bring them into line with inflation.

• Final-average salary plan. This method is similar to the career-average salary plan except the benefit is based on an employee's *average* salary for the last three or five years with the employer. In some plans, the highest five consecutive years out of the last 10 are used. Employers using this plan sometimes credit a smaller percentage of employees' salaries than they would if they used the career-average salary plan.

The number of small defined-benefit plans has declined in recent years, although the number of large defined-benefit plans has remained fairly stable. Most of the growth of qualified plans has come in the form of defined-contribution plans.

Under most *defined-contribution* plans, contributions are fixed, but the actual benefit you receive is not known until you retire. For example, a plan might require an employer to contribute 7 percent of each employee's salary each year to the fund. Profit-sharing plans, 401(k) plans, thrift plans, money-purchase plans, and ESOPs are all types of defined-contribution arrangements. Some profit-sharing plans and ESOPs leave the contribution up to the employer's discretion and give guidelines on how contributions are to be allocated among all the participants. Under most 401(k) plans, employees elect to defer part of their salary and have it contributed to the plan, along with the employer's matching contributions, if any, which are equal to some percentage of the employee's deferrals.

Each individual's account receives, at least annually, his or her share of the plan's investment income plus any appreciation in the market values of the underlying investments. Thus, the actual benefits you receive depend on the amount that has accumulated in your account.

Unlike defined-benefit plans, there are generally no benefit formulas associated with defined-contribution plans. Whatever is in your account when you retire becomes your benefit. Your plan may use the money to buy an annuity, or it may give you the money as a lump sum.

The kind of plan that has experienced the largest growth in recent years is the 401(k) plan. In 1984, there were about 17,000 401(k) plans; they covered 7.5 million people and had about $92 billion in assets. In 1997, there were about 250,000 401(k) plans; they covered 25 million people and had about $750 billion in assets.

YOUR PLAN A summary of your pension plan, given to you by your plan administrator when you first begin employment, outlines the type of plan you have and the benefit formulas that are applicable (if you are in a defined-benefit plan). We suggest that you consult this document, known as the *summary plan description,* years before you begin to contemplate retirement. Because you may not have access to all your salary records for each year you worked, your plan administrator can probably estimate the amount of pension you will receive.

Under the Employee Retirement Income Security Act (ERISA), the law that governs many pension plans, you are entitled to a statement of your pension benefits once a year. If your plan doesn't provide this information automatically, request it. The law requires that you make your request in writing. If you have any trouble with your plan or employer, you can seek help from: Division of Technical Assistance and Inquiries, Pension and Welfare Benefits Administration, U.S. Department of Labor, 200 Constitution Ave., N.W., Room N 5625, Washington, DC 20210.

VESTING To be eligible for a benefit funded by employer contributions, you must be *vested*; that is, you must have worked a certain number of years for the same employer.

At one time, 10-year "cliff" vesting was the norm for most pension plans, which meant employees had to work at the same company for at least 10 years. However, the 1986 tax law liberalized the rules. Now employees who work for a single employer earn the right to a pension after they have been on the job for only five years. The 10-year rule still applies to multiemployer plans—those collectively bargained plans to which two or more employers contribute.

Instead of cliff vesting, your company may use graded vesting, which means 20 percent of your pension is vested after three years of service. Under this arrangement, an additional 20 percent of your pension is vested each year until 100 percent is vested after seven years. Other plans allow benefits to vest more rapidly, some even providing for 100-percent vesting immediately, as soon as an employee joins the plan.

As you prepare to retire, review all the companies you have worked for during your career that maintained a pension plan. Check to see whether you're eligible for a pension from any of them. If you worked for one employer less than 10 years, or if you previously received your benefit as a lump-sum distribution, you probably won't be eligible. But if the plan provided for more rapid vesting, you might qualify for a small benefit. If you've worked fewer than five years in any one job, you probably won't get anything. Because of the vesting rules and the fact that many employers do not maintain pension plans, it's possible to work for many employers and walk away with nothing at retirement. If you're not sure, check with the pension administrators at your former employers.

The vesting rules apply only to plans funded by employer contributions. In plans that are funded with your own contributions, such as 401(k) plans, your pension is vested immediately. However, the portion of your account attributable to your employer's matching contributions remains subject to the normal vesting rules.

YEARS OF SERVICE Generally under defined-benefit plans, the more years you have worked, the larger your pension. But not every year you work is necessarily counted as a year of service for purposes of figuring your benefit. For example, you earn a full year of credit if you belong to the plan for an entire year and partial credit if you work half-time or for half of the year. If you worked fewer than 1,000 hours during the year, you may have earned no pension credits for that year. Or if you worked for an employer that did not have a pension plan for some of the years you were employed, your plan may or may not count the years before the plan started.

In calculating your pension, your employer also considers any breaks in service in your years with the company. A break in service is a year in which you did not work more than a minimum amount, usually 500 hours. For example, you work for an employer for four years and leave the company for a period of five years. When you eventually come back to work, you may have lost the credit for the four years you worked there previously.

There are exceptions to this rule, however. If you left because of pregnancy or the birth or adoption of a child, up to 501 hours of your leave does not count as a break in service. If you serve in the armed forces during a war or in a national emergency, that time away from your job is not considered a break in service. But if you had a break in service before 1976 for reasons other than military service, your employer may not give you credit for some of those years.

SOCIAL SECURITY BENEFITS AND YOUR PENSION

Some pension plans, especially those defined-benefit plans that use benefit formulas based on an employee's salary, are likely to be integrated with Social Security. That means your employer has considered the amount of your Social Security benefit in designing its pension plan so that the combination of both will provide a certain percentage of your preretirement income. An integrated plan is also referred to as a plan with permitted disparity.

Some employers also use integrated plans to give more pension benefits to higher-paid employees. As noted in Chapter 2, Social Security is designed to replace a larger percentage of pay for lower-paid workers. Partially to make up for this, many integrated pension plans provide higher-paid workers with a larger percentage of their preretirement earnings than lower-paid workers.

To mesh pension benefits with Social Security, a plan may subtract part of an employee's Social Security benefit from his or her pension benefit, or it may provide more pension benefits for earnings above a certain level. That level is usually the "wage base"—the amount of your earnings on which your employer has paid Social Security taxes.

In the past, integration rules often resulted in lower-paid workers receiving a very small pension or none at all. However, now plans must leave you with at least one-half of your pension benefit after accounting for Social Security. But this rule applies only for the years worked after 1988. If your plan subtracts Social Security benefits, you may still find yourself without a pension for those early working years. Because the integration rules are complicated, you should consult your plan administrator to find out how they affect your benefits.

WHEN YOU CAN TAKE YOUR BENEFITS

Under most defined-contribution plans, you may choose to receive the vested portion of your pension-account balance whenever you terminate your employment. You can get it in a single sum or leave it invested in the plan. For account balances of $5,000 or less, you may have to take your money in a lump sum.

All defined-benefit plans pay out pensions when you retire on or after your normal retirement age, usually 65. Most defined-benefit plans also provide benefits to those taking early retirement. (ERISA doesn't require all plans to offer early-retirement benefits, however.) Your plan may also allow you to take a reduced benefit at 55 or 60 instead of a full pension beginning at normal retirement age. Your pension is smaller because you have fewer years of service and you do not have the benefit of the salary increases you might have received if you had continued working until you were 65.

In addition, if your benefits begin before the normal retirement age, there is a reduction for early retirement that varies from plan to plan. It reflects the fact that the pension begins sooner and is expected to be paid for more years. Usually count on losing up to 7 percent of your benefit for each year you are under 65 when payments begin.

Example: If you ordinarily receive a monthly pension of $1,000 at 65 but choose to take your benefit at 60, you could lose about one-third of your monthly benefit and only receive $667. If you begin to collect your pension at age 55, it may be reduced by half or even more than half. In this example, you'd receive $500. But you do have the advantages of receiving the benefit sooner and receiving it for more years.

A few plans offer early-retirement benefits without the usual reduction to employees who have been with the company for 20 or 25 years. Even if you are in one of these plans, you may still have to meet further eligibility requirements. For example, you must only be doing work covered by the plan when you reach early-retirement age. Similarly, the plan may allow employees with 20 years of service to receive a pension at age 60 without any reduction, but the employee must actually be working in order to collect benefits. Someone who quits at 58 will not receive the unreduced pension even if he or she has worked the required 20 years.

TAKING EARLY RETIREMENT Should you take your pension early? It depends on your continued satisfaction with your job, whether or not you can afford to leave the work force, and your employer's plans for keeping you on in the company. If your employer forces you to take early retirement, you have little choice. In that case, you must decide whether or not to take an unreduced deferred pension or a reduced pension that begins immediately.

Employers often increase your pension benefits as an added inducement to take early retirement. If your employer is not offering improved benefits and still wants you to leave, try to negotiate better terms. Try at least to obtain an unreduced immediate pension.

If you leave your employer but intend to collect your pension later, consider whether those benefits will continue to grow indefinitely. If you are a member of a defined-benefit plan, your pension, payable at the normal retirement age, is generally fixed. The main advantage to delaying your pension payout in this case is to get an unreduced benefit instead of the reduced early-retirement pension. If you are in a defined-contribution plan, the money in your account will continue to share in investment gains (or losses) of the plan.

DELAYING RETIREMENT Under the Age Discrimination in Employment Act (ADEA), an employer cannot force most employees to retire because of age. As a result, you may be able to postpone retirement past your employer's normal retirement age, which is usually 65. Under current law, unless you are a 5-percent owner of your company, you are not required to begin withdrawing your money from a qualified plan until April 1 following the year you retire. If you're in good health and want to continue working, your pension obviously will be larger.

If you are a 5-percent owner, you are required to begin taking distributions no later than April 1 of the calendar year following the year in which you reach age 70½. A 5-percent owner is a person who owns, or is considered under the tax law to own, more than 5 percent of the stock or more than 5 percent of the voting power of all the stock of a corporation. In addition, a person who is a sole proprietor or owns more than 5 percent of the capital or profits of a partnership, limited liability company, or other business is a 5-percent owner. As a result, if you own an interest in a small business, you may be a 5-percent owner.

All taxpayers must begin taking distributions from traditional IRAs by April 1 of the calendar year following the year they turn 70½. However, no distributions need be taken from a Roth IRA before death.

PENSION PAYMENT OPTIONS

One of the most difficult and important decisions you face at the time of retirement is how to take your pension benefits. This decision will affect your financial well-being for the rest of your life.

Most defined-contribution plans make the money available as a lump sum, and many such plans also allow payment in installments or in various forms of annuities. You may be able to choose among a lump-sum payment and several annuity options. (If your benefits have a value of $5,000 or less, the plan may require you to take a lump-sum payment.) Each option has its advantages and disadvantages, and tax considerations may also affect your decision.

ERISA says that defined benefit plans must pay your pension as some form of an annuity unless you elect otherwise. Most plans first determine the amount of your pension as a monthly annuity payable for your lifetime, with no benefits payable after your death. This is called a life annuity or straight life annuity and is the plan's normal benefit form. However, most plans offer other options.

A plan must pay married participants in the form of a *qualified joint-and-survivor* annuity unless the participant elects otherwise with the consent of his or her spouse. A qualified joint-and-survivor annuity provides an annuity for as long as the retired employee lives. This annuity also provides the retiree's surviving spouse with a benefit equal to at least 50 percent of the benefit the retiree received; payments to the surviving spouse must continue for the rest of his or her life. This arrangement is called a *50-percent joint-and-survivor* annuity. Some plans also offer married participants a *100-percent joint-and-survivor* annuity, which provides the surviving spouse with the same payments the retiree received. Within the 90-day period before the "annuity starting date" for a married participant (the first day of the first period for which the participant would receive an annuity payment), the plan administrator must provide the participant with a written explanation of a qualified joint-and-survivor annuity as well as an opportunity to waive the survivor benefit for his or her spouse. The administrator may also provide the participant with the opportunity to take a lump-sum benefit. (Similarly, the administrator may provide unmarried participants with the opportunity to take a lump sum.)

If a participant is married, his or her spouse must consent in writing to the participant's waiver of a qualified joint-and-survivor annuity. The IRS has suggested that the plan administrator also provide the spouse with a detailed written explanation concerning the consent in addition to the actual consent. On page 60 is a typical consent form provided by most pension plans. If your spouse asks you to waive your rights to a qualified joint-and-survivor annuity, be sure you understand how you will be protected if you survive your spouse.

There are differences between the 50-percent joint-and-survivor annuities offered through pension plans and those offered by life-insurance companies (see Chapter 4). Pension annuities pay benefits to a retired participant for his or her lifetime and pay 50 percent of that amount to the survivor when the retiree dies (assuming a 50-percent joint-and-survivor arrangement). Insurance-company annuities usually pay benefits to both persons jointly and then reduce the monthly benefit to the survivor when either of the parties to the annuity dies.

There are other kinds of annuities. Your plan, for example, may offer a *life annuity with a 10-year period certain.* Under this arrangement, the retiree receives payments for the rest of his or her life. But if the retiree dies before receiving 120 payments (in other words, within 10 years of retirement), his or her beneficiary continues to receive the payments until a total of 120 payments has been made, to either the retiree, the surviving spouse, or another named beneficiary. Payments then stop, and the surviving spouse receives nothing more. Sometimes, you may find a plan that offers an annuity with a 5-year period certain. In this case, payments to a surviving spouse continue for only five years. If you choose a form of annuity other than a life annuity, your monthly payments are lower to reflect the possibility that payments will be made to your survivors.

Many plans also allow you to take your pension as a lump-sum

FORM 1·

RETIREMENT BENEFIT PLAN

Spousal consent to waive qualified joint and survivor annuity

I, _(name of participant's spouse)_, am the spouse of _____.
I understand that I have the right to have _____(name of plan)_____ pay my
spouse's retirement benefits in the special QJSA payment form and I
agree to give up that right. I understand that by signing this agreement, I may receive less money than I would have received under the
special QJSA payment form and I may receive nothing after my spouse
dies, depending upon the payment form [or beneficiary] that my
spouse chooses.

I agree that my spouse can receive retirement benefits in the
form of a _(insert form of benefit selected)_. [I also agree to my spouse's choice of
_____(name)_____ as beneficiary who will receive _____ percent of
the survivor benefits from the plan after my spouse dies.] I understand
that my spouse cannot choose a different form of retirement benefits
[or a different beneficiary] unless I agree to the change.

I understand that I do not have to sign this agreement. I am
signing this agreement voluntarily.

I understand that if I do not sign this agreement, then my spouse
and I will receive payments from the plan in the special QJSA payment.

_____   _____
Date   Signature of participant's spouse

WITNESS BY EITHER PLAN REPRESENTATIVE OR NOTARY PUBLIC

WITNESS BY PLAN ADMINISTRATOR

_____   _____
Date   Signature of plan representative

WITNESS BY NOTARY PUBLIC

On this ____ day of _____, 19____ personally appeared before me the above-named Participant's spouse, know to me (or satisfactorily proven) to be the person whose name is subscribed to the above instrument, and in my presence signed and sealed the same, and acknowledged that he (she) executed the same for the purposes therein contained and acknowledged the same to be his (her) act.

IN WITNESS WHEREOF, I hereunto set my hand and official seal.

_____

Notary public

payment that is equal to the value of the annuity payments you would have received if you had chosen that option. The plan determines the amount of your lump-sum distribution by calculating a number of factors that are spelled out in your plan document. These factors differ from plan to plan and often change when interest rates change. Consult your plan document to see how a lump-sum distribution is calculated under your pension plan.

Table 7 shows what you and your surviving spouse can expect to receive from different pension options. In this example, we have assumed that both husband and wife are 65 and the retiree is entitled to a $1,000 monthly payment under his or her plan's normal form.

SURVIVORS' BENEFITS

ERISA requires that pension plans offering retirement benefits in the form of annuities also offer survivors' benefits. There are two kinds of survivors' benefits—those available after you have retired and those available before. After you have begun collecting your pension, your surviving spouse is eligible for a portion of your benefits so long as you have selected a joint-and-survivor annuity.

Under defined-contribution plans, your full account balance is usually provided as a death benefit when you die, regardless of whether or not you are vested. Under a defined-benefit plan, if you have not retired and your benefit is vested, the amount your surviving spouse would receive, called a *preretirement survivor* annuity, depends on whether you died after becoming eligible for early retirement benefits or before. *Example:* You die at age 57, two years after you first become eligible for early retirement. You have accrued a monthly pension benefit of $1,000 payable at 65. The plan calculates the survivors' benefits as if you had retired and received an early-retirement benefit under a qualified joint-and-survivor annuity on the day before you died, and then death immediately followed. Your early retirement benefit, payable as a single life annuity, would have been $500. The plan then assumes you had selected a qualified joint-and-survivor annuity (ordinarily a 50-percent joint-and-survivor annuity) and reduces the $500 by approximately 10 percent. Your monthly pension is now $450 and is further reduced by half to reach the amount that your spouse is entitled to under a 50 percent joint-and-survivor option. In this example, your surviving spouse would receive $225 each month for life as a preretirement survivor annuity. As you can see, if you die very soon after reaching your plan's early-retirement age, your spouse cannot expect a very large benefit from your pension plan. The benefit becomes larger the closer you are to the plan's normal retirement age, usually 65.

TABLE 7 · PENSION INCOME COMPARED

▶ *How much a retiree and his or her survivor would receive each month under various pension options.*

	Monthly benefit	
Pension option	**Retiree**	**Survivor (if payable)**
LIFE ANNUITY (NORMAL FORM)	$1,000	0
100% JOINT-AND-SURVIVOR ANNUITY	820	$820
50% JOINT-AND-SURVIVOR ANNUITY	900	450
LIFE ANNUITY WITH 120 PAYMENTS GUARANTEED (LIFE ANNUITY WITH A 10-YEAR PERIOD CERTAIN)	910	910
LUMP-SUM DISTRIBUTION (SINGLE PAYMENT)	100,000	0

If you have a vested benefit but die before you reach early-retire-ment age, your spouse's benefit is even lower. In calculating this benefit, the plan assumes you had: (1) terminated employment immediately prior to your death; (2) lived to your early-retirement age, typically 55 or 60; (3) elected to receive early retirement under the plan's qualified joint-and-survivor annuity; and (4) immediately died. Many plans also will not pay a benefit to a survivor until the date when the deceased spouse would have reached the plan's early-retirement age. Thus, if you die at 50, your spouse may have to wait until you would have been 55 or 60 to collect a benefit.

Preretirement survivors' annuities are not likely to provide much income for widowed spouses unless the employee died when he or she was close to retirement. In planning for a spouse's income after your death, be sure to consider the amount of the benefit and when your spouse is eligible for it. For most people, it's wise not to count too much on your defined-benefit plan alone. A combination of Social Security, a defined-contribution plan, group life insurance, and person-al savings often provides sufficient benefits.

If you are working somewhere else when you die and have a fully vested pension from another employer, your spouse is still eligible for a preretirement survivor annuity from your first employer. However, these benefits are usually not available to people who have left pension plans before 1985 (or before 1987 in some collectively bargained plans). Check with the plan administrators at your former employers to see if your spouse is eligible.

If you are not vested, your spouse ordinarily receives nothing from the defined-benefit plan when you die.

DISABILITY BENEFITS

Defined-contribution plans usually pay the balance of the employee's account when he or she becomes disabled. Defined-benefit plans, on the other hand, handle disability benefits in one of three ways, assum-ing that the employer maintains a separate long-term disability-insur-ance program.

First, the pension plan may provide no disability benefit until the employee is 65, when the insurance benefit stops. At that point, the pension plan may pay the pension earned up to the time of disabil-ity, or it may pay the pension the employee would have received if he or she had continued working to age 65. Second, the pension plan may pay a disabled worker an immediate pension equal to the benefit that he or she has accrued to date, with or without a reduction for early retirement. (These benefits tend to be very small.) Third, a plan may pay an immediate pension benefit that's larger than the worker's accrued benefit, assuming the disabled worker had worked until 65. Obviously, a person would do better under the latter arrangement.

Pension plans generally specify no minimum age for receiving disability benefits. Payments may continue as long as the employee is disabled, or they may stop when a worker turns 65, when the plan begins paying regular retirement benefits. Survivors' benefits are usually available to spouses of workers who had been receiving disability benefits.

Each pension plan has its own rules for determining eligibility benefits for disabled workers. Some, for example, may use the same standard that the Social Security Administration uses for determining disability benefits (see Chapter 2). Others may use more liberal or even stricter tests.

COST-OF-LIVING INCREASES

Most pension plans don't provide for cost-of-living increases once monthly payments start. That means the monthly benefit you receive at retirement remains the same until your death. This lack of adjustment for inflation is a significant drawback of private pensions. *Example:* You receive a monthly pension of $100 at age 65. Inflation runs 4 percent a year, so your pension is worth only $68 by the time you are 75. If you're lucky enough to have cost-of-living increases, be sure to consider them when you complete the worksheets discussed in Chapter 1.

Some pension plans occasionally do give ad hoc increases to retirees. Check to see whether employees who have retired before you have received any such increases, although there's no guarantee that the plan will continue to give cost-of-living adjustments when you retire.

HOW PENSION PLANS ARE TAXED

Payments from pension plans are generally taxable in the year you receive them. With certain exceptions, they are added to your income in determining your federal and state income taxes. If your employer funded the plan and you contributed nothing, all of your pension is taxable under current law. But any part of your pension payments that represents amounts on which you have already paid taxes (your after-tax contributions) is not subject to additional taxes. Various payment options are taxed in the following manner:

LUMP-SUM PAYMENTS Prior to 1987, the tax law provided special 10-year averaging and capital-gains benefits for lump-sum distributions from qualified plans (other than traditional IRAs), including lump-sum distributions paid out before retirement. The purpose of these provisions was to reduce the effect of progressive tax rates on a taxpayer receiving a large distribution in a single year. That is, if a taxpayer received such a distribution, he or she would land in a higher tax bracket than he or she would have had the payment been received in installments over several years.

Beginning with the Tax Reform Act of 1986, Congress began to cut back the availability and benefits of the special-averaging rules. However, Congress did make it easier for taxpayers to roll over their distributions into traditional IRAs. Congress believed that a taxpayer should be encouraged to roll over a lump-sum distribution to a traditional IRA, particularly a distribution received prior to retirement. The taxpayer could then defer tax on the distribution until he or she began withdrawing it from the IRA in installments on retirement.

Accordingly, beginning in 2000, plan participants born after 1935 will no longer be able to use any special-averaging method. These taxpayers will generally want to roll over their lump-sum distributions to defer the tax otherwise payable.

Under a transition rule, 10-year averaging (and a special capital-gains benefit described below) remains available to plan participants born before 1936 (as well as their beneficiaries). In addition, under a second transition rule, these participants as well as other taxpayers receiving lump-sum distributions after reaching age 59½ (and the beneficiaries of such participants) can use a five-year averaging formula for distributions received prior to January 1, 2000.

Under 10-year averaging, your pension payment is generally taxed (1) as if you were single, (2) you received one-tenth of the amount each year for 10 years, and (3) you had no other income. *Example:* You receive a lump-sum pension distribution of $100,000 and are eligible to choose 10-year averaging. Your employer funded the plan. You made no after-tax contributions. The $100,000 distribution is taxed as if you were a single taxpayer, had received payments of $10,000 a year for 10 years, and had no other income. The tax rates required for 10-

year averaging are the higher rates that were in effect in 1986, when the Tax Reform Act of 1986 was enacted.

Five-year averaging is similar to 10-year averaging except that the distribution is treated as if it were distributed over five years. The tax rates used in this computation are the tax rates now in effect.

Five- or 10-year forward averaging almost always results in your paying less tax than if you take a lump sum and pay all the taxes that are due the year you receive the money. Thus, if you are eligible to use one of these provisions, you should obtain IRS Form 4972, "Tax on Lump-Sum Distributions," to calculate the tax on your distribution.

To use either averaging method, you will, however, have to meet a few requirements in addition to the requirements described above:

• You must take all of your assets from a qualified plan (other than an IRA or SEP) in a lump sum in a single year.

• You must not roll over any portion of your distribution into an IRA, and you must not have rolled over any portion of any prior distribution from such plan into an IRA.

• The payment must be made after you reach age 59½.

• You must have been in the plan for at least five calendar years, not counting the year in which the distribution is made, unless payment is made as a result of your death.

• You must not have previously elected averaging for any year after 1986.

Example: You were born in 1933. In 1999, you retire after 20 years with your employer and receive a lump-sum distribution of $90,000 from your employer's qualified profit-sharing plan. You roll over $15,000 of the distribution into a traditional IRA. You are not eligible to use any type of forward averaging for the balance.

What if you receive lump-sum distributions from two or more plans in a single year? For tax purposes, these plans may still be considered a single plan. But even if the plans are considered separate, you may not use forward averaging for the distribution from *either* plan if you elect to roll over *any* portion of the distribution from one plan. Forward averaging is available only to taxpayers electing (and qualifying) to use this method for all lump-sum distributions received during the year.

If you were born before 1936 and were a member of a pension plan before 1974, the portion of the benefits you earned before 1974 may be taxed at a flat 20-percent capital-gains rate. (To calculate your tax on this portion, you again must use IRS Form 4972.)

If your company has funded your pension plan over the years with its own stocks or bonds, your lump-sum payment may be eligible for favorable tax treatment. This means if you take a lump sum in the form of employee securities, an amount equal to the employer's cost for the securities must be included in your income. But you usually don't have to pay tax on the appreciation until you sell the securities, when that appreciation is taxed as a capital gain. In contrast, if you don't receive employer securities in a lump-sum distribution, in most cases, you would have to pay taxes on the securities' value when you received them, just as if you had received the distribution in cash. But if you made contributions to purchase the securities, again you may defer tax on the appreciation.

ANNUITIES Taxation of pensions taken as annuities can be complicated. How pensions are taxed depends largely on whether the money has been taxed before it went into the pension plan.

If your pension plan was noncontributory, that is, your employer funded the plan and you contributed nothing, all of your annuity payments are usually taxed as ordinary income. But you may be covered by a contributory plan in which you make all the contributions or by a contributory plan in which both you and your employer make contributions. In these cases, the portion of each annuity payment that represents a return of your employer's contribution, if any, as well as the earnings from contributions made by both you and your employer, are taxable. But contributions you made with money that was already taxed to you (after-tax contributions) will come back tax-free. If you previously recognized taxable income representing the cost of insurance protection provided by the plan, these previously taxed amounts are treated as if they were nondeductible employee contributions.

Note: If your employer provides a 401(k) or other salary-reduction plan, the salary reductions put into the plan are treated the same way as your employer's contribution, and you have to pay taxes on the amount when you begin to withdraw it.

If your annuity starting date is after November 18, 1996, the nontaxable portion of each payment is determined according to tables provided by the IRS. You have no choice on apportioning the payment. The nontaxable portion of each payment is determined by dividing your total after-tax contributions to the plan by the total number of expected payments shown in the IRS table. Once you have received the total number of expected payments (and thus have excluded an amount from your income equal to the amount of your after-tax contributions), any additional payments are fully taxable. The nontaxable amount should be shown on Form 1099-R.

If your annuity starting date was on or before November 18, 1996, you should ordinarily continue to use the method you previously used for determining the nontaxable portion of each payment. Again, if your annuity payments began after 1986, the cumulative amount you may exclude from your income may not exceed your after-tax contributions.

TAXATION OF DISTRIBUTIONS FROM IRAS

TRADITIONAL IRAS The taxation of distributions from traditional IRAs resembles that of distributions from qualified plans. However, five- or 10-year averaging is not allowed for these IRA distributions. If you have not made any nondeductible contributions to the IRA, the full amount you receive is taxable as ordinary income. If you did make nondeductible contributions, a portion of a distribution is not subject to tax. Since the nondeductible contribution was made with money that was taxed when earned, the portion of your withdrawal representing the contribution is not subject to tax for a second time. You must usually prorate any withdrawal between the taxable and nontaxable portions. Consult a tax adviser for further assistance with the calculation.

ROTH IRAS In the Taxpayer Relief Act of 1997, Congress provided taxpayers with a new retirement-savings vehicle—the Roth IRA. In contrast with contributions to traditional IRAs, contributions to a Roth IRA are not deductible under any circumstances. However, qualified distributions from the Roth IRA are tax-free.

A qualified distribution is a distribution that is made to you after the five-year taxable period beginning with the first taxable year for which you made a Roth IRA contribution. In addition, to be treated as a qualified distribution, the distribution must be (a) made to you on or after you reach age 59½, (b) made to your beneficiary (or your estate) on or after your death, (c) made upon your disability, or (d) exempt from the 10-percent early-withdrawal penalty (described in this chapter), because it is for first-time home-buyer expenses.

A distribution from a Roth IRA other than a qualified distribution is subject to tax. The tax law provides a very favorable rule for determining what portion of your distribution represents the return of your contribution. Distributions from a Roth IRA are generally treated as made from contributions first, and for this purpose, all of your Roth IRAs are treated as a single IRA. Thus, no portion of a distribution from a Roth IRA is included in your income until the total of all distributions exceeds the total of all of your contributions to all your Roth IRA accounts. However, if a portion of a distribution is included in your income and you have not reached 59½, the portion may also be subject to the 10-percent penalty for early withdrawals (described in this chapter).

Special rules apply if you have converted a traditional IRA into a Roth IRA. Under these rules, the IRS considers that you have first withdrawn your regular Roth IRA contributions, then amounts you have converted (rolled over) from your traditional IRAs. Withdrawals of converted amounts are generally treated as coming first from converted amounts that were includible in your income.

If your adjusted gross income is $100,000 or less for a year (and you do not file separately, if married), you may convert (roll over) your traditional IRA into a Roth IRA. If you make the conversion in 1998, 25 percent of the amount converted (less the amount of your non-deductible IRA contributions, if any) is ordinarily included in your income in each of 1998, 1999, 2000, and 2001. After 1998, the 4-year spread will no longer apply. The amount you convert is included in your income in the year of the conversion. Amounts included in income are not taken into account in determining whether you exceed the $100,000 threshold. Nor does the 10-percent penalty for early withdrawals (described in this chapter) apply to your conversion.

Special rules do, however, apply if you withdraw amounts from your converted IRA within a five-year period beginning with the year of your conversion.

First, if you converted your IRA in 1998 and are reporting the resulting income under the 4-year spread rule described above, a special rule applies to any amounts you withdraw from the Roth IRA before 2001. If you make such a withdrawal, you must ordinarily include in your income for the year of the withdrawal an amount equal to the amount of the withdrawal. This amount is in addition to the amount otherwise included in your income for the year under the 4-year spread rule. However, you are not required to include in income an amount greater than the remaining taxable amount of the conversion (that is, the taxable amount of the conversion which you have not yet included in income under the 4-year spread rule in the current or a prior taxable year). In the remaining years until 2001 (assuming you make no further withdrawals), the amount you must include income under the 4-year spread rule is the lesser of (1) the amount otherwise required to be included (determined without regard to the prior withdrawal), or (2) the remaining taxable amount of the conversion.

A second special rule applies to amounts you withdraw from a Roth IRA that are attributable to a converted IRA, regardless of when the conversion takes place. If you withdraw a converted amount within the 5-year period beginning with the year of conversion, then, to the extent the amount withdrawn represents an amount that you included in income on the conversion, the amount withdrawn will be subject to the 10-percent tax on early withdrawals. (*Note:* The amount withdrawn is not otherwise included in your income.) Of course, if you are over 59½ when you make the withdrawal or one of the otherwise available exceptions to the early withdrawal tax applies, the tax will not be imposed.

Example 1: In 1998 your adjusted gross income exceeds $100,000. However, in 1999 your adjusted gross income is $100,000 or less (excluding any income from conversion of an IRA). You convert your traditional IRA to a Roth IRA in 1999. The amount converted is $50,000. No portion of this amount is attributable to nondeductible contributions you made to the IRA. You must include an additional $50,000 in your income for 1999.

Example 2: Same facts as Example 1 above except that in 2001 you withdraw $10,000 from the Roth IRA. You have made no other contributions to this IRA. The distribution is treated as made from the amount you converted in 1999 and included in your 1999 income. As a result, for 2001, you do not have to include the $10,000 in your income. However, because the $10,000 is allocable to a conversion contribution made within the previous 5 years, that amount is now subject to the 10 percent penalty tax on early withdrawals, as if it were included in your income for 2001, unless an exception to the penalty applies.

ADDITIONAL TAX CONSIDERATIONS

TAXES AFTER DEATH Benefits payable to your beneficiaries or to your estate after your death are generally taxable in a manner similar to the taxation of your own benefits while you are alive. If you die with a relatively large estate, your estate may be subject to estate tax as well. Your taxable estate also includes your vested account balance in a defined-contribution plan and the value of future payments under a joint-and-survivor annuity or other annuity that began, or could have begun, prior to your death. However, most estates do not have to pay any tax (see Chapter 18).

TAX PENALTIES FOR EARLY WITHDRAWAL Pension distributions are subject to various additional taxes in certain circumstances. These additional taxes can cut deeply into your pension accumulations and affect your financial well-being. Keep them in mind as you begin planning for retirement.

TAKING PAYMENTS TOO EARLY If you take a distribution from a qualified plan, including an IRA, before you're 59½ and do not roll the distribution over into another qualified plan or IRA, you may have to pay a penalty of 10 percent of the amount included in your income. However, no penalty tax applies to: (1) amounts paid as an annuity over your lifetime or your life expectancy; (2) amounts paid after you reach 55 if paid from a qualified plan after separation from service with the employer maintaining the plan; (3) amounts paid upon death or disability; or (4) amounts paid from a qualified plan under a qualified domestic-relations order.

If none of these exceptions applies, then in most cases you'll have to pay ordinary income taxes on the amount included in your income and pay the penalty. If you're in this situation, you may want to minimize the tax bite by taking a life annuity that avoids the penalty and spreads out the ordinary income tax over your lifetime. Or, for a distribution from a qualified plan, you might want to roll over the money into an IRA and defer taxes on monies withdrawn until you're at least 59½ and begin taking distributions. But the IRA option is feasible only if you have other money to live on in the interim. If you need the money from your pension, your choices may be between a life annuity, installments over your life expectancy, or a lump-sum payment with a tax penalty. Unfortunately, none of these options may be ideal.

Recent legislation has provided additional exceptions for early withdrawals from IRAs in hardship and other cases. Under current law, you may withdraw amounts from an IRA to pay certain medical expenses or, if you have been unemployed, to pay health-insurance premiums. You may also withdraw amounts to pay qualified higher-education expenses (including those related to graduate-level courses) for yourself, your spouse, or any child or grandchild of you or your spouse. A penalty-free withdrawal may also be made for up to $10,000 of first-time home-buyer expenses.

If a distribution from a Roth IRA is included in your income, the distribution may also be subject to the 10-percent penalty discussed in this section. However, the same exceptions that apply to early withdrawals from a traditional IRA apply to withdrawals from a Roth IRA.

Moreover, even if a distribution from a Roth IRA is not included in your income, if the distribution represents proceeds from a traditional IRA converted into a Roth IRA within the past five taxable years, the 10-percent penalty may be imposed. The application of the penalty in this instance is discussed in the section above regarding Roth IRAs.

MINIMUM-DISTRIBUTION RULES

The tax code encourages your savings for retirement by providing deductions for contributions to qualified plans and deferring taxes on the earnings from the contributions until you withdraw them. However, Congress has decided that this deferral should not be permanent. Once you reach 59½, you may withdraw the funds without paying any 10-percent penalty. Moreover, once you reach retirement, you must begin withdrawing funds from qualified plans.

TAKING TOO LITTLE Unless you are a 5-percent owner of a company, you need not begin taking money from a qualified plan until April 1 following the later of, first, the year you turn 70½ or, second, the year you retire. (The IRS specifies a minimum amount that must be withdrawn.) A further distribution must be taken for each succeeding year. Therefore, if you wait to take your first distribution until the April 1 deadline, you will have to take your second distribution by December 31 of that same year.

If you fail to take out the required amount for any year, you may have to pay a stiff 50-percent penalty on the amount of the shortfall for that year.

Example: The minimum withdrawal is $1,250, and you take out only $750. You have to pay a tax of $250 on the shortfall of $500 in addition to the regular tax. Bear in mind that this tax is not deductible.

A 5-percent owner of a company must begin taking required minimum distributions by April 1 following the calendar year he or she turns 70½ even if he or she is still working. In addition, the same age-70½ rule applies to all taxpayers who have established traditional IRAs. But no minimum distribution is required from a Roth IRA while the taxpayer who established the Roth IRA is alive.

The minimum-distribution requirement is satisfied if you receive your entire benefit in a lump-sum distribution by the required starting date, or if you begin to receive your entire benefit by that date in the form of a life annuity payable over your lifetime or the combined lifetimes of you and your spouse (or other beneficiary).

In the latter case, your required minimum distribution each year is ordinarily equal to the amount determined by dividing the balance in your qualified plan (or traditional IRA) as of December 31 of the immediately preceding year by the applicable life-expectancy factor. You can find these factors in IRS Publication 590, "Individual Retirement Arrangements (IRAs)."

If, as permitted under the tax code, you make your first distribution for the year you turn 70½ (or retire) after December 31 of that year and on or before April 1 of the following year, a special rule applies. This rule is illustrated in the following example.

Example: You are unmarried and turn 70½ on February 6, 1998. The balance in your traditional IRA on December 31, 1997, is $100,000. According to the IRS tables, your life expectancy as of your 71st birthday is 15.3 years. Dividing $100,000 by 15.3 years results in a minimum payment for 1998 of about $6,536, which must be paid to you by April 1, 1999. On December 31, 1998, your account balance is $110,000 and, using the recalculation method described below, your life expectancy is 14.6 years. Reducing this by the $6,536 required to be distributed for 1998 on the following April 1, only $103,464 must be considered in determining the required distribution for 1999. The amount you must withdraw for 1999 is $103,464 divided by 14.6 years, or $7,086. You must make this withdrawal of $7,086 by December 31, 1999, in addition to the $6,536 withdrawal required by April 1, 1999.

Thus, two minimum-withdrawal amounts are required in 1999, the first year of required withdrawals. Each year thereafter, a new minimum-withdrawal amount must be calculated and withdrawn by December 31.

Planning under
the minimum-distribution rules

If you take your pension in the form of an annuity, complying with the minimum-distribution rules is ordinarily not a concern. However, if you decide not to take an annuity or a lump-sum distribution, the minimum-distribution rules become more significant. Likewise, the minimum-distribution rules determine the amount you must take from your traditional IRAs each year once you reach 70½.

From the tax standpoint, in these cases, it's generally a good idea to minimize your required annual minimum distribution so that the assets in your qualified plans (and traditional IRAs) can continue to grow on a tax-deferred basis. You can always withdraw more than the required minimum distribution any time you need additional funds.

Determining the smallest minimum distribution you must take depends on two factors: (1) the person (or persons) you select as your designated beneficiary, and (2) the method you use to calculate the applicable life expectancy. By April 1 following the year you turn 70½, you must ordinarily notify your plan trustee or IRA custodian in writing of your designated beneficiary and the method to be used to determine the applicable life expectancy.

If you are married, you will probably want to select your spouse as your designated beneficiary so that the funds in your plans will be available for him or her. The tax code also provides certain tax benefits if you do select your spouse.

Assuming you do select your spouse, you must then determine the applicable life expectancy to use. As a practical matter, while you may choose to compute minimum distributions over your life expectancy, ordinarily you will want to compute them over the joint life expectancy of you and your spouse because this produces a lower annual minimum distribution. You have three choices for determining your joint life expectancy. First, you may use the recalculation method. Unless your plan provides otherwise or you select a different option, your life expectancy and the life expectancy of your spouse will be recalculated annually.

Example 1: On March 1, 1998, you turned 70, and on August 1, 1998, your spouse turned 65. According to the tables provided by the IRS, for purposes of determining the amount of any minimum distribution from your qualified plans or traditional IRAs, your joint life expectancy in 1998 is 23.1 years. You will therefore be required to withdraw the amount in your plan or IRA as of December 31, 1997, in equal increments over that 23.1-year period.

For purposes of determining your minimum distribution for 1999, under the recalculation method, your joint life expectancy will be refigured based on the joint life expectancy of persons 71 and 66 years old. According to the IRS tables, this is 22.2 years. As you can see, using this method, you can never outlive the funds in a qualified plan or IRA. Your life expectancy increases the longer you live. However, use of the recalculation method can produce an undesirable result if your spouse dies before you. In this case, beginning with the year following the year your spouse dies, you can use only your own life expectancy to determine your minimum distribution each year.

Example 2: Same facts as Example 1, except that your spouse dies in 1999. In 2000, you turn 72. According to the IRS tables, your life expectancy is then 14.6 years. Your minimum distribution for 2000 is your account balance as of December 31, 1999, divided by 14.6.

Technically, a similar problem arises if you die before your spouse. However, if your funds are in an IRA, your spouse may choose to treat the IRA as his or her own following your death. To do so, your spouse must roll over the amounts in your IRA into an IRA in his or her name before taking any distributions. In this case, the minimum-distribution rules are applied as if your spouse had originally established the account. Your spouse need not begin taking minimum distributions from the "new" IRA until he or she reaches age 70½. Moreover, as explained below, if your spouse designates a new beneficiary, such as a child or grandchild, the minimum distributions can be stretched out over an extended period that does not end on the death of your spouse.

To avoid the acceleration of distributions if your spouse dies before you, you may choose one of the two remaining methods of computing life expectancies. If you decide to choose one of these methods, be sure to notify the trustee or custodian in writing prior to the deadline. First, you may select the term-certain method. Under this method, the joint life expectancy of you and your spouse is calculated for the year you turn 70½. Each year thereafter, this initial expectancy is reduced by one year.

Example 3: Same facts as Example 1, except that you choose the term-certain method. Your applicable life expectancy for 1999 is 22.1 years (23.1 years initial life expectancy less one year).

The disadvantage of the term-certain method is that either you or your spouse or both of you may outlive your plan benefits. Therefore, you may want to choose the so-called hybrid method. Under this method, you recalculate your life expectancy but not that of your spouse. Consequently, even if your spouse dies before you, the remaining portion of his or her original life expectancy continues to enter into the calculation of your applicable life expectancy each year for an additional number of years. If you select this method, you should refer to IRS Publication 590, "Individual Retirement Arrangements (IRAs)," or seek the assistance of a tax professional to calculate the applicable life expectancy for each year.

What if you select a person other than your spouse as a designated beneficiary? For example, you may provide that following your death, benefits are to be distributed to your children for life. In this case, the joint life expectancy you use cannot last longer than the combined life expectancies of you and the beneficiary with the shortest projected life span (usually the oldest beneficiary). Moreover, where your spouse is not your designated beneficiary, the amount of the minimum distribution you must take each year while you are alive is determined using a hypothetical individual not more than 10 years younger than yourself. Refer to Publication 590, "Individual Retirement Arrangements (IRAs)," for the rules used to calculate your minimum in this instance.

Following your death, however, the rules become more liberal. The 10-year limitation no longer applies, and distributions of amounts in the qualified plan or IRA may be stretched out over many years, yielding significant tax-deferral benefits to your beneficiary. Technically, the applicable life expectancy your beneficiary uses depends on whether you used the recalculation or term-certain method to calculate minimum distributions during your lifetime. For example, if you used the recalculation method, your beneficiary first calculates his or her life expectancy as of the year you turned 70½ and then initially reduces such life expectancy by the number of years you received distributions to determine the applicable life expectancy for purposes of calculating the minimum distribution for the first year after your death. The applicable life expectancy is then reduced one year for each calendar year thereafter.

Example: You have designated your son as the beneficiary of your IRA. In 1999, you reach age 70½. You take your first minimum distribution prior to April 1, 2000, and your second distribution prior to

December 31, 2000, using the recalculation method in each instance. On February 1, 2001, you die. For purposes of calculating the minimum distribution from this IRA for 2001, your son first determines his life expectancy as of 1999, when you turned 70½. If your son was 40 in 1999, his life expectancy was then 42.5 years, according to the IRA tables. This expectancy is then reduced by 2 (the number of years you received distributions) to 40.5 to determine the applicable life expectancy for 2001. For each year thereafter, the applicable life expectancy is reduced by 1. In other words, following your death, your son can continue the IRA for another 40.5 years. Your son must, however, continue to maintain the IRA in your name.

Finally, what if you want to select a designated beneficiary for your plan or IRA other than an individual? As a general rule, it is never advisable to select your estate as your beneficiary. Your estate is not considered a designated beneficiary for tax purposes. If you do select your estate, you will be treated as if you had not selected a beneficiary and will be required to take minimum distributions over your life rather than over the life of yourself and a beneficiary. Furthermore, at your death, the entire remaining balance in the account will have to be distributed to your estate by the end of the year following the year of your death.

In certain cases, trusts are allowed as designated beneficiaries. You will need the assistance of a tax professional in this case to ensure that your selection of a trust does not unnecessarily accelerate distribution from a qualified plan or IRA at your death.

As noted above, you are not required to take minimum distributions from your Roth IRA while you are alive. Following your death, the entire balance in your Roth IRA must be distributed either by the end of the fifth calendar year after the year of your death or over the life expectancy of a designated beneficiary beginning before the end of the calendar year following your death. If your beneficiary is your spouse, he or she may delay distributions until you would have reached 70½ or, as described in the previous section, choose to treat the Roth IRA as his or her own.

How do you want your money?

In choosing a payment option, you have to consider both the nontax and the tax aspects of each payment method.

NONTAX ASPECTS If your plan gives automatic cost-of-living adjustments to retirees or has given ad hoc adjustments in the last five years, you probably should not take a lump sum distribution. Of course, if you choose not to take the lump sum, on the death of the survivor of you and your spouse, your heirs receive no further benefits. If you do take a lump sum, the balance at that time is payable to your beneficiaries, but you would lose out during your lifetimes on any future increases in pension benefits, which could be vital to your financial well-being. If you don't expect any benefit increases in pension benefits, consider the additional following points:

1. If you are married and your plan offers a 100-percent joint-and-survivor annuity that provides an income to your spouse after your death, we recommend that you take it. It is important to provide a continuous income for your spouse after your death, especially if he or she has no independent income. As we have pointed out before, your plan may automatically give you a joint-and-survivor annuity unless your spouse elects in writing to give up the benefit. Be careful, though: The plan may give you a 50-percent joint-and-survivor annuity rather than a 100-percent joint-and-survivor. Though two people can live together more cheaply than each alone, the reduction in living expenses is not 50 percent.

2. Compare the annual investment return you receive under a 100-percent joint-and-survivor plan with the annual return you receive by investing a lump-sum distribution. The return under the annuity is the amount the lump sum would have to earn to fund the annual annuity payment, assuming the lump sum and earnings thereon were paid out over the life expectancy of you and your spouse. Determine what you can earn on the lump sum, and choose that option if it will give you a larger return.

3. Don't choose a joint-and-survivor annuity if your spouse is in ill health and has only a short time to live.

4. Don't be tempted to give up a joint-and-survivor annuity in favor of a life-insurance policy. In Chapter 5, we point out that life-insurance agents often try to persuade prospective retirees to give up a joint-and-survivor annuity and buy life insurance instead. That's usually not a good idea.

5. Consider taking a lump-sum payout if your plan offers only a 50-percent joint-and-survivor annuity. The 50-percent plan may give your spouse too little to live on, and you may do better investing the lump sum and allowing your spouse to live off the income. Work through several calculations to make sure that your spouse will do better under the lump-sum option.

6. Consider your personality and possible propensity to spend a lump sum. If you feel you may quickly use up your pension distribution, then an annuity is a better option for you. With most annuity options, you will have money coming in on a regular basis for the rest of your life.

TAX CONSIDERATIONS You also must give some thought to the tax treatment of various distribution options from qualified plans.

If you choose a lump sum, you may roll it over into a traditional IRA and defer taxes on the lump sum (and subsequent earnings on that amount) until you reach age 70½, when you must begin withdrawing a minimum amount each year. As discussed on pages 68-70, the entire amount you then withdraw each year is ordinarily taxable when withdrawn. If you choose the rollover option, you have only 60 days from the time you get your distribution to complete the rollover process. Any pension proceeds you have failed to roll over are fully taxable.

Lump-sum payments from a qualified plan are subject to a federal withholding tax of 20 percent. The plan trustee must deduct this 20-percent tax from any distributions you might roll over unless you ask the plan trustee to make payment directly to the custodian of your IRA (or the trustee of another qualified plan). If a distribution check is made payable to you, the tax will be withheld even if you indicate that you intend to roll over the distribution.

If you roll over only the 80 percent of the distribution you actually receive by check, you will be required to include the 20 percent withheld in your income. If you wish to roll over an amount equal to your entire distribution, you will have to dig into your pocket for the other 20 percent and contribute it to your IRA (or the new qualified plan) within 60 days of your receipt of the distribution check. To avoid this problem, have your plan trustee make payment directly to the custodian of your IRA (or new plan).

If you choose a lump sum and elect not to roll it over into an IRA, consider the various tax treatments we have described previously in this chapter. Remember, if you were born after 1935, you will no longer be eligible to use forward averaging after 1999. Moreover, you can use forward averaging only once in your lifetime. If, for example, you are eligible to pay taxes on a lump-sum distribution you receive in 1998 using 10-year averaging, you cannot use it again when you withdraw the balance from another qualified plan a few years later. It makes no sense to roll your pension money into an IRA and then withdraw the money as a lump sum. Forward averaging may not be used for IRA distributions.

We recommend that you figure the present value of a stream of income after taxes under each arrangement and see which way you come out best. If you can't make the calculations yourself, get help from your employer's benefits administrator or a tax adviser. The following illustrates some tax comparisons among various options:

1. You retire on January 1, 1999, when you turn 65. You receive a lump-sum distribution of $125,000. You made no nondeductible contributions to the plan. You are considering either taking the lump sum and paying all the taxes that are due using 10-year averaging or taking the money and rolling it over into an IRA.

If you choose to take a lump sum and pay the taxes, 10-year averaging will reduce the tax on the amount you receive as if you had earned the $125,000 over a period of 10 years. After you make the calculation using IRS Form 4972, the taxes on your distribution amount to $19,183. Subtracting this sum from the $125,000 lump sum results in $105,817, the present value of your distribution after taxes. (We have not considered state income taxes in this calculation.)

Now consider a rollover to a traditional IRA. Assuming you don't need the money in your IRA for living expenses, you can let it earn interest inside an IRA for another six years and three months— until April 1 following 2004, the year when you turn 70½. If you earn 7 percent on your IRA, it grows to about $188,000 by December 31, 2004. At that point, you must begin withdrawing your money, although the withdrawal for the first year, 2004, is not due until April 1, 2005. Assuming the remainder of your funds continue to earn 7 percent and you withdraw money in level annual installments over your life expectancy of 16 years (according to the IRS tables), you have an annuity of $18,558. Assuming you are in the 28-percent tax bracket (again, ignoring state taxes), your annual income after taxes comes to $13,362. The present value on your retirement date of this stream of income that begins in 2005 is about $113,000.

As you can see in this example, you are better off rolling over the distribution, as far as taxes are concerned. However, whether or not you come out best tax-wise depends on the amount of your pension, tax bracket, life expectancy, and your assumptions of how much your money can earn inside the IRA.

2. Now compare a lump-sum payment of $125,000 with an immediate life annuity from your company pension plan. Again, choosing a lump sum with 10-year forward averaging, you'll have

$105,817 after paying taxes. If you choose the life annuity, the monthly amount you receive will be based on factors specified in the plan document. Whether this option is better or worse than a lump sum depends on what those factors are and how long you actually live.

Another alternative is to choose the lump sum if you think you can invest it profitably at a higher rate. You could also receive a lump-sum distribution and roll it over into an individual retirement annuity, providing a lifetime income. There is no tax on the rollover, but the monthly annuity payments are taxable as they are received, and this may give a higher monthly life annuity than your company's plan (see Chapter 4).

HOW SAFE IS YOUR PENSION?

In recent years, some financially strapped companies have discarded a number of financial benefits for their workers, including pension plans. If a company decides to terminate its pension arrangements and has enough assets to pay the benefits promised, the federal government allows the company to end the plan. The company then provides for the benefits by giving employees a lump-sum payment upon retirement or by buying annuities from life-insurance companies equal in value to the employee's accrued benefit.

If your employer is in this group, you and your fellow workers should investigate the insurance company that your employer is using. It may have chosen a carrier that is financially unstable or one that puts its money in high-risk investments, such as junk bonds. You may, in the end, have little say in your employer's decision. But you should at least check the insurance company's ratings from Moody's, Standard & Poor's, and A. M. Best and make your feelings known to your plan administrator.

If your employer terminates a pension plan and has insufficient assets to pay all the promised benefits, then it's up to the federal government to make sure workers get their benefits. The government also gets involved if your employer goes into liquidation or bankruptcy reorganization. Sometimes the government's pension agency, the Pension Benefit Guaranty Corporation (PBGC), makes its own determination that an employer and its pension plan are in bad financial shape. Sometimes, the PBGC even initiates a plan termination.

Most tax-qualified defined-benefit plans set up by private corporations are insured by the Pension Benefit Guaranty Corporation, which was set up in 1974 to protect workers' pensions. Your money in defined-contribution plans, and money in some defined-benefit plans established by state and local governments, church and fraternal organizations, and professional organizations, is not protected by the PBGC.

If a pension plan insured by the PBGC cannot pay vested benefits to workers, the agency becomes the trustee of the plan and continues to pay pension benefits up to a maximum specified by the law. In 1998, the agency was allowed to pay up to $2,880.68 each month to a worker in a single-employer plan who retired at the plan's normal retirement age. For workers in multiemployer plans, the maximum limit is lower. The maximum limit is smaller still for benefits to workers who retired early or who took their benefits in a form other than a life annuity.

The agency also pays survivors' benefits. If a surviving spouse is receiving benefits before a pension plan is terminated, the PBGC will continue to pay them. If a plan ends before a worker has reached the plan's normal retirement age and the worker dies, the agency will pay the surviving spouse's benefits.

If your pension plan terminates, your plan administrator must notify you in writing at least 60 days beforehand. If your employer is terminating the plan and has enough assets to pay benefits, you will receive a second notice that tells you the amount of the benefit, how it has been valued, and the assumptions used in the calculation. If the company has purchased an annuity from a life-insurance company, be sure you receive a certificate from the carrier.

If your plan has insufficient assets to pay benefits and the PBGC takes over the plan, it must notify you of this action. The PBGC keeps records of plan participants and their benefits. If you are about to receive retirement benefits, the PBGC pays them directly to you.

A·N·N·U·I·T·I·E·S

ANNUITIES SERVE MANY PURPOSES. THEY can act as investment vehicles, allowing you to continue saving money and taxes at the same time. Or they can provide you with a guaranteed income each month for the rest of your life. You might even have an annuity that does both. Some annuities are deferred; others give you immediate payment.

An *immediate* annuity begins to pay off as soon as you invest in it. You can set up such an annuity at retirement either by investing your accumulated savings or by electing to have your company's pension benefits paid to you as a lifetime stream of income. The advantage of such an annuity is that you can never outlive your money.

A *deferred* annuity is one that you invest in now and draw on later. You can buy a deferred annuity by investing a lump-sum payment or by making periodic payments. Later, you can convert that money into an income stream. Deferred annuities have two phases—an *accumulation* phase, during which you save money at a stated rate of interest, and a *payout* phase, when the insurance company in which you have invested your money returns your accumulation in the form of monthly or yearly payments. You don't have to take your payment from the insurance company where you saved your money. You can shop around for a company that offers the highest payout and most favorable terms. This chapter will tell you how to do that.

THE ACCUMULATION PHASE

The main factors affecting the value of an annuity between the time you pay the premium and the time you start getting something back are (1) the interest rate, (2) the terms governing your ability to cash in the policy, and (3) administrative charges.

INTEREST RATE Each month or so, an insurance company declares the interest rate it will credit on new annuity contracts, a rate determined primarily by the investment opportunities the company has for new money coming in. This rate is called the current rate. In mid-1998, these rates were in the 5½-percent range.

The current rate is usually good for an initial guarantee period. Some policies let you choose one of several guarantee periods, ranging from one to as many as 10 years. Some annuities offer higher rates if you choose a longer guarantee period. Once a guarantee period is over, companies offer a new current rate good for the next period, which may be shorter or longer than the period you first selected.

Although you don't know at the start of one period what rate will be declared for the next period, there is a contractual minimum rate, which may also vary over the life of the annuity. An annuity contract might specify, for example, a minimum of 5 percent for the first 10 years and a minimum of 3 percent after that.

A few companies credit your money with a certain interest rate during the accumulation phase but actually pay those rates only if you convert to the payout phase of the contract. If you take your money in a lump sum rather than annuitize the accumulation phase, the company recomputes your earnings using a lower rate.

In recent years, insurance companies have promoted annuities by touting a high current rate. Don't buy merely on the basis of that high rate, and don't ignore the other elements of the contract.

CASHING IN YOUR POLICY Sellers promote annuities by emphasizing their total accumulated value to prospective buyers after five, 10, 15, and 20 years. But in many cases, you can't cash in your annuity and receive that particular sum. You receive instead the *cash surrender value*, your total accumulation after the insurance company deducts surrender charges.

The surrender charge, designed to discourage you from cashing in your contract before the company has recouped its expenses, is usually expressed as a percentage of the accumulation value. A few annuities express surrender charges as a percentage of the premium. That's a more favorable arrangement, since policyholders who cash in the annuity pay a penalty only on the original investment, not on the interest earnings.

Usually, surrender charges are high if you cash in early, but they decline over time and disappear after seven or eight years. Typical surrender charges start at 6 percent of the accumulation value and disappear by the seventh or ninth year. Some charges may be much higher and last much longer. Surrender charges can be important if you have recently bought an annuity but sudden poor health forces you to take early retirement and you need the money for immediate living expenses. Many annuities waive the surrender charge if you take a distribution as an annuity rather than a lump sum.

Obviously, a surrender charge that's glued to an annuity for the entire accumulation phase is more onerous than one that decreases after seven or eight years. For example, one that remains level at 7 percent for seven years is less desirable than one that starts out at 7 percent, tapers off, and disappears in the eighth year.

Some plans guarantee that you won't lose any principal if you cash in early. In effect, they promise that the surrender charge will not exceed the interest you've earned. That's helpful to those who must cash in soon after investing in an annuity.

All companies waive surrender charges if the annuitant dies. Beneficiaries receive the entire accumulation value. (If the person actually owning the annuity is different from the person named as the annuitant, surrender charges are not waived.)

ADMINISTRATIVE CHARGES Some companies deduct annual administrative charges, usually $12 to $30, from your accumulation value. These charges often apply only to small accounts, such as those less than $10,000, and effectively reduce the accumulation value. A $25 charge equals a one-quarter of one percentage point reduction in the interest rate on a $10,000 accumulation. Other companies forgo an administrative charge but offer lower rates on small accounts, which has a similar effect.

READING THE FINE PRINT A number of other contract clauses can affect the size of your accumulation.

• Market-value adjustment. When interest rates fall, the market value of the insurance company's assets (usually bonds) rises. If you cash in during a period when the surrender charge is in effect and rates are down, the company increases your accumulation value; in effect, it shares the gain on its assets with you. Even though you would have to pay applicable surrender charges, the market-value adjustment in this case produces a higher cash-surrender value. Conversely, when interest rates rise, the value of the company's assets goes down, and you share in the loss if you surrender early.

In theory, a market-value adjustment should give an insurance company more flexibility to invest for higher returns, and thus credit higher rates to policyholders, producing higher accumulations over the years. In practice, other factors have a greater influence on an annuity's performance.

• Persistency bonus. If you keep your annuity for a certain number of years, the company adds a specified amount to the annuity's accumulation value. This might be 5 or 10 percent of the premium. That percentage might increase as the years go on. Some companies entice you to stay by offering higher rates at the beginning of each new guarantee period. These rates are higher than those companies offer new customers.

PARTIAL WITHDRAWALS   Annuities are not meant to be sources of ready cash. For that reason, you can't borrow tax-free against your accumulation value if your annuity is "nonqualified" (a commercial annuity that you have purchased with after-tax dollars from an insurance company). Contributions to a qualified annuity, such as a tax-sheltered annuity (TSA) or other annuity distributed by a qualified plan, ordinarily have not been taxed, and you may borrow against your accumulation in these types of accounts.

Most companies do allow "free" partial withdrawals from nonqualified annuities—that is, you can take part of your money without paying a surrender charge. The free-withdrawal provision doesn't mean you can use an annuity as a checking account, though. Insurance companies limit either the number of withdrawals or the minimum size of a withdrawal. Some companies also impose a charge, usually $25, on partial withdrawals. Most contracts allow you to withdraw up to 10 percent of your accumulated value without incurring a surrender charge. Some contracts offer cumulative free withdrawals, which can aggregate up to 50 percent of the contract's value.

Sometimes the free-withdrawal provision applies only to the first withdrawal you make in any year. A company might apply a surrender charge to a second withdrawal even though the total for the year does not equal 10 percent of the accumulation value.

THE PAYOUT PHASE

For people about to retire, the *payout* phase is the most important aspect of a deferred annuity.

When you're ready to cash in your annuity, usually at age 65 to 70, you can withdraw the accumulated value in a lump sum or in monthly payments as lifetime income. The lump sum is yours to invest, spend, or pass on to your heirs. But monthly annuity payments are usually higher than the income you could earn by investing a lump sum yourself. They may even be higher than the amounts you could receive if you arranged your investment so that you drew both interest and some principal in the expectation you won't live very long (see *Table 8*, How Long Will $100,000 Last?, on page 88).

By turning all or a portion of the accumulated value into monthly payments for life, or *annuitizing*, you strike an irrevocable bargain with the insurance company. You no longer have the money to do with as you please, but you also have the security of knowing that you cannot outlive the payments.

You can annuitize your accumulation from a deferred annuity into a lifetime income stream from the same company, or you can take your accumulation in a lump sum and go to another company and buy an immediate annuity. In either case, insurance actuaries compute the size of the monthly annuity payment by applying a settlement-option rate, expressed as dollars of monthly income per thousand dollars of accumulated value. Settlement-option rates depend on how long the actuary believes the company will be making payments to you and on the company's forecast of how well it can invest the money during that period.

The actuary figures two settlement-option rates. One, called the guaranteed settlement-option rate, is spelled out in every deferred-annuity contract and represents a minimum. The other, called the current settlement-option rate, is not written into the contract, but it will apply when the time comes to annuitize your accumulation if it's higher than the guaranteed rate written into the contract. In recent years, companies' current settlement-option rates have been much higher than the guaranteed rates.

The difference between the current and the guaranteed settlement-option rates can be substantial. In recent years, a typical current settlement-option rate for a 65-year-old man who took a life annuity

TABLE 8 .   HOW LONG WILL $100,000 LAST?

▶ *Example of how annuity and investment options compare*

	Monthly payment	When money runs out	Probability of outliving the money	Estate left if man died at					
				Age 67	Age 70	Age 75	Age 80	Age 85	Age 90
Annuity options									
LIFE ONLY	$742	NEVER	0%	0	0	0	0	0	0
LIFE WITH 10 YEAR CERTAIN	704	NEVER	0	$94,191	$84,139	0	0	0	0
Investment options									
INTEREST ONLY	447	NEVER	0	100,000	100,000	$100,000	$100,000	$100,000	$100,000
INTEREST + SOME PRINCIPAL	529	AGE 100	3	97,932	94,383	87,041	77,446	64,906	48,516
INTEREST + SOME PRINCIPAL	560	AGE 95	11	97,148	92,255	82,132	68,902	51,611	29,012
INTEREST + SOME PRINCIPAL	607	AGE 90	26	95,960	89,028	74,689	55,948	31,454	0
INTEREST + SOME PRINCIPAL	681	AGE 85	45	94,090	83,949	62,970	35,552	0	0
INTEREST + SOME PRINCIPAL	810	AGE 80	65	90,829	75,094	45,542	0	0	0
INTEREST + SOME PRINCIPAL	1,079	AGE 75	81	84,030	56,628	0	0	0	0

Chance of outliving from 1983 Individual Mortality Table. Annuities are: life annuity, life annuity with 10-year period certain option. Interest rate assumed for investment options: 5.5 percent.

was about $7.40 a month per $1,000 of accumulated value. A typical guaranteed rate found in many newly issued deferred-annuity contracts was about $5.85 a month per $1,000. On a $100,000 accumulation, that works out to a lifetime income of $8,900 a year at current rates, compared with $7,000 annually at guaranteed rates.

Just as the typical current and guaranteed settlement rates vary widely, so do the rates offered on any given day vary from one company to the next. Obviously, it pays to shop carefully for settlement-option rates. Note, however, that companies usually offer a better settlement rate to policyholders converting from the accumulation phase of a contract than to people buying an immediate annuity with money that they've saved elsewhere. That's meant to discourage shopping. Nevertheless, some companies specialize in immediate annuities and offer high monthly payments on your accumulation.

The longer a company figures it must pay benefits, the lower each payment is. Thus, for the same accumulated value, the payments for a 60-year-old just beginning to annuitize are lower than for a 70-year-old. Payments to a woman beginning to receive an income stream are lower than for a man of the same age, since women live longer. For example, one company recently offered 65-year-old men an annuity rate of $7.42 for each $1,000 of accumulated value. It offered women the same age a rate of only $6.68. Some companies have unisex rates; that is, the settlement-option rate for men and women is the same. If you're annuitizing from a qualified plan, the company must use unisex rates. If the plan is nonqualified, the company usually uses sex-distinct rates.

PAYOUT OPTIONS When it comes time to annuitize your accumulation, you are in effect placing a bet with an insurance company. You are betting that you'll live long enough to receive the value of your accumulation in the form of monthly or yearly payments. The insurance company is betting that you won't.

These are your payments options:

• Life annuity. With a life annuity, you receive payments for the rest of your life. When you die, the payments stop and your heirs receive nothing. A life annuity provides you with the most monthly income.

Example: A 65-year-old man annuitizing $100,000 would receive around $740 a month, or $8,880 a year, if the company paid an interest rate of about 5.9 percent.

• Life annuity with periods certain. Under this arrangement, the company agrees to make your monthly payments for the rest of your life. But if you die within a certain period, usually in five or 10 years, your heirs continue to receive your payments until the specified periods end. Monthly payments for a life annuity with a 10-year period certain, for example, are generally 5 to 10 percent lower than for a life annuity.

Example: The same man converting a $100,000 accumulation into an annuity with a 10-year period certain from the same company at the same interest rate would receive around $704 each month. If he died within 10 years of taking the annuity, his beneficiary would receive the balance of the payments through the tenth year. If he chose a life annuity with a five-year period certain, his monthly payment would be around $732.

• Joint-and-survivor annuity. This annuity is written on both your life and the life of another person, such as your spouse. Full payments are made so long as you and the joint annuitant are alive. When one annuitant dies, the insurance company reduces the amount of the payments by one-third or one-half (depending on the option you choose) and continues to make reduced payments to the survivor until he or she dies. You can also elect a 100-percent joint-and-survivor option in which your survivor receives your full benefit. As we note in Chapter 3, this type of joint-and-survivor annuity is different from the ones available from your company pension. In those arrangements, payment is made to a survivor when the retiree dies.

The amount of the payment under a joint-and-survivor annuity may be dramatically or only slightly lower than the monthly payment under a life annuity, depending on the ages and sexes of the two annuitants. If the other annuitant is older than you or close to your age, the initial payment may not be much different from the payments under a life annuity on your life alone. If the other annuitant is much younger, the monthly payments will be considerably lower.

Example: A 65-year-old man annuitizes $100,000. If he chooses a two-thirds joint-and-survivor annuity for himself and his 64-year-old wife, his monthly payment will be around $558 if the company pays an interest rate of about 5.85 percent. When either he or his wife dies, the insurance company reduces the monthly payment to around $372. When the second spouse dies, payments stop. With a 50-percent joint-and-survivor annuity, the same man receives $695 a month. When either he or his wife dies, the company lowers the payment to about $348.

The advantages and disadvantages of joint-and-survivor options are obvious. You receive less money while you are alive, but when you die, your spouse has a guaranteed income. If your spouse would otherwise have to live only on income from Social Security, a joint-and-survivor annuity is a desirable option. It's important to calculate carefully how much income you both will need to live and how much your spouse will need after you're gone. The larger the payment to a spouse, the lower your payments during retirement. You might also consider an annuity with a period certain as a way to have more money during retirement but still provide for your spouse if you should die within 10 years. This option is appropriate if both you and your spouse are in the later years of your retirement.

OTHER WAYS TO GET YOUR MONEY These include:

• Systematic withdrawals. Systematic withdrawals give you a periodic income from the money you've accumulated in your annuity without annuitization and without incurring a surrender charge. Withdrawals typically take three forms: a monthly withdrawal of earned interest; a flat dollar amount withdrawn on a periodic basis regardless of the amount of interest earned; and an amount withdrawn based on life expectancy. In a systematic-withdrawal plan, the insurance company calculates a monthly payment based on your life expectancy, sex, and the amount of money in your account. This arrangement allows you to obtain the money saved through a deferred annuity without actually annuitizing your accumulation. The money remaining in your account continues to earn income, tax-deferred, at a rate of interest determined by the insurance company.

Systematic withdrawals have several advantages. Because the annual income from the annuity is less than what it would be under other payout options, you save income taxes (part of your accumulation is taxable when you begin to take monthly payments). Withdrawals are also attractive to people who need a monthly income but still wish to leave money to their children. If you later decide to annuitize the remaining accumulation, most insurance companies let you do that. (Income is based on a recalculation of your life expectancy, based on IRS mortality tables.) Many insurers also give you a choice of systematic-withdrawal options that allow you to tailor payments to your needs.

Example: A man turning 65 in 1998 began to take systematic withdrawals from his $100,000 accumulation. He could take those payments in one of two ways (see Tables 8 and 9 on pages 88 and 93). Under one arrangement, he would receive a monthly payment of $416.67; under the other, he would receive $660.97 each month. Under the first plan, his monthly payments continue until he is 85 and rise to $645.16. With the second, the payments decline through the years until, when he reaches 85, they have dropped to $421.63 a month. If he takes a life annuity, he'll receive $742 a month and somewhat less if he takes other annuity options (see Table 8 on page 88).

With a life annuity, the monthly payment is fixed until you die. But with systematic withdrawals, annual payments can increase or decrease depending on how much the fund grows and on IRS rules. As we explain in Chapter 3, in the case of a qualified plan (including a qualified annuity), on or before April 1 following the calendar year you turn 70½, you must begin withdrawing a minimum amount each year based on your life expectancy or the life expectancy of you and your beneficiary. (The IRS imposes no such requirement if you withdraw money from a nonqualified annuity.) The size of your accumulation also changes as you withdraw money and earn an investment return. As a result, your payments may go up or down each year.

Suppose, for example, you want to retire at 55 but must tap your savings for living expenses. You might want systematic withdrawals that let you take larger monthly payments when you first retire and lower ones when you begin receiving Social Security benefits. In this case, you must also consider whether your proposed systematic withdrawals will be exempt from the 10-percent penalty tax on withdrawals prior to age 59½. (See next section.)

Or suppose you decide to retire at 70 but don't need the money in your annuity right away. In that case, you might prefer a plan that lets you withdraw smaller amounts in the early years and larger ones later to pay any medical or nursing-home expenses.

Systematic withdrawals can also be calculated for joint lives. As with the joint-and-survivor options, monthly payments are lower. When you die, payments continue to your spouse as long as he or she lives. When your spouse dies, money remaining in the account becomes part of his or her estate. If payments are to be made only to you, any money in your account passes to your estate when you die.

The following tables show different types of systematic withdrawals. Both tables assume a person retiring at age 65 who has a $100,000 accumulation on which to base withdrawals. Table 9 illustrates lower annual payments in the early years of retirement and higher ones in the later years. Table 10 shows higher payments early and lower ones later. Both arrangements assume the company will credit a 5.5-percent rate on funds remaining in the account.

    • Lump-sum payments. At the end of the accumulation phase of an annuity contract, you can take the money as a lump sum, invest it,

TABLE 9 • FIGURING ANNUITY INCOME: SYSTEMATIC WITHDRAWALS WITH MINIMUM PAYMENTS

Age	Projected monthly payment	Cumulative payment	Accumulation value
65	$416.60	$5,000.00	$100,353.66
66	434.29	10,211.44	100,507.06
67	453.86	15,657.78	100,427.03
68	474.11	21,347.15	100,092.36
69	495.04	27,287.57	99,480.77
70	516.61	33,486.90	98,568.96
71	535.30	39,910.45	97,376.14
72	554.17	46,560.51	95,884.48
73	573.16	53,438.46	94,076.11
74	592.18	60,544.56	91,933.38
75	611.09	67,877.69	89,439.03
76	624.49	75,371.56	86,641.99
77	642.77	83,084.79	83,465.24
78	654.25	90,935.80	79,971.89
79	664.48	98,909.56	76,160.02
80	666.11	106,902.92	72,118.32
81	673.29	114,982.37	67,765.68
82	670.31	123,026.08	63,210.45
83	664.82	131,003.96	58,472.46
84	656.54	138,882.50	53,576.17
85	645.16	146,624.41	48,551.26

First withdrawal is one month after policy is issued. Interest rate of 5.5 percent assumed. Source: Jackson National Life Insurance Co.

possibly at high rates that carry some risk, and try to live on the interest alone, leaving the principal to your heirs. You gamble, of course, that you'll die before the money is used up. If, on the other hand, you choose an annuity-payout option, you can never outlive your money.

Table 8 shows a number of ways a 65-year-old man in good

TABLE 10 · FIGURING ANNUITY INCOME: SYSTEMATIC WITHDRAWALS WITH MAXIMUM PAYMENTS

Age	Projected monthly payment	Cumulative payment	Accumulation value
65	$660.97	$7,931.69	$97,336.16
66	656.46	15,809.24	94,578.39
67	653.80	23,654.84	91,701.84
68	650.89	31,465.50	88,703.06
69	647.70	39,237.95	85,578.69
70	644.22	46,968.63	82,325.48
71	637.70	54,621.07	78,973.92
72	630.73	62,189.82	75,524.19
73	623.26	69,668.94	71,977.01
74	615.26	77,052.10	68,333.64
75	606.66	84,331.96	64,596.06
76	593.83	91,457.89	60,811.50
77	584.07	98,466.72	56,939.37
78	569.51	105,300.86	53,034.15
79	554.13	111,950.44	49,104.17
80	533.51	118,352.56	45,212.84
81	516.67	124,552.62	41,315.55
82	494.10	130,481.76	37,482.85
83	470.75	136,130.77	33,727.82
84	446.61	141,490.03	30,064.58
85	421.63	146,549.58	26,508.48

First withdrawal is one month after policy is issued. Interest rate of 5.5 percent assumed.
Source: Jackson National Life Insurance

health might deal with a $100,000 accumulation. If this man chooses a life annuity, he receives $742 a month for life, but none of the accumulation passes to his heirs. A life annuity with a 10-year period certain provides $704 per month, but leaves something over if he dies before reaching age 75.

If he takes the accumulation and lives on the interest alone, he has only $447 a month for life, assuming a 5.5-percent effective annual interest rate earned on safe investments, such as certificates of deposit. But the entire nest egg passes to his heirs.

To increase the monthly payment to himself, he has to draw on the principal. The table shows how long the money lasts at increasingly larger monthly payment amounts, what the chances are of outliving the money under each assumption, and how much of an estate remains as time passes.

If a woman takes a life annuity or a life annuity with a 10-year period certain, her monthly payments are smaller. If she chooses to withdraw only interest and principal, the chances of outliving her money are greater.

Example: A 65-year-old woman buys a life annuity from one company. Her monthly payment is $668. If she buys a life annuity with a 10-year period certain, she has $650 a month. If she "annuitizes" on her own, withdrawing interest and principal, her chances of outliving her money at age 80 are 50 percent. At age 90, her chances are 78 percent.

• Split-funding techniques. You can take a sum of money and divide it into two annuities—an immediate annuity to provide an income stream and a deferred annuity that continues to grow at some rate of interest, tax-deferred. This arrangement may be useful for people taking early retirement.

Example: You decide to retire at age 55, too early for Social Security benefits. But for the next 10 years, you need additional income to supplement your company pension. If you have saved $100,000, for example, you can take around $39,000 of that sum and buy an immediate annuity with a 10-year period certain, which will provide about $402 each month or more than $4,800 a year, assuming a 5.75-percent rate. The remaining $61,000 can be invested in a deferred annuity. When you turn 65, you can annuitize the new accumulation, which will have grown back to $100,000 based on an interest rate of 5 percent. This can in turn supplement your Social Security benefits.

HOW ANNUITIES ARE TAXED

If you annuitize from a qualified annuity (an annuity on which you already took some tax reduction, such as an IRA or Keogh account), your monthly payments are fully taxable. But if you annuitize from a nonqualified plan, only a part of your payments are taxable. With these plans, the IRS considers part of your monthly payment a return of principal and the other part a return of interest earnings. You pay taxes only on the interest. You don't have to figure the interest yourself—the insurance company sends a statement showing what percentage of each annuity payment can be excluded from income.

In estimating your tax bill (see Chapter 6), be sure to include the taxable portion of any annuity income. A word of warning: Once you have recovered all of your principal, your entire monthly payment is considered interest and is fully taxable for the rest of your life. When you are shopping for annuities, ask the agent for an estimate of your yearly tax.

If your spouse is the beneficiary of your annuity or will be the new owner of the policy upon your death, the IRS taxes the proceeds the same way as when you were alive. If you have named a child or someone else as the owner or beneficiary, the IRS requires that he or she take the proceeds from the annuity within five years of your death. Otherwise, the amounts not withdrawn are subject to a penalty. At the time of your death, the value of the annuity is usually included in your estate and is subject to federal and state estate taxes.

PENALTIES If you withdraw your money before age 59½, the IRS imposes, in addition to income taxes, a 10-percent penalty tax on the amount by which the value of the annuity exceeds the premium that you paid in. This rule assumes that the annuity is nonqualified. For qualified annuities, the entire amount withdrawn is taxed, as we've noted.

There are, however, exceptions for both qualified and nonqualified annuities. If you choose a systematic withdrawal and meet certain conditions, you may be able to avoid IRS penalties. For example, once payments begin, they must continue for at least five years and until you turn 59½. Payments must be based on your age on your birthday nearest the first withdrawal. This rule, which is applicable only to qualified plans, requires the insurance company to recalculate the amount withdrawn every year until you reach 70½. Payments must be based on your account values on December 31 of the year preceding the date of the withdrawal. That means you cannot split the annuity accumulation among several investments unless you plan to take comparable, systematic withdrawals from all investments. If you are annuitizing from a nonqualified plan, your payments can remain level, since there is no requirement that you begin withdrawing money at age 70½.

If you fund your payments with money saved in a qualified plan, the IRS imposes a penalty each year of 50 percent of the difference between the amount you should have taken for that year and the amount you took for that year if you don't withdraw the minimum amount required beginning April 1 following the year you turn 70½. This penalty is similar to the one described in Chapter 3 for failing to withdraw money from an IRA or a Keogh account. If you stay on the job, you don't have to take distributions from a tax-qualified plan until you're 75.

If you take a partial withdrawal from a nonqualified annuity purchased after 1982, the IRS considers that you withdrew all interest before any principal and taxes you accordingly. If your withdrawal exceeds your total interest earnings, you are taxed only on the interest, not on the principal.

Example: Your $10,000 annuity has grown to $15,000. If you withdraw $5,000, the IRS treats that $5,000 as interest subject to taxes. But if you withdraw $6,000, you are taxed on only the $5,000 that's considered interest. (Different rules apply to annuities funded before 1982. Check with your tax adviser.)

VARIABLE ANNUITIES

So far, we have described only fixed annuities. During the accumulation phase, your money grows at a specified rate of interest determined by the insurance company. During the payout phase, your monthly payment is also fixed; the insurance company calculates the settlement-option rate, and your payments never change. This can be a major drawback if inflation increases significantly. With a *variable* annuity, however, neither the rate of interest during the accumulation phase nor the monthly payment during the payout phase is fixed.

During the accumulation phase of a variable annuity, the insurance company usually gives you a choice of one or more stock, bond, or money-market funds in which to invest your money. The amount in your account rises or falls depending on the fortunes of the fund you select. Many annuities also offer a fixed-account option, which provides about the same rates as a fixed-dollar annuity. You can divide your money among the various investment options, and you can usually switch investments every 30 days.

Investing in a variable annuity is very much like investing in mutual funds outside an annuity. You assume the same market risks as any investor. But there are important differences. Because the investments are inside an annuity "wrapper," there is no tax on any dividends, interest, or capital gains until you withdraw your funds. As with any annuity, there's a 10-percent penalty tax on any withdrawal made before age 59½. This tax advantage is partly offset by fees that range anywhere from 1.5 to 2.5 percent of your fund's assets each year and by surrender charges discussed previously.

Though you have the flexibility to allocate your money among several types of investments inside the annuity, the number of funds may be limited. When investing outside an annuity, you may choose among hundreds of stock, bond, and money-market funds, most with no sales fees.

At the end of the accumulation phase of a variable annuity, you have the same options as with a fixed-dollar arrangement. You may withdraw the accumulated value or convert to a guaranteed monthly pension for life. You may also opt for a variable payout—a monthly pension whose size can vary from month to month according to investment results.

With variable monthly payments, you cannot predict your income. Some months, your income will go up; other months, it may go down, depending on the performance of the funds you select. Therefore, choosing a variable payment is a gamble. If you do decide to play the odds, it helps to know how a variable payment is figured.

With a fixed annuity, you receive a certain number of dollars each month. With a variable annuity, you receive the value of a fixed number of annuity units. The value of those units fluctuates according to the performance of the underlying investments. To calculate the number of units you will receive, the insurance company uses what is known as the assumed interest rate, or AIR. Using the assumed interest rate and a mortality table, the company computes a net single premium for an annuity that would be paid if the underlying funds earned exactly the AIR. The company then divides your account value on the day you annuitize your accumulation by the net single premium. The result is the number of annuity units you will have during your retirement.

The value of those annuity units fluctuates monthly as the investments in the funds you selected change. If the net earnings of those funds is greater than the AIR, the value of each unit rises to reflect the excess earnings. If the funds earn a rate less than the AIR, the value of your annuity units goes down.

Shop carefully for a variable-annuity payout. Don't automatically take the plan from the company offering the highest AIR. *Example:* One company is offering an AIR of 6 percent, and another offers an AIR of 4 percent. At the beginning, the higher AIR will pay higher monthly payments. But if you live a long time, the 4-percent AIR will produce higher payments in the end. That's because changes in the annuity unit values reflect the differences between the interest rate the funds assumed and the rate they actually earned. Since there's no way to know when you'll die, your choice is between smaller payments in the early years, when you may have other sources of income, or smaller payments in the later years, when you may have high medical expenses.

In choosing an immediate annuity with a variable payout, be sure to compare annuities at the same AIR. Ask the agents to show you illustrations using the same assumed interest rate. Of course, your monthly payments will be smaller from companies with higher mortality and expense charges.

INDEXED ANNUITIES

This is a relatively new product that offers the safety of a fixed annuity while providing growth potential through participation in a portion of the gains of a selected stock-market index, usually the Standard & Poor's 500. With these arrangements, your principal is guaranteed to grow at least 3 percent a year, but it can go much higher, depending on the stock-index performance. *Example:* Suppose a person deposited $100,000 and chose an annuity period for nine years. At the end of the period, he or she would be guaranteed a return of $130,477. If the stock market (and the index) declined during that time, the person would always receive that sum. However, if the index grew by 10 percent, the person would have accumulated $235,468.

If you want to be conservative with your money in retirement, an indexed annuity might be a good compromise between safety and capital appreciation. If CDs are yielding in the 5-percent range, you would give up about 2 percent of your return in exchange for the unlimited potential return from the stock market.

You may also be able to buy an indexed immediate annuity, which guarantees a monthly income slightly below what a traditional immediate annuity would pay. If the index value increases by more than the guaranteed interest rate, your monthly income increases. *Example:* A 65-year-old man choosing a traditional life and 10-year certain immediate annuity would get a fixed monthly income of $704. But if the S&P 500 Index increased 10 percent a year, his monthly income would be $765 in the tenth year. Although the monthly income would go up and down over the years, it would never drop below $684.

How safe is your annuity?

Some years ago, several large insurance companies experienced financial trouble. Thus, it is important to check the insurance company's rating in a resource such as A.M. Best's Insurance Reports, available in most public libraries. A.M. Best rates the financial stability of insurance companies on a scale from D (weak) to A++ (superior) and lists only companies that have been under the current owner at least five years. If a company is a wholly owned subsidiary of a parent company that has a rating, Best assigns the parent company's rating until the subsidiary has the required experience. Best's ratings are far from perfect, however, and should be used only as a rough guide. Moody's, Standard & Poor's, and Duff & Phelps also rate most major life-insurance companies. Ratings range from CCC to AAA. Ratings from one agency don't necessarily correspond to ratings from another.

You might also check to see how the insurance company invests its money. If it is promising very high rates—perhaps much higher than other companies—it may be putting its funds in risky investments, such as junk bonds.

Most states have guaranty associations that make good on the promises of an insolvent life-insurance company. In most cases, when a court liquidates a company, the guaranty association in each state where the company did business collects money from other companies that write policies in that state. The guaranty funds then pay the claims made by policyholders from the troubled company. (Policyholders must usually collect from the guaranty association in the state where they live.) Guaranty associations do have their limitations, however. Policyholders may not recover their entire investment, and there may be long delays in receiving payment.

All states now have life-insurance guaranty associations.

5

L · I · F · E

INSURANCE

LIFE INSURANCE HAS TWO PURPOSES IN retirement planning. It can provide income for your surviving spouse or other dependents, and it can be an estate-planning tool. In this chapter, we explore the use of life insurance for income protection. In Chapter 18, we discuss life insurance in estate planning.

Insurance agents try to make a compelling case for maintaining or even buying a life-insurance policy in your retirement years. On the surface, their arguments sound sensible. After all, when you die, your spouse has the proceeds from the policy to supplement his or her income. But if you analyze this argument, you will see why holding on to a life-insurance policy in your later years may not always be wise.

Life insurance is a way to provide income for dependents if the family breadwinner dies. For that reason, we recommend that families with young children carry large amounts of life insurance on the adult family members. But as children grow up, a family's needs for protection diminish. By the time you reach retirement, for example, your children are probably through with college and on their own. In that case, does it make sense to keep your life insurance in force?

For most people, keeping a life-insurance policy during retirement years doesn't make economic sense. If you have a term policy, it probably isn't renewable once you reach age 65 or 70. Even if it is, the premiums are high. For example, a 47-year-old man who bought a

$75,000 term policy in 1991 from New York Savings Bank Life Insurance (SBLI), a company offering low-cost insurance, will pay close to $2,000 a year for his coverage by the time he is 65.

If you have a term policy, the insurance carrier may encourage you to convert it to a cash-value form of insurance when you are near retirement. We don't recommend that option for most people. If you own a cash-value policy, the premiums are also high. Paying high premiums for life insurance could mean your family has less money for more pressing immediate needs, such as health insurance, long-term-care insurance, or medical bills. If you keep the policy, you're gambling that one spouse will die early enough so the proceeds from the policy will supplement what may be a meager income for the other.

In deciding whether to keep a life-insurance policy, consider your total annual outlay for all your insurance needs. Premiums for Medicare, a good Medicare-supplement policy, and a good long-term-care policy may take a very large chunk of your income.

If you own term insurance, you can invest or put into a savings account the money you would otherwise pay in premiums for cash-value forms of insurance. If you have a cash-value policy, you should cash it in and invest the cash. Remember, if you do cash in a policy, the amount you receive is net of any outstanding policy loans. Check to see if you have an old loan you have forgotten about. If you do, the loan, plus any unpaid interest, is subtracted from the policy's face amount so that your surviving spouse receives less than the face value if you die while the policy is still in force.

If you have a paid-up cash-value policy and are no longer paying premiums, it might make sense to keep the policy, especially if the company is paying high dividends. Some people who own small paid-up policies like to leave the proceeds to their children. In that case, be sure to name your children as the policy's beneficiaries (see Chapter 18). You also may want to keep one or more policies in force if your estate is exceptionally large and tied up in real estate or a family business you do not want your kids to sell, for example—and there won't be enough in it to pay the taxes.

You may also want to retain a policy if cashing it in results in high tax bills for a particular year. The interest that builds up inside a cash-value policy is tax-deferred until the day you withdraw it, and then only a portion of it is taxed. The IRS ordinarily collects tax on the amount by which the cash value exceeds the sum of the premiums you paid over the years minus any dividends you received. That portion is called your *gain,* on which you pay ordinary income taxes. The gain may not be trivial if your company has consistently paid high dividends through the years. *Example:* If your gain is $12,000 after owning the policy for 20 years, your tax bill could be well over $3,000 (assuming a 28-percent marginal tax rate). If you want to cash in a life-insurance policy and doing so will result in a large tax bill, you might consider cashing in the policy in a year when you have a smaller tax liability. For example, it may be unwise to cash in a policy the same year that you take a large withdrawal from your IRA or pension plan.

LIFE INSURANCE OR ANNUITY?

Your employer will probably offer you several options for taking a pension. These options include a life annuity, which gives you payments so long as you live but provides nothing for your spouse after you die, or a joint-and-survivor annuity, with lower payments but monthly checks for your spouse after your death. You can choose a 50-percent joint-and-survivor annuity, which provides your surviving spouse with half the monthly income you receive when you are alive, or a 100-percent joint-and-survivor annuity, which gives your spouse the same monthly payments you receive during your lifetime. The latter option, however, gives you the lowest monthly payment of all.

In recent years, life-insurance agents have developed a new argument for selling policies to people about to retire. If you are married and expect a sizable pension from your employer, an agent may try to persuade you that buying a life-insurance policy is a better option than the joint-and-survivor annuity offered by your company. Why should you take a reduction in your monthly income when you can buy a life-insurance policy? But unless your spouse is terminally ill when you retire, you're almost always better off taking a joint-and-survivor annuity.

In the long run, buying a life-insurance policy is far more costly. For one thing, the insurance company must pay its usual expenses to put the policy on the books. These expenses, which include the agent's commission, can run as high as 100 percent of the first year's premium. Usually, there are no similar expenses with the annuity.

Insurance companies also charge higher premiums to people who have health problems. By the time you retire, your health may have deteriorated, perhaps to the point where the company classifies you as a "substandard" risk and charges a very high premium for coverage. If the insurance company charges you "substandard" rates, you're better off choosing the annuity option that provides your spouse with the most income until he or she dies. Insurance companies also charge higher premiums to older people, whatever their health, so you may be unable to afford much coverage. The smaller the policy, the less money your spouse has to live on after your death.

To determine which is the better option, fill out *Worksheet 5*, "Life insurance versus annuity," in the back of the book. Our example uses an employee eligible for a $1,000 monthly pension taken as a life annuity or a $900 monthly pension taken as a 50-percent joint-and-survivor annuity. The employee is 65 years old, and the spouse is 62. The rates are from a major life-insurance company that does not pay dividends. If you're offered a lower-cost whole-life policy than the one used here, the resulting calculation may be slightly more favorable for life insurance. But it's still doubtful that life insurance will turn out to be better in the long run than a joint-and-survivor annuity. In the example, the joint-and-survivor annuity pays $450 a month; the annuity bought with the life-insurance proceeds pays $200 a month. If the insurance buys less monthly income than the joint-and- survivor annuity, which is often the case, the annuity is the better deal.

TAPPING YOUR CASH VALUES

If you find yourself with an old cash-value policy and are ill, you might want to consider tapping the cash values in the policy to use for medical expenses. You can approach your insurance carrier and apply for accelerated or living-needs benefits, you can do business with a company that will buy your insurance policy for something less than its face value (see pages 107–108), or you can take out a policy loan.

LIVING-NEEDS BENEFITS

Living-needs benefits are often marketed to people approaching retirement who are starting to think about their potential need for long-term care and the devastating financial effects of a catastrophic illness.

Often added as riders to existing life-insurance policies, this coverage works similarly to other cash-value policies, such as whole life and universal life, except that part of the death benefit is paid when a specific event, other than death, occurs. That event might be a serious illness such as cancer, a heart attack, kidney failure, or a stroke. Or part of the death benefit might be paid if you are confined to a nursing home.

Policies specify how much of the death benefit is payable when a specific triggering event occurs. For example, a policy might pay 25 percent of the death benefit in the case of a heart attack or stroke. If the policy carries a $100,000 death benefit, the company pays $25,000. At the same time, the company reduces all the elements of the policy by 25 percent. Thus, the new face amount becomes $75,000, and the cash value and premium are similarly reduced by 25 percent. Once part of the death benefit is paid, you can cash in the policy and take the remaining cash value, or you can keep the policy in force and allow the cash value to continue to accumulate. Policies that call for the death benefit to be paid when you enter a nursing home work a little differently. Such policies usually pay 2 percent of the death benefit per month, subject to a maximum amount. It's possible that you could stay in a nursing home long enough to exhaust all of the policy's nursing-home benefits. In that case, there would be no death benefit payable to your survivors.

Remember that when you access your death benefits, your beneficiary will no longer receive the original face amount of the policy. This point is worth keeping in mind. If you decide to access a living-needs benefit, you may have to choose between paying for medical expenses today or providing money for your family after you die. It may not be an easy decision.

However, in one respect, Congress has made it easier for you to access a living-needs benefit. As we note on pages 102–103, if you cash in a life-insurance policy or receive dividends or other amounts under the policy (other than policy loans) during your lifetime, and the aggregate amount you receive exceeds the premiums you have paid, you will be subject to tax on the excess. In contrast, life-insurance proceeds your estate or beneficiaries receive on your death are usually free from this tax. In the Heath Insurance Portability and Accountability Act of 1996, Congress generally extended this exclusion to accelerated death benefits paid on policies insuring persons who are terminally or chronically ill. Similarly, under the new rule, amounts received on the sale of a policy insuring a terminally or chronically ill person to a viatical-settlement firm are usually exempt from income tax.

The tax code considers an individual terminally ill if he or she has been certified by a doctor as having an illness or physical condition that can reasonably be expected to result in death within 24 months after the date of certification. An individual is considered chronically ill if he or she has been certified by a licensed health-care practitioner as unable to perform (without substantial help) at least two activities of daily living for a period of 90 days or more because of a loss of functional capacity or if he or she requires substantial supervision due to severe cognitive impairment. If you are considering accessing a living-needs benefit or selling your policy to a viatical-settlement firm, you should consult your tax adviser to determine whether the proceeds you receive will be taxed.

Living-needs benefits seem like a sensible idea on the surface. But they are not without cost if you ever use them. Insurers exact a price for early access to your death benefit, and that affects what your survivors will receive. To calculate that price, insurers use one of two methods. With the lien method, the company specifies the percentage of your death benefit you can take. Typically, that's 25 to 40 percent. For example, if your policy's death benefit is $100,000, you might be able to take $25,000. The company computes interest, often at 8 percent a year, on the amount taken. When you die, it subtracts the sum you received, plus interest, from your death benefit. If, in the above example, you were to die a year later, your beneficiary would receive about $73,000 ($100,000 minus $25,000 minus about $2,000 in interest). The longer you live, the more the interest adds up and the less money your survivors would ultimately receive.

The other method is called the discount method. The money you take out is discounted—that is, interest is deducted in advance, based on your life expectancy. If you want $25,000 and you're expected to live another year, you might only receive about $23,000, not the full $25,000. The rest of the death benefit remains intact for your beneficiaries regardless of whether you die before or after the one-year period has elapsed. Companies reserve the right to determine the amount of the discount, but many don't give policyholders much information beforehand.

Insurers typically charge a processing fee, usually $100 to $300, for accessing the living-needs benefit.

The cash-value accumulation and the guaranteed cash-surrender value are all reduced if the policyholder accelerates the benefits. If the policy is structured as a universal-life contract, the policyholder might be able to pay extra premiums to increase benefits, but if partial withdrawals have been made, the benefits are reduced. Outstanding policy loans also lower the benefits.

Like other cash-value insurance, accelerated death benefit policies carry a high price tag, especially if you buy them when you're older. You may also be able to buy an accelerated death benefit policy that combines term insurance with whole life or universal life as a way of lowering premiums. Sometimes companies let you buy a policy with a single, large premium.

Premiums for an accelerated death-benefit policy, whether it is structured as whole-life or universal-life, remain level for your life—they don't increase as you get older. However, the mortality charge that comes out of your accumulating cash values may increase if the insurance company has paid substantial nursing-home claims and finds that the mortality charge has been too low. If that happens, your cash values build more slowly. Companies that sell regular long-term-care policies also have a way to adjust for increases in the cost of nursing-home care and bad claims experience. They simply raise the premiums, as we point out on pages 103–104.

Deciding whether to buy a new policy that accelerates the death benefit should hinge solely on whether you need life insurance at all. As we've noted, people approaching retirement or those already retired rarely need life-insurance coverage. Therefore, we don't recommend that you buy an accelerated death-benefits policy on the gamble that a misfortune listed in the policy will befall you. Instead, spend your money on good health insurance that provides benefits for more illnesses, or on a good Medicare-supplement policy, or on long-term-care insurance.

VIATICAL SETTLEMENTS

In recent years, companies have sprung up that offer to buy the value of your life-insurance policy and give you the money to spend on medical care. These transactions are called viatical settlements, and they require some very careful consideration before you take one. Companies try to target people who have cancer, heart disease, or AIDS, and typically offer to pay only 60 to 80 percent of the policy's face value. The amount a viatical-settlement firm is willing to give generally depends on your medical condition and how long doctors say you have to live. The longer your life expectancy, the smaller the payout. Many firms will do business with policyholders who have as long as four years to live.

The viatical-settlement industry is competitive, so it pays to shop for the best payout. If you use a broker, a commission of 5 to 7 percent will come out of the amount you receive. To receive a list of companies, call the Viatical Association of America, 800 842-9811, or visit *www.viatical.org/viatical*.

GUARANTEED ACCEPTANCE POLICIES

Some companies specialize in small life-insurance policies for older people, arguing that anyone can buy a policy regardless of health conditions. The coverage may sound tempting, but when you dig deeper into what's offered, policies come up short. Sellers of low-value life insurance, as this coverage is known in the industry, usually offer $2,000 to $15,000 worth of benefits through TV commercials and mail solicitations. The ads may be aimed at particular groups, such as the American Legion, and appeal to patriotism. Flags appear on the envelopes, or sometimes the envelope even looks like a flag. The ads also appeal to fear—fear of not having money to pay burial expenses or fear of saddling your survivors with the cost of your funeral.

Once past patriotism and fear, the solicitations get to the heart of the sales appeal: guaranteed acceptance regardless of a person's health. Promises such as "guaranteed acceptance . . . you cannot be turned down for any reason," "no medical exam," and "no health questions are asked" are designed to win new policyholders, many of whom would be uninsurable at other carriers or would have to pay exhorbitant rates if they were eligible for a policy. "As long as you're between 45 and 79 years of age, your acceptance is guaranteed regardless of past or present health conditions," reads one advertisement. After age 80, companies may offer very small amounts of coverage, something in the $1,000 to $2,000 range. Furthermore, they may also offer reduced benefits the first few years. That's a company's way of protecting itself from paying out too many benefits if a newly insured person is sick and about to die. Disclosure of the reduced benefit may not be obvious.

What's more obvious, however, is the pitch for benefits payable if you die in an accident, an unlikely occurrence for most older people. For women age 60 to 69, just 7.4 percent of all deaths are due to accidents; for men age 60 to 69, only about 11 percent. Accidental-death coverage is a kind of insurance lotto that pays twice the benefits if a policyholder dies in an accident. It's a waste of money. If you need life insurance at all, you need it no matter what the cause of your death may be.

Even though annual premiums are low, perhaps $400 or $500 a year, we don't recommend that you buy these policies. This coverage is akin to that offered by hospital-indemnity policies that we discuss in Chapter 12. In fact, they may even be sold by the same companies or their subsidiaries.

T·A·X·E·S

THE FIRST TAX RETURN YOU FILE AFTER retiring is usually different from those you filed during your working years. You may have no wages, salary, or tips. Instead, your return will show income from a variety of sources: pensions, Social Security, dividends, and interest. If you sold your home and are now renting, deductions for mortgage interest and real-estate taxes will disappear. If you bought a smaller home, those deductions may be lower. And if you have moved from a state that has an income tax to one that doesn't, it may not pay to itemize deductions.

In addition, there will be no taxes withheld by your employer, and you may have to pay estimated taxes each quarter to both the IRS and your state tax department. These payments are due on January 15, April 15, June 15, and September 15, and you need to file the appropriate forms when you pay them. If you don't pay estimated taxes, the IRS and your state tax department can impose tax penalties equal to the current interest rate charged for underpayments. (That rate varies every quarter.)

HOW YOUR INCOME IS TAXED

After retirement, there is no change in the way your income from interest and dividends is taxed. But special rules apply to payments from Social Security, disability insurance, and pensions.

SOCIAL SECURITY BENEFITS If your only source of income is Social Security, your benefits probably won't be taxable. But if you have other income, be prepared to pay taxes on as much as 85 percent of your benefits. (In some states, you have to pay state income taxes as well.)

To determine whether you owe any taxes on your benefits, add your regular adjusted gross income from Form 1040 (without including for this purpose any taxable Social Security benefits), any interest earned on tax-exempt bonds, any interest earned on Series EE educational bonds, which is excluded from tax, and half of your Social Security benefits. If the sum exceeds $25,000 for a single person or $32,000 for a married couple filing jointly, then a portion of your benefits will be includible in your income. Refer to Chapter 2 to calculate the taxable portion of your benefits

As explained there, if the sum of your adjusted gross income (not including any taxable Social Security benefits) plus your nontaxable interest and half your benefits does not exceed $34,000 if you are single or $44,000 if you are married filing jointly, then not more than 50 percent of your benefits will be taxed, and your calculation of the taxable portion of your benefits is complete. However, if the sum exceeds the applicable threshold, then up to 85 percent of your benefits are subject to tax

The tax described above applies to Social Security retirement, monthly survivors' and disability benefits, and to Tier 1 Railroad Retirement payments. It does *not* apply to Supplemental Security Income (SSI) or the lump-sum death benefit paid to a surviving spouse.

If your Social Security benefits are taxable, restructuring your investments may be in order. For example, interest earned on municipal bonds, though normally tax-free, is counted in figuring the taxable portion of your Social Security benefits. If you earn substantial interest from these bonds, you might consider selling them and putting your money into taxable but higher-yielding investments. You may end up with a higher income even after paying taxes. But remember, if you sell the bonds at a profit, the capital-gains tax reduces the amount available to reinvest.

Another strategy to avoid paying taxes on Social Security benefits is to defer the income from some of your investments. You might, for example, consider investing in Series EE savings bonds. You do not have to pay current income taxes on earnings from these bonds. Be sure, however, to check the yields on Series EE bonds. They may be too low to justify giving up some of the income you would otherwise earn from other investments.

If you continue to work while receiving Social Security benefits, carefully consider the impact on your tax bill. You must continue to pay Social Security taxes on your earnings, and the income from your job may push your Social Security benefits into the taxable range. If your earnings are high enough, you could even lose part of those bene-fits. As explained in Chapter 2, if you're at least 65 but under age 70 and continue to work in 1998, you lose $1 in benefits for every $3 of earnings above $14,500. If you're under age 65 and receive Social Security benefits, you lose $1 for every $2 in earnings that exceed $9,120. After you reach age 70, your benefits are no longer reduced if you keep working.

DISABILITY PAYMENTS Most of the time, disability pay-ments are not taxable. However, in some cases they are.

If you are receiving workers' compensation because you were injured at work, your benefits receive the same tax treatment as dam-ages awarded in a lawsuit to compensate victims for their personal physical injuries; that is, they are not usually taxable. But sometimes they are. If you are well enough to go back to work but still receive workers' compensation, those payments are considered income, and the IRS takes its share. Also, if the workers'-compensation benefits replace Social Security benefits, the benefits may be taxed. *Example:* You're injured on the job and eligible to receive Social Security disability ben-efits of $1,500 per month. You also receive workers' compensation pay-ments of $1,000 a month for 1998. Because of that payment, Social Security reduces your monthly disability benefit by $1,000 per month. When tax time comes, the $12,000 paid in workers' compensation benefits for 1998 are treated as if they were the Social Security pay-ments they replaced and are subject to the same rules as all Social Security benefits. Depending on your other income, you may or may not pay taxes on the $12,000.

If you have purchased a disability-income policy and paid the premiums yourself, you do not have to pay taxes on any benefits you receive. But if you and your employer split the cost of a disability poli-cy, only part of your benefits are taxed. (The insurance company will send Form W-2 showing the taxable portion.) If your employer has paid the full premiums, payments made under the policy to pay med-ical expenses and to compensate for a permanent disability or the loss of use of any part of your body are not considered income and thus aren't taxed. But benefits paid to replace lost wages are.

If you receive disability payments from your employer's qualified-pension plan, the government usually taxes those payments as income. However, the credit for the elderly and disabled may partly offset any taxes (see following section). Any payments you or your family receive from the Veterans Administration as disability compensation or as pension payments for disabilities are not taxed.

PENSION INCOME How income from your pension is taxed depends on whether you take your money in a lump sum or as an annuity, and on whether any money you put into the plan was previously taxed. The rules are complex. How these rules work and strategies for taking your pension are explained in Chapter 3.

YOUR TAX DEDUCTIONS AFTER RETIREMENT

THE STANDARD DEDUCTION The standard deduction, an amount you subtract to arrive at your taxable income, is available at retirement to almost everyone. You can, of course, itemize your deductions in lieu of claiming the standard deduction if your itemized deductions exceed your standard deduction.

The amount of the standard deduction varies according to your filing status, your age, and whether you're blind. For 1998, the basic deduction for a single person with no dependents is $4,250, for a single head of household $6,250, and for a married couple filing jointly $7,100. You can, however, claim a larger standard deduction if you're over 65, blind, or a qualifying widow or widower.

But if someone else can claim you as a dependent on his or her tax form—your child, for example—your standard deduction is reduced. Your standard deduction will be limited to the greater of (1) the sum of your earned income (wages and salary) plus $250 (but only up to the amount of the regular standard deduction), or (2) $700. In addition, you may still claim the additional standard deduction for age or blindness.

MEDICAL EXPENSES Medical expenses are generally deductible only in an amount by which they exceed 7.5 percent of your adjusted gross income. If you are single, over 65, and have an adjusted gross income of $25,000 in 1998, for example, you can deduct any medical expenses above $1,875. But unless your medical expenses in excess of this amount plus your other itemized deductions exceed your standard deduction ($5,300 for 1998), you will claim the standard deduction and thus derive no tax benefit from the payment of the medical expenses.

You may deduct any medical expenses you have paid for yourself and your dependents. You cannot, of course, deduct amounts reimbursed by an insurance company. In general, you may deduct expenses for the diagnosis, cure, treatment, or prevention of disease, and the cost of transportation to and from the place of treatment. You can also deduct the amount you pay for health-insurance premiums so long as the policy is the type that reimburses you for actual expenses. You cannot deduct the premiums for hospital-indemnity policies that pay a fixed amount per day. (See Chapter 10 for a description of these kinds of policies.)

The Health Insurance Portability and Accountability Act of 1996 now allows you to deduct certain premiums paid for "qualified long-term-care insurance" as medical expenses. Only the amount of the premium up to a specified annual limit is treated as a medical expense. For 1998, the annual premium limits are $210 per year for persons age 40 or less as of the end of the year; $380 per year for persons older than 40 but not older than 50; $770 per year for persons older than 50 but not older than 60; $2,050 per year for persons older than 60 but not older than 70; and $2,570 per year for persons older than 70. (See Chapter 12 for a discussion of these policies, including a comparison of these policies with other long-term-care insurance policies.)

These are some expenses you can deduct: hospital charges; doctor bills, including those from dentists, chiropractors, and Christian Science practitioners; guide dogs for the blind; Medicare Part B premiums and Part A premiums if you must pay them yourself; premiums to health-maintenance organizations; special equipment such as wheelchairs, braces, and oxygen; special items such as false teeth, hearing aids, and eyeglasses; nursing services; and prescription drugs. Experimental or unorthodox procedures are usually deductible so long as they fit the general definition of "medical expenses."

You cannot take deductions for expenses that enhance your general well-being. For example, the IRS doesn't allow a deduction for health-club dues, but if your doctor prescribes daily whirlpool treatments to relieve an arthritic condition, that expense is acceptable. You can't usually deduct these expenses: general household help, illegal operations or treatment, cosmetic treatments, life-insurance premiums, nonprescription drugs (even if your doctor recommends them), toiletries and cosmetics, weight-loss programs, and trips that are supposed to improve your overall health.

The following items are deductible except for the caveats mentioned:

- Transportation. If you travel by car, taxi, public transportation, or ambulance to obtain medical treatment, you can deduct transportation costs. If you use your car, the deduction for 1998 equals actual expenses or 10 cents per mile. If you travel to another city for medical care, you can deduct up to $50 per night for lodging costs. If someone else travels with you, the government lets you deduct another $50 per night.

But to claim lodging expenses, you must receive treatment at a nearby medical facility, or the treatment must be for a specific medical condition. If you and your spouse spend the winter in the Caribbean because the warm weather helps your arthritis, you can deduct the cost of your transportation but not your spouse's. You cannot deduct food and lodging expenses for either yourself or your spouse. If your trip has nothing to do with a specific medical problem—you go to Florida to avoid the cold-and-flu season in Maine—you can deduct no expenses whatsoever.

- Nursing homes. According to the IRS, expenses incurred for care in a nursing home can be deducted so long as you can prove that medical care is one of the principal reasons for confinement. For example, if you are bedridden and unable to care for yourself as a result of an illness, your nursing-home costs are deductible as medical expenses. If you are ambulatory but need help with activities of daily living, such as eating, bathing, and dressing, due to your reduced mobility, most nursing-home expenses usually aren't deductible. In this case, if you receive nursing services at least part of the time you're in a nursing home, those costs can be deducted. You need to get an itemized bill from the facility showing what portion of the total expense is actually for skilled care.

If you move into a continuing-care retirement community (CCRC) that provides nursing care and you pay in advance for that care as part of a nonrefundable entrance fee, you can deduct the portion of the payment that funds the care. Part of your monthly fee is also deductible. The CCRC will tell you how much to deduct (see Chapter 17).

In connection with the adoption of rules for deduction of premiums paid for "qualified long-term-care insurance," Congress did add one further exception, to allow deduction of certain costs paid to nursing homes and similar costs for home-health care as medical expenses. However, to claim a deduction under this exception, you will need to obtain various certifications from your doctor or other health professional.

Under this new exception, the costs of nursing home-care, or home health or other care, are deductible if paid for "qualified long-term-care services." Such services mean necessary diagnostic, preventive, therapeutic, caring, treating, mitigating, and rehabilitative services, and maintenance or personal-care services that are required by a chronically ill individual and are provided according to a plan of care prescribed by a licensed health-care practitioner. A chronically ill individual is generally defined in the new law as a person who has been certified within the last 12 months by a licensed health-care practitioner as unable to perform (without substantial assistance from another person) at least two activities of daily living for a period of at least 90 days due to a loss of functional capacity. Such activities are eating, toileting, transferring, bathing, dressing, and continence.

In addition, a chronically ill individual means a person requiring substantial supervision to protect him or her from threats to health and safety due to severe cognitive impairment. In other words, a person who is suffering from Alzheimer's disease may be considered chronically ill under this provision.

In effect, under current law, you may deduct the costs of benefits that could be provided under a tax-qualified long-term-care policy. See Chapter 12 for further discussion of these policies.

• Home improvements needed for medical conditions. Part of the cost of renovations to your house or apartment can be deducted as a medical expense so long as they are prescribed by a doctor to remedy a specific condition, they are not lavish or extravagant, and they have not been made primarily for personal convenience or enjoyment. Moreover, if the renovation increases the value of your home, that increase must be subtracted from the deduction. *Example:* You live in a two-story house, but a heart condition prevents you from climbing stairs. You need to install a new bathroom on the first floor. The bathroom costs $5,000 and increases the value of your home by $3,000. You must subtract the value of the increase, or $3,000, leaving you with a deduction of $2,000.

Many types of improvements don't increase the value of your home, so you can deduct their full cost. These include adding exit and entrance ramps, widening doorways, and modifying stairways; installing railings or support bars in bathrooms; modifying kitchen cabinets and other equipment; relocating or modifying electrical outlets or fixtures; and installing lifts (but not elevators, which do raise your home's value). In the case of elevators, operating costs may be deductible.

• Nursing services. Payments for nursing services are deductible so long as they are medically necessary. They need not be performed by a registered nurse. Payments to a practical nurse or to an attendant (even a relative) are deductible if he or she changes bandages, bathes you, gives medication, or renders other medically necessary nursing services. Besides the nurse's salary, you may deduct expenses for the attendant's food and lodging. If you move to a larger apartment to provide space for a live-in helper, the extra rent and utility costs are deductible. If your attendant also does household chores, you cannot claim those costs as medical deductions.

SPECIAL TAX CREDITS

If you meet certain criteria, you may qualify for tax credits (extra deductions) on your income taxes. If you are at least 65, are permanently or totally disabled, and have a relatively low income, you may qualify for a special tax credit of up to $1,125. If you are a single taxpayer, your adjusted gross income cannot exceed $17,500; if you're married filing a joint return, your adjusted gross income cannot be more than either $20,000 or $25,000, depending on your age, your spouse's age, and whether one of you is permanently and totally disabled. *Table 11* shows you if you're eligible. If you are, file Schedule R. The IRS will help you fill it out.

To figure the credit, first determine your "base amount." For instance, if you file a joint return and both you and your spouse are over 65, your base amount is $7,500. That means any nontaxable Social Security benefits, nontaxable pensions, or disability benefits cannot exceed $7,500. After figuring the base, reduce it by the total of your nontaxable Social Security benefits, nontaxable pensions, disability benefits, and one-half of your "excess" adjusted gross income. The excess is the amount by which your adjusted gross income exceeds $10,000 if you are married filing a joint return, or $5,000 if you are married, filing a separate return, and you and your spouse didn't live in the same household anytime during the year.

If the answer is zero or less, you can't claim the credit. If the result is greater than zero, multiply it by 15 percent to arrive at the amount of your credit. If the credit exceeds your tax liability, the excess is not refunded to you and cannot be carried over to other tax years.

As a practical matter, the credit has become less significant in recent years. While Social Security benefits increase with inflation, the base amount has not been increased. Similarly, the threshold for determining excess adjusted gross income has remained fixed. Furthermore, some taxpayers who might previously have claimed the credit no

TABLE 11 · INCOME LIMIT FOR ELIGIBILTY TO RECEIVE A TAX CREDIT FOR THE ELDERLY OR PERMANENTLY AND TOTALLY DISABLED

Situation	Nontaxable pension, disability, or Social Security benefits less than this	Adjusted gross income less than this
SINGLE, UNMARRIED HEAD OF HOUSEHOLD, OR WIDOW OR WIDOWER		
65 or older	$5,000	$17,500
Under 65 and retired on permanent and total disability	5,000	17,500
MARRIED, FILING JOINT RETURN		
Both 65 or older	7,500	25,000
Both under 65 and one retired on permanent and total disability	5,000	20,000
Both under 65 and both disabled retired on permanent and total disability	7,500	25,000
One 65 or older and the other under 65 and retired on permanent and total disability	7,500	25,000
One 65 or older and the other under 65 and not retired on disability	5,000	20,000
MARRIED, FILING SEPARATE RETURN, DID NOT LIVE WITH SPOUSE		
65 or older or under 65 and retired on permanent and total disability	3,750	12,500

longer owe taxes as a result of increases in the standard deduction and personal exemption.

See *Table 12* to help you calculate the credit. It assumes you and your spouse are both over 65 and file a joint return.

TABLE 12 · INCOME-TAX CREDIT

▶ *A sample calculation*

INCOME (add taxable income)		
TAXABLE INTEREST		$8,000
PART-TIME WAGES		+ 7,500
ADJUSTED GROSS INCOME		$15,500
NONTAXABLE SOCIAL SECURITY BENEFITS		$2,500

CREDIT (Subtract income figure from base amount. If result is greater than zero, credit is 15%.)		
BASE AMOUNT		$7,500
TOTAL SOCIAL SECURITY	$2,500	
½ ADJUSTED GROSS INCOME OVER $10,000 ($15,500 − $10,000 = $5,500)	+ 2,750	− $5,250
RESULT: ($7,500 − $5,250)		$2,250
		x 15%
MAXIMUM CREDIT		$338
TAX BEFORE CREDIT		$195
ALLOWABLE CREDIT		$195

WHO MANAGES YOUR
M·O·N·E·Y
WHEN YOU CAN'T?

SOONER OR LATER, WE ALL HAVE TO THINK about the unthinkable—who will handle my financial affairs if I'm incapacitated?

Deciding who will manage your finances is as much a part of retirement planning as learning where to get a Medicare card. The tools for accomplishing this task include: joint accounts, powers of attorney, living trusts, and conservatorships and guardianships.

JOINT ACCOUNTS

JOINT TENANTS WITH RIGHT OF SURVIVORSHIP Establishing a joint account with right of survivorship at a bank or brokerage firm is an easy way to enable someone to share in managing your money. When you set up a joint account by signing an authorization card, you give one or more joint owners the right to deposit funds into or withdraw funds from the account. If the account has two owners, either can withdraw all the assets in the account for any reason, although in general, an owner who didn't contribute to the account can't keep more than half. In any case, when one owner dies, the remainder of the account immediately belongs to the other. In some states, however, the surviving owner may need tax waivers to use the money if the account is large. The surviving owner may also have to pay applicable estate taxes out of the account (depending on whether the owner who died contributed to the account and the size of his or her estate).

Setting up a joint account allows the joint owner, who may be your spouse or your children, to make deposits and write checks to pay your bills if you can't. If, for example, you're confined to a nursing home, the joint owner can use funds from your account to pay for your care. Joint accounts also provide a way to transfer money to someone without having the account go through probate at your death. If a husband and wife establish a joint account, the surviving spouse has the money right away. That is a significant advantage if your spouse has no other immediate funds to live on.

Joint accounts do have a few drawbacks:

• The person you choose as joint owner can close the account at any time and withdraw all of the money. It's a good idea to have some money in another account that's solely in your name. Put only enough money in the joint account to cover the bills you will have to pay if you become incapacitated or the expenses your spouse will have immediately upon your death. Put the rest of your assets in a separate account in your name alone—but remember, at your death the distribution of that account will have to await the probate of your will.

• By setting up a joint account, you could unwittingly circumvent your will. Suppose your will gives equal shares of your estate to all your children, but most of your estate is in bank certificates of deposit that are held jointly with only one of your children. Since your will only governs property that goes into probate, that is, property in your name only, the certificates of deposit pass to the child who is the joint owner and not to the other children you thought you provided for in your will. You can avoid potential problems by making sure a substantial portion of your assets are outside the joint account or by setting up joint accounts of equal value with each of your children.

• If you later seek Medicaid to pay for costs of your stay in a nursing home or for home health care, setting up a joint account does not automatically protect your money from Medicaid. The determination as to what part of the account is includible in your assets for Medicaid purposes is generally made on the state level. In many states, the presumption is that the account belongs totally to the Medicaid applicant (even though under state banking law, 50 percent of it may belong to each joint owner). In some states, this presumption can be rebutted if you can show actual contributions by the other joint owner.

There are special rules regarding what constitutes a "transfer" for Medicaid purposes in creating a joint account, and it is best to consult a specialist in this area to determine what the rules are in your state.

Joint tenancy should not be confused with *tenancy in common,* which is another form of joint ownership. Under this arrangement, each person owns half of the assets, but at the death of one owner, the survivor is entitled only to his or her half. The other half of the assets passes under the will of the deceased owner. This device is a preferable form of ownership where each party wants to leave his or her share of the property to individuals other than the co-owner. It is also often used in connection with the ownership of real estate, especially for business purposes.

Joint accounts are not the same as accounts that are held "in trust for" someone else. With these accounts, you retain control over the money while you are alive. At your death, the person you are holding the money in trust for becomes the owner of the account. That person cannot touch the account during your lifetime. Thus, "in trust for" accounts are not useful devices for managing your money.

POWERS OF ATTORNEY

A power of attorney is a legal tool under which you give another person the power to act for you. The person you invest with this power is called an "agent" or an "attorney-in-fact," but does not have to be a lawyer. You can name more than one person as your agent, in which case you must designate whether both agents must act together or if each one can act separately. Some forms permit you to designate a successor if the agent initially named cannot act.

To set up a power of attorney, you simply sign a prepared form obtained from a bank or brokerage house, a legal supply store, or your attorney, and list the powers you want your agent to have. A power of attorney may be limited or extensive. For example, you may want someone to sign papers for you only at a real-estate closing or manage your finances while you are on vacation. Or you can give someone broader powers—to sign checks, to deal with your broker, to make gifts on your behalf, or to get into your safe-deposit box.

Powers of attorney cannot be used after your death. Nor can they be used if you become disabled unless the form of power you sign clearly grants this power to your agent. If you give your agent the power to act on your behalf when you're incapacitated, you are establishing a *durable power of attorney.*

Powers of attorney are easy to set up and can be especially useful if you include the durability feature. If you have only a few assets, such as bank CDs or perhaps a mutual fund or two, a power of attorney can be a useful management tool if you become disabled. Powers of attorney are not necessarily permanent documents, however. If you change your mind, you can prevent your agent from using it by simply tearing up the piece of paper assigning the powers. You can then sign a new power of attorney appointing someone else as your agent.

Powers of attorney have some pitfalls. Your agent can act while you are alive and make decisions for you even though you can make your own decisions and don't want any interference.

Although an agent is required to make decisions for your benefit, there are few safeguards to prevent him or her from misusing your funds. If that happens, your only recourse may be an expensive lawsuit that may come too late to recover your money. Because powers of attorney are easy to use, financial institutions in some states may not accept standard-form documents. In that case, use a form provided by the institution.

Some of the potential abuses of a power of attorney can be prevented by retaining the original power of attorney (or having someone you trust hold it for you for safekeeping) and not giving a copy to your agent until you became disabled. Be sure someone such as your lawyer or a trusted family member knows where you have stored your powers of attorney. They should be accessible if you become disabled.

An alternative is to grant your agent a "springing" power of attorney that will only go into effect if you become disabled. Under this type of power, before your agent can act, a physician or other person named in the form must certify in writing that you are no longer competent to manage your own affairs. The need to obtain the certification could, however, result in unwanted delay.

LIVING TRUSTS

The most complicated way of assigning someone the task of managing your money is to set up a living trust. These trusts, which are explained in greater detail in Chapter 19, provide for a trustee or trustees to sign checks, give instructions to brokers, and otherwise manage the assets you put into the trust. Under some arrangements, you may also be one of the trustees.

You need a lawyer to set up a trust, and the cost can run several hundred dollars or more. But if you have several types of investments, or assets in real estate or a business, a living trust may actually be more practical than a durable power of attorney.

You might not want to put all of your assets into a revocable trust now, but may want the benefits of trust management if you become disabled. You can accomplish this by establishing a revocable trust now, naming a trustee, and funding the trust with a minimal amount of property. You should also execute a durable power of attorney and give your designated agent the authority to transfer all of your assets into the trust if you become disabled. If you never become disabled, you retain full, independent management of your assets. This type of trust is often referred to as a "standby" or "disability" trust.

GUARDIANS, CONSERVATORS, AND COMMITTEES

If you don't arrange for someone to take care of your financial affairs and you become incapacitated, the state may have to appoint someone to do it. States are also empowered to appoint someone to personally supervise people who are unable to care for themselves. States have different names for those who perform these tasks—guardians, conservators, committees, curators—but their duties are similar.

They may collect all or part of your assets, manage them, pay your bills, collect income from your property and accounts, including Social Security, and periodically report to the court on how they are carrying out these functions. Guardians are also entitled to commissions that are generally governed by state law and are based on the value of your assets. These commissions are usually awarded and paid at the time the guardian renders his or her accountings. If a guardian is called on to perform particularly difficult jobs, such as running your business or managing investment real estate, the judge may award additional compensation. Some states require guardians to post a bond, the cost of which is paid out of your funds. The bond insures you against losses from wrongdoing on the part of the guardian.

HOW GUARDIANS ARE APPOINTED If a guardian is to be appointed, a family member or another person acting for you files papers with the court requesting a hearing. The papers usually specify the relevant facts about your mental and physical condition and your assets and liabilities and request that a particular individual be named as your guardian. An application for guardianship may also set out a plan for managing your money and caring for you. Your doctor may be asked to testify about your mental and physical condition and provide evidence that you are incapable of handling your own affairs. In some states, the appointment of a guardian amounts to a legal declaration of incompetency. In other states, it does not.

In some states, you must give permission before a guardian is appointed; in others, you have little say in the matter. Nevertheless, there are legal procedures in place to protect you and your money. For instance, you have the right to be represented by a lawyer. In addition, the court will generally appoint someone to act on your behalf. This person is called a "guardian ad litem" or a "special guardian." This special guardian reviews all of the documents and evidence presented and renders a report to the court stating why the proposed guardianship is (or is not) in your best interests.

WHO CAN BE A GUARDIAN? Anyone can be a guardian. Most states allow you to choose your own guardian or at least recommend someone to the court. If you have not made any other arrangements and feel that at some time in the future a guardian may be appointed, see your lawyer and make your preferences known while you are still able to do so. Some states allow you to designate a committee to act on your behalf. Check with your lawyer to see if this option is available to you.

If you do not tell the court whom you want as a guardian, most state laws leave the choice up to the judge, who usually appoints a family member, following this order: spouse, adult children, parents, brothers and sisters, and other blood relatives, especially those you have been living with for some time. Some states require the guardian to reside in your state. Even so, in some circumstances the judge may have to choose a blood relative who lives far away.

Appointing a guardian is a complicated and costly procedure that often involves emotional pain. It's best to avoid the need for one. If possible, establish a joint account, power of attorney, or living trust instead.

PART TWO

HEALTH CARE

8

M·E·D·I·C·A·R·E

WHEN LYNDON JOHNSON SIGNED THE MEDICARE Act in the summer of 1965, he promised that older Americans would never be denied "the healing miracle of modern medicine," nor would "illness crush and destroy the savings they had so carefully put away." For the last quarter century, the federal government has struggled to keep that promise, spending ever-increasing sums on health care for the elderly. In 1967, the first year benefits were paid, the government spent $3.2 billion on Medicare. By 2002, Medicare is projected to spend $246 billion. For elderly patients, the cost of medical services not fully covered by Medicare has also risen dramatically, now threatening to "destroy the savings they had so carefully put away."

The seeds of Medicare's cost explosion, as well as the explosion in all health-care costs, were sown the day Congress embraced fee-for-service reimbursement plans as the model for Medicare. For years, Medicare paid whatever health-care providers demanded.

But in the early 1980s, Medicare stopped payment on the blank checks it had given hospitals. Medicare now tells hospitals what it will pay for an inpatient diagnosis and care. Almost all hospital services today fall into one of 490 diagnostic-related groups (DRGs). Hospitals are reimbursed according to the diagnostic group for which you are admitted. A hospital usually receives a fixed dollar amount for a given diagnosis, no matter how long you stay or what treatment is given.

To some extent, the DRG schedule (sometimes called the prospective-payment system) has slowed the growth in expenditures for inpatient hospital claims. Hospitals have become somewhat more efficient, since they can no longer automatically pass on their costs to Medicare. But Medicare has been unable to cut costs for physicians' or hospital outpatient services to the same degree. The Balanced Budget Act of 1997 will slow the growth in Medicare spending, although program expenditures will continue to grow faster than overall federal spending. The act limits the rate of increase in payments to medical providers, sharply increases the premiums beneficiaries will pay in the future, and offers a bewildering number of options that will begin to shift more of the financial burden to those receiving care. Medicare was never meant to cover all the hospital and medical bills for the elderly. Medicare beneficiaries pay their share of the costs through premiums, deductibles, and coinsurance; figuring out how to cover those costs is becoming much more complex. This chapter and those that follow will help you find your way around the new world of Medicare choices.

MEDICARE BASICS

Medicare's prospective payments for hospital inpatient care are designed to cover 100 percent of the costs of medically necessary services for Medicare beneficiaries. (Patients do pay a hospital deductible, however.) For most physicians' services, outpatient hospital services, and supplies, Medicare pays 80 percent of what it determines is the "allowable charge."

The portion of the allowed charge not paid by Medicare is called *coinsurance* and is paid by the beneficiary. Beneficiaries also pay *deductibles,* those amounts that they must pay before Medicare benefits begin. Beneficiaries also may pay *excess charges,* that is, an amount above Medicare's allowed charge that physicians can bill to the beneficiaries. Congress has limited that amount to 15 percent above the allowable charge. Most doctors don't find it worthwhile to bill you repeatedly for additional amounts. Charging you extra is called "balance billing." Whether doctors balance bill often depends on where you live.

PART A COVERAGE: HOSPITAL SERVICES This covers various levels of care provided by hospitals.

• Acute care. For the first 60 days you are in a hospital in each benefit period, Medicare pays your entire bill except for a deductible.

In 1998, the hospital deductible is $764. (Each year, it is adjusted to account for rising costs.) If you are hospitalized for 61 to 90 days, you pay coinsurance for each day you are in the hospital. In 1998, that amount is $191 per day. If your stay exceeds 90 days, you can use your lifetime reserve days—each beneficiary gets 60 lifetime reserve days to use for long hospitalizations—and pay a daily copayment of $382 in 1998. Once you have used those days, however, they are gone forever. And if you're unfortunate enough to have a very long hospitalization and you've used up those reserve days, you'll be responsible for the charges unless you have a Medicare supplement policy that picks up all the daily coinsurance costs. The hospital automatically uses your reserve days for extended stays unless you request in writing that those days should not be used. Medicare pays nothing if you are hospitalized longer than 150 days in any benefit period, although most supplemental policies pay for at least another 365 days. Hospital stays are so short these days that most beneficiaries never need that coverage.

A "benefit period" begins when you enter a hospital and ends when you've been out for 60 consecutive days. If you are hospitalized for, say, 15 days, discharged, then readmitted 20 days later, you are still in the same benefit period and don't have to pay the deductible again.

For Medicare to pay your hospital bills, a doctor must prescribe the care, and the care must be given in a hospital that participates in Medicare. (Almost all hospitals do.) There's no coverage for care in a nonparticipating hospital except in an emergency, and even then, Medicare may not pay the entire bill.

Medicare picks up the tab for most hospital expenses, including the cost of a semiprivate room, lab tests, X-rays, nursing services, meals, drugs provided by the hospital, medical supplies, appliances, and the cost of operating and recovery rooms. Telephones and televisions are not covered; neither is the cost of private-duty nurses or private rooms unless they are medically necessary.

If you need blood, Medicare pays the entire cost of replacing the blood, but only after you have used three pints. The blood deductible applies for each benefit period.

• Skilled-nursing care. Medicare imposes strict eligibility requirements for these benefits. It pays only if care is provided in a Medicare-approved facility, if a doctor certifies that such care is needed daily, and you have been in a hospital for at least three days prior to needing skilled-nursing care. If your stay is approved, Medicare picks up 100 percent of the cost of a semiprivate room, meals, nursing services, medical supplies, and appliances for the first 20 days. For stays lasting from 21 to 100 days, you must pay coinsurance. In 1998, that amount is $95.50 a day. If you require skilled-nursing care for longer than 100 days, you must pay out of your own pocket or with the proceeds from a long-term-care policy (see Chapter 12). So don't count on Medicare paying much of your bill for skilled-nursing care, especially if you need it for a long time. Most people use this benefit for about 24 days on average.

• Home health care. There are strict eligibility rules for home health benefits, and they may get stricter. Medicare pays if care is provided by a Medicare-certified home-health-care agency, if you require intermittent skilled-nursing care or physical or speech therapy, if a doctor orders and regularly reviews such care, and if you are homebound. There will soon be a new definition of what "homebound" means. However, Medicare does not consider a hospital or a nursing facility to be a beneficiary's home and will not pay home-health benefits if someone is confined in those places. Under Part A, you are entitled to 100 home health visits after you've been in the hospital for three days for each spell of illness. Additional home health visits fall under Part B (see page 133).

As long as you need what are considered "skilled" nursing services, you may qualify for Medicare home-health benefits. To qualify as a skilled service, it must be so complex that it can be safely and effectively performed only by or under the supervision of professional or technical personnel. If you qualify for this kind of care, Medicare will pay for physical, occupational, or speech therapy, medical social services, home health aides, medical supplies, and durable medical equipment, such as hospital beds and oxygen tanks. Contrary to what you may have heard, if you need some skilled care, Medicare does cover services provided by home health aides even if the service is considered to be personal or custodial in nature, such as help with bathing, dressing, or getting in and out of bed. Note, however, that Medicare does not cover home-delivered meals, transportation, housekeeping, and personal-chore services. If you need that kind of help, the place to contact is your local Area Agency on Aging (see Appendix A). You may be eligible for those services under the federal Older Americans Act.

The Balanced Budget Act also limits the amount of home health care you can receive. The law restricts skilled nursing and home-health-aide services to a combination of less than eight hours per day and a maximum of 28 hours a week (35 hours if reviewed on a case-by-case basis). Furthermore, each agency providing these services will be reimbursed a set amount for each patient regardless of medical need. It's hard to say what this will mean for care in the long run.

• Hospice care. A hospice is a facility that provides inpatient, outpatient, and home care for the terminally ill. Unlike hospitals, hospices don't try to cure patients but focus on counseling, symptom control, and pain reduction. To qualify, you must carry Part A, your doctor and the hospice must agree that you have fewer than six months to live, and you must agree in writing that you are giving up standard Medicare benefits for your terminal illness and treatments for curing the illness. You can, however, receive Medicare services for other conditions and can revoke the hospice benefit at any time and return to regular Medicare.

Hospice benefits last 210 days if a physician says you are terminally ill and have elected the hospice benefit instead of regular Medicare coverage. Medicare usually will not pay for 24-hour care, and the amount it covers will depend on how sick you are. When Medicare does pay, it covers all expenses for nursing and doctor services, supplies, appliances, social services, counseling, and home health and homemaker services in Medicare-approved hospices. As part of the hospice benefit, Medicare beneficiaries also pay 5 percent or $5 toward each prescription, whichever is less.

• Inpatient psychiatric care. Medicare pays the entire cost for inpatient care, less the yearly hospital deductible. Coverage is limited to a total of 190 days during your lifetime.

PART B COVERAGE: MEDICAL SERVICES Part B of Medicare, an optional program for which you must apply, covers medical services outside the hospital and hospital care provided to you as an outpatient. Under Part B, Medicare pays 80 percent of the allowed charge. You pay the remaining 20 percent. You are also responsible for paying the annual deductible, that is, the first $100 of your medical bills each year, before Medicare starts paying for Part B services. You can meet the deductible requirement in one doctor's visit or by using a combination of services.

• The allowed charge. Understanding how Medicare figures the allowed charges (all called the approved amount) is central to understanding your coverage under Part B. When a doctor submits a Medicare claim, the claim goes to an insurance company that works under contract with Medicare to process claims. This company, known as the *carrier,* determines the allowed charge for the particular service you needed. The allowed charge is the portion of the doctor's charge that Medicare will pay. In 1992, Medicare began paying doctors according to a national fee schedule based on the relative value of the services performed. The effect of this fee schedule is to compensate general practitioners more fairly and reduce fees to more highly paid specialists, such as radiologists and ophthalmologists. (Medicare determines the value of each service by calculating the amount of work, overhead costs, and malpractice insurance expenses needed to provide the service.)

• Excess charges. Medicare gives doctors the option of accepting the allowed charge based on the new fee schedule as payment in full or requiring you to pay the difference between the allowed and the actual charge. That gap, as we explained earlier, is called the excess charge. If a doctor bills for that amount, he or she is said to engage in "balanced billing." A doctor can bill no more than 15 percent of the allowable charge. Suppose, for example, Medicare determines that the allowable charge for a particular procedure is $2,000. A doctor can bill you no more than $300 extra (15 percent of $2,000).

A doctor who agrees to accept the allowed charge in all cases is called a *participating* physician and signs an annual contract with Medicare. In Medicare parlance, such a physician "accepts assignment." (Doctors who don't sign contracts are "nonparticipating.") About 80 percent of the doctors serving Medicare beneficiaries are participating physicians. The rest may accept assignment on a case-by-case basis, for example, if they believe you cannot pay the extra charges. In effect, doctors are free to provide their own "means test," accepting the allowed fee for some patients and billing others a higher fee. The likelihood of your doctor accepting assignment depends on where you live, the doctor's specialty, and your age. Surgeons and nephrologists are more likely to accept assignment than are anesthesiologists and general practitioners. And doctors are more apt to take assignment from patients who are 85 than from those who are 65. Doctors who do not take assignment for elective surgery must give you a written estimate of your out-of-pocket costs if the charge is likely to total more than $500 and if Medicare may not cover the procedure. If a doctor fails to give you this estimate, you are entitled to a refund of any amount you paid over Medicare's allowed charge.

To find a participating doctor, consult the *Medicare-Participating Physician/Supplier Directory,* which you can find at your local Social Security Administration office. You can also obtain the directory free of charge from the insurance company that handles Medicare claims for your area. Your local Social Security office or Area Agency on Aging can tell you the name of your carrier. The carrier is also listed in *The Medicare Handbook* you receive when you sign up for the program. The insurance counseling program in your state might also be able to help you find participating doctors. Be sure to ask if a doctor is still participating when you call for an appointment. The HealthCare Financing Administration is now letting doctors opt out quarterly. As we went to press, there was no system in place to alert beneficiaries if a participating doctor has opted out.

• Doctors' fees. Part B benefits cover services furnished in a doctor's office or in your home as well as those provided in an inpatient or outpatient hospital setting. Services include anesthesia, radiology, pathology, surgery, some podiatric treatment, second-opinion consultations, dental care if it involves jaw surgery or setting broken facial bones, and chiropractic treatment to correct an out-of-place vertebra shown on an X-ray.

• Outpatient hospital coverage. These benefits cover outpatient hospital services, including those required in an emergency room or outpatient clinic. Generally, whatever the hospital bills is the amount Medicare pays, and in recent years, hospitals have been using oupatient services as an escape hatch from restrictions on amounts Medicare will pay for inpatient services. As they've tried to recoup their costs, the price of outpatient services has been rising. If you don't have a Medicare-supplement policy, the 20-percent coinsurance can become a huge expense. Blood transfusions are also covered under Part B, but the deductible is different from the one under Part A. If you use three pints and have paid the $100 annual deductible, Medicare picks up 80 percent of the allowed charge. You pay the 20-percent coinsurance plus replacement costs for the first three pints of blood you use.

• Physical and occupational therapy. For you to be eligible for this coverage, your doctor must prescribe a treatment plan for you and periodically review it. If therapy is provided in an outpatient hospital facility or skilled-nursing facility or by a home-health-care agency, clinic, or Medicare-approved rehabilitation agency, the usual cost-sharing arrangement applies. New rules limit the amount Medicare will spend for physical and occupational therapy to $1,500 each year.

• Psychiatric care. Medicare pays for care in either a doctor's office or outpatient hospital facility, but the benefits are different depending on where the service is performed. If care is given in an outpatient facility, Medicare pays 80 percent and you pay 20 percent, but if it's given in a doctor's office, Medicare pays about 50 percent of the allowable charge, up to a maximum annual benefit of $1,000. Medicare also pays for psychiatric care in skilled-nursing facilities. Unscrupulous providers have offered "services" to dementia patients and have billed Medicare, which could begin cracking down on such abuses.

• Laboratory fees. Medicare pays 100 percent of the allowed charge for clinical diagnostic tests (such as for blood and urine) performed in independent laboratories certified by Medicare. If tests are done in a noncertified lab, you must pay for them yourself. Neither laboratories nor doctors who perform clinical-lab tests in their offices can bill you for excess charges. For other diagnostic tests, such as X-rays, EKGs, and tissue biopsies, Medicare's usual cost-sharing applies, and nonparticipating physicians can bill more than the allowed charge.

• Ambulance services. If the following conditions are met, Medicare pays 80 percent of the allowed charge: You must have a medical need for an ambulance; the ambulance and its equipment must meet Medicare's standards; and the use of an alternative vehicle could endanger your life. Ambulance services are frequently denied, and you may have to go through the appeals process to get payment.

• Drugs. Medicare does not cover self-administered prescription drugs like those you purchase from a pharmacy. There is an exception, however, for immunosuppressive drugs that are taken within one year after an organ transplant that Medicare has covered. Medicare does cover drugs while you are in a hospital or skilled-nursing facility if your stay is covered. It also covers certain injections in physicians' offices.

• Durable medical equipment. Medicare pays 80 percent of the approved amount for the rental or purchase of things like oxygen, hospital beds, wheelchairs, and walkers. Durable medical equipment has been the subject of considerable fraud and abuse, so don't be surprised if you find it's difficult to get coverage for certain items, and be suspicious if you're offered any of these items free.

• Preventive services. Medicare now pays for some preventive services, including yearly mammograms, which are not subject to the Part B deductible, Pap smears and pelvic exams, also not subject to the

Part B deductible, diabetes-glucose monitoring, diabetes education, colorectal-cancer screening, bone-mass measurement, and shots for flu and pneumococcal-pneumonia. (Medicare covers the entire cost of the shots.)

WHAT MEDICARE DOES NOT COVER

Medicare does not pay for in-hospital private-duty nurses or for private rooms in hospitals or skilled-nursing facilities unless a doctor says your condition is so serious that you need such services. Nor does it pay for televisions, telephones, or personal items such as hearing aids, eyeglasses, or orthopedic shoes.

In general, it pays only for services that are reasonable and medically necessary to help you recover from an illness. You can't submit a claim for setting a broken arm and then bill Medicare for a routine chest X-ray, too. Nor does the program pay for preventive care, such as routine annual physicals. However, as we've noted, Medicare is now beginning to pay for some screening tests. (See above.) It does not pay for insulin injections that patients can administer themselves. It doesn't pay for ordinary foot or dental care, almost all chiropractic services, or cosmetic surgery.

There are no benefits for skilled care in nursing homes that you need for more than 100 days. Nor are there benefits for meals delivered to your home through local meals-on-wheels programs. If you become sick while visiting a foreign country or on a cruise ship, Medicare won't cover your expenses. The program pays for treatment only in some Canadian and Mexican hospitals, and then only in certain situations.

FILING A CLAIM

The federal government does not pay your medical bills directly. It contracts with private insurance companies to process claims and pay health-care providers. The companies that pay claims for Part A coverage are called intermediaries; those that pay Part B claims are called carriers. After you are dismissed from a hospital, the facility bills Medicare directly. You receive a Medicare Summary Notice that tells you what services were billed to Medicare. For services covered under Part B, your doctor or medical-supply company must submit your claim to the carrier even if they don't accept assignment. Neither a doctor nor a medical-supply company can charge extra for preparing your claim form. If your doctor refuses to prepare your claim form, contact the carrier. If the doctor or supplier accepts Medicare's payment as payment in full, the carrier pays the doctor directly. If the doctor refuses to accept assignment on your claim, Medicare pays you, and you pay the doctor. Medicare will send you an Explanation of Medicare Benefits or an EOMB, which shows the services that were billed to Medicare, the charges Medicare approved, how much was credited toward your $100 deductible, and the amount Medicare paid. Medicare will soon be phasing in a new notice called a Medicare Summary Notice (MSN) that will explain what it paid for both Part A and Part B services.

If you disagree with the amount Medicare pays or dispute coverage for certain services, you can appeal the decision. The EOMB will tell you how to do that, or consult *The Medicare Handbook*, which is sent annually. You can also try to call Medicare's hotline: 800 638-6833.

WHAT YOU PAY FOR MEDICARE

Part A is financed through payroll taxes. Most beneficiaries pay no additional premiums for their Part A coverage. However, some people must pay monthly premiums for hospital coverage, including disabled persons who have gone back to work but are still disabled and people who have not worked the required 10 years to obtain Social Security benefits. If you do not have the required work history, you may still be eligible for Part A benefits based on your spouse's work record. However, if you and your spouse divorce before being married 10 years, you have to pay the Part A premiums to continue your coverage. The Part A premium in 1998 was $309 per month if you have less than 30 quarters of work experience and $170 if you have between 30 and 39 quarters.

Part B is financed through general tax revenues and premiums paid by beneficiaries. The U.S. Treasury pays about 75 percent of the cost of the program; beneficiaries pay the rest. In 1998, beneficiaries pay $43.80 a month; in 1999, they will pay $48.70; in 2000, $53.20; in 2001, $58.90; in 2002, $64.80; and in 2007, $105.40. Premiums are deducted from your Social Security checks. If you don't sign up for Part B during the initial enrollment period, you'll pay more later. In addition, you can't sign up until the following January, when a new enrollment period opens, and then benefits won't begin until July. Almost everyone signs up for Part B. It's a terrific insurance buy.

SIGNING UP FOR MEDICARE

If you elect early-retirement benefits from Social Security, you automatically receive a Medicare card in the mail when you turn 65. If you sign up for Social Security benefits when you are 65, you receive your Medicare card at the same time. However, if you have turned 65 and want to delay your Social Security benefits, you have to apply for Medicare. In that case, do so during the first three months of your initial enrollment period, which is the seven-month period that begins three months before the month you are first eligible for Medicare. *Example:* You turn 65 on October 1 and become eligible for Medicare on that date. Your initial enrollment period begins on July 1 and lasts through January of the following year. If you don't enroll during the three months before your eligibility date, your benefits may be delayed from one to three months. If you don't enroll during the seven-month initial enrollment period, the delay could be as long as 16 months.

Furthermore, if you do not enroll in Part B during your initial enrollment period but later decide you want benefits, you can sign up during the general enrollment period held each year from January 1 through March 31. Your benefits won't begin until July 1, however. If you delay enrolling, your monthly premium goes up by 10 percent for each 12-month period you are not enrolled in the program.

VETERANS' BENEFITS

If you have served in the armed forces, you may be eligible for a variety of veterans' benefits. The ones of most interest to retirees are usually medical and burial. Some veterans' homes also offer long-term-care services that may be more desirable than nursing-home care.

• Medical. Many veterans can receive care for a non-service-related medical condition in a Department of Veterans Affairs facility. Admittance depends on your income level and if space is available in the veterans' hospital.

• Burial. Any person who has completed the required period of service and has been discharged under other than dishonorable conditions can be buried in any of the 113 national cemeteries operated by the Veterans Department.

For more information about benefits or the location of the nearest VA facility, contact the regional VA office in your state.

MEDICARE AND COVERAGE FROM YOUR EMPLOYER

Special rules apply if you work past age 65 and your employer, who has at least 20 employees, continues to provide health insurance for you. The rules also apply if your spouse is employed and his or her employer provides health-insurance coverage for both of you. You can continue coverage under your employer's plan or your spouse's and enroll in Medicare. However, Medicare pays only after the employer's plan does. In other words, Medicare is the second payer.

If you are covered under an employer's plan when you become eligible for Medicare, you can delay Medicare coverage without paying a penalty and without waiting for a general enrollment period when you finally decide to take the coverage. Check with your Social Security office to find out how soon you have to apply after your employer's coverage stops. Your company may offer a monetary incentive to opt out of its group health plan in an effort to shift its own health-care costs to Medicare. If that's the case, be sure your company offers the same deal to all those who are eligible for Medicare. If the company doesn't, it may be fined $5,000, and you may be at a disadvantage. Carefully weigh such offers. If your employer picks up most of the cost for your health care, it may be cheaper to stay in the plan rather than pay the Medicare Part B premium plus a premium for a supplemental policy.

When Medicare is the secondary payer, it will not pay more than the difference between what your employer's insurance company approves and what your employer's insurance pays, up to the amount Medicare would have paid if it were primary. *Example:* Let's say a doctor charges $100, and your employer's insurance company approves $80 for payment and pays 80 percent of that amount, or $64. Medicare approves $60 for payment. Medicare pays the difference between what the employer's insurance approved ($80) and what the employer actually paid ($64). In other words, Medicare pays $16.

IF YOU ARE DISABLED

Medicare pays the health-care bills for disabled persons under age 65 who qualify for Social Security disability benefits and have been disabled for at least two years. However, if you have been receiving Medicare benefits as a disabled person and then go back to work before you turn 65, you can continue to receive Medicare benefits only if you are still disabled. After you start working, Part A benefits continue for at least 48 months, and Part B benefits continue for the same time as long as you pay the Part B premium. Once your hospital benefits run out, you can continue buying both Part A and Part B benefits as long as you are disabled.

MEDICARE AND LOW-INCOME BENEFICIARIES

Medicare offers two programs for low-income people over age 65: the Qualified Medicare Beneficiaries program and the Specified Low-Income Medicare Beneficiary program.

In the first program, people with incomes below the federal poverty level, around $10,000 for a single person in 1998, do not have to pay the Medicare premiums, deductibles, and coinsurance. The state picks up those costs through its Medicaid program, although the amount it pays may not cover the full amount.

In the second program, the state pays the Part B premium for those with incomes at or 20 percent above the poverty level. The costs are split between the federal and state governments, but the federal government's share is limited over time. The money runs out in 2002, when the program is no longer available. The money available in the next few years is insufficient to help everyone who is eligible for the program. Nevertheless, if you or someone you know is eligible, it doesn't hurt to contact your local Department of Social Services or Area Agency on Aging for assistance. You can also call the Medicare hot line: 800 638-6833.

HEALTH INSURANCE
FROM YOUR
E·M·P·L·O·Y·E·R

IF YOU'RE LIKE MOST WORKERS PREPARING for retirement, you may have counted on your employer to pay for your health insurance after you leave the work force. But the number of employers offering such coverage is dropping, and the rules are changing. In 1991, 80 percent of all large employers offered retiree health coverage. By 1996, only 71 percent did.

The explosion in health-care costs and new government rules have made many employers reluctant to fund health insurance for retirees. Corporations now have to show on their books the expected cost of retiree health benefits and account for a potentially huge liability that will take a large chunk of their pretax earnings. Consequently, employers are now requiring their retirees to pay a greater portion of their medical bills, and they are tightening eligibility rules. Furthermore, some workers will have no coverage at all when they retire.

If your employer won't pay for your health insurance, it's important to know what options you have for buying your own coverage. Health insurance is vital, and if you have few options, you may have to postpone your retirement.

The first step in assessing your health coverage is to know what your employer will provide and how much you will have to pay. Then you can compare that coverage and premium with other policies on the market.

A common mistake retirees make is buying too much health insurance or the wrong kind. One good policy that supplements Medicare, whether from your former employer or from a private insurance company, is enough. Coverage from a former employer is often cheaper and more comprehensive than a policy purchased from an insurance company. But if coverage from your employer is skimpy or too expensive, a Medicare-supplement policy from a private carrier is the better choice.

Sometimes a combination of policies is appropriate. For example, if your employer offers coverage only for inpatient hospital stays and no benefits for outpatient or other medical services, or you have a plan that pays just for prescription drugs, you will need a supplemental policy.

IF YOU RETIRE EARLY

Whether your employer offers retiree health coverage usually depends on your age when you leave the work force. Many companies used to offer benefits to workers who were at least 55 years old and had five years of service. Now, however, those employers are becoming rarer. Most now require their employees to be older and have completed 10 or 15 years of service. Some companies provide no benefits for workers who retire before age 65. Others give early retirees health coverage for only a short time. For example, your employer may offer health coverage for only three years. That's fine if you plan to retire at age 62 and will have three years' worth of coverage before becoming eligible for Medicare. But if you retire at age 60, your benefits will run out before Medicare picks up your medical bills, and you'll have to find your own insurance to cover the two remaining years. In addition, when coverage ends for you, it may end for your nonworking spouse as well.

Obviously, it's important to see if your employer will continue coverage for your spouse when you retire and after you become eligible for Medicare. If your spouse will have no coverage and also must wait several years before becoming eligible for Medicare, he or she will have to find other health insurance.

If your employer offers no coverage and you retire several years before you're eligible for Medicare, you (and your spouse) have four options: (1) continue existing coverage from your employer for a short time; (2) convert to an individual health-insurance policy offered by the same carrier that provided your group coverage; (3) buy a new policy from another carrier; or (4) buy coverage from your state's high-risk pool, if there is one. The best choice is the plan that gives you the greatest coverage at the lowest price for the longest time.

COVERAGE UNDER COBRA If you worked for a business with 20 or more employees, the Consolidated Omnibus Budget Reconciliation Act of 1985 (COBRA) entitles you and your dependents to continued coverage for at least 18 months under your former employer's plan. If you are disabled and eligible for Social Security disability benefits when your employment ends, you get an additional 11 months of coverage, or a total of 29 months. Your COBRA coverage can last up to 36 months if you are insured through your spouse's plan at work and your spouse dies, if you divorce or separate, or if your spouse becomes eligible for Medicare.

Such coverage isn't free. You have to pay 102 percent of the premium (the 2 percent is for administrative expenses). If you're disabled, you pay 150 percent for the extra 11 months of coverage. If you were not paying for any of your health insurance before leaving the company or were only paying for part of the premium, you will undoubtedly have to pay a hefty bill for this coverage.

Employers pay an average of $4,000 a year to insure workers and their dependents and anywhere from $1,800 to $2,200 to insure employees who are single. Depending on the plan, your bill could be more or less. If you choose to buy insurance under your COBRA rules, find out well in advance what your premiums will be so you can accommodate them in your retirement budget. Also plan for premium increases. The U.S. has yet to tame health-care inflation; premium hikes are inevitable.

You can lose COBRA coverage if you don't pay your premiums, if you become eligible for Medicare, if your employer discontinues health benefits for employees still working, or if you join another plan. However, if you or your spouse join another plan that imposes a waiting period for preexisting health conditions, you can keep your COBRA benefits until they normally would run out. By that time, your preexisting condition may be covered under the new plan. You could be without coverage for that condition if your benefits stop before the waiting period on the new plan is over.

An increasingly common way to lose benefits is for your former employer to drop coverage for employees still working or to change insurance carriers. Sometimes the new carrier "underwrites" all employees, active and retired. This means it scrutinizes your health and decides whether it wants to insure you. If it doesn't, you may have no coverage. The new plan may also provide fewer benefits.

Despite such uncertainties, COBRA coverage can be vital. If you retire early and are too young for Medicare unless you are seriously disabled, a preexisting health condition may make it difficult or impossible to buy insurance. If you want to or must retire early, try to coordinate your retirement with the length of time you'll receive COBRA benefits. If you can wait until you are 63½ to retire, you'll have protection until Medicare begins. When you do qualify for Medicare, your spouse can continue COBRA coverage for an additional 18 months, assuming he or she is not yet eligible for Medicare. Coverage for your spouse is a crucial factor in choosing the best time to retire.

If you work for a company that has self-insured its workers' health coverage, you are entitled to COBRA benefits even though such plans are normally exempt from other insurance regulations.

If you are not eligible for COBRA because your former firm employs fewer than 20 workers or is a church organization, you may still have some protection under state laws. Some states provide for continuation of benefits, and you may be able to stay on your employer's group policy for as long as 18 months. (But in others you may get coverage for only three months.) These continuation benefits are usually not available to workers in self-insured plans or in states without comprehensive-continuation laws. These states include: Alabama, Alaska, Arizona, Delaware, the District of Columbia, Hawaii, Idaho, Indiana, Michigan, and Pennsylvania.

Many employers don't like to offer COBRA coverage, claiming it is an administrative nightmare and costs them too much money. Consequently, some employers offer you the option of taking an accident-only policy instead of full-fledged health benefits under COBRA. These policies do not cover illness; they pay only if you're injured in an accident. Even though such a policy is much cheaper, you give up valuable protection; we don't recommend those substitutes.

CONVERSION POLICIES If COBRA benefits stop before you qualify for Medicare, your employer must give you the right to convert to an individual policy. If you're not eligible for COBRA, your state's insurance laws may require your employer to offer conversion policies, although limitations and coverages vary from state to state. All states except Alabama, Alaska, Connecticut, Delaware, the District of Columbia, Hawaii, Idaho, Massachusetts, Michigan, Mississippi, Nebraska,

New Jersey, North Dakota, and Oklahoma require such policies.

Conversion-policy coverage is almost always inferior to what you received from your group plan when you were working. Only 29 states require companies to offer conversion policies with major-medical or comprehensive benefits. A major-medical policy usually covers hospital and surgical charges, outpatient care, and physicians' fees, but a conversion policy is likely to provide only hospital and surgical benefits and pay only a fixed amount each day for hospital room and board and surgical procedures.

The price of a conversion policy is high, because people in poor health usually buy this coverage.

Despite low benefits and high premiums, a conversion policy may be your only option if you have chronic health problems. Insurers aren't allowed to underwrite conversion coverage, so you can always get it no matter how bad your health. If you are unable to buy an individual policy or obtain coverage from your state's high-risk pool, if it has one, you may have to pay the price for conversion coverage or risk going uninsured until you turn 65.

YOUR RIGHTS UNDER THE HEALTH INSURANCE PORTABILITY AND ACCOUNTABILITY ACT In 1996, Congress passed the Health Insurance Portability and Accountability Act, sometimes referred to as the Kennedy-Kassebaum law, named for its sponsors. The act provides some help to employees who leave an employer group plan and must buy coverage on their own. It allows you to use evidence of prior coverage to reduce or eliminate the wait normally imposed by a preexisting-conditions clause, which the act limits to 12 months. But in order to eliminate the wait for coverage for medical conditions you have when you buy a policy, you must be mindful of the barriers the law imposes. If you have had coverage from an employer and are buying an individual policy, you must have had group coverage for at least 18 months, use up your COBRA coverage for another 18 months, and then find a new policy within 63 days after your coverage runs out. If you are eligible for Medicare, the protections of the Kennedy-Kassebaum law don't apply.

BUYING A POLICY ON YOUR OWN If you retire early and your employer does not provide health insurance, you can always forgo your COBRA benefits and try to find a policy in the private market. If you have health problems, you may not be able to do this. But if your health is good and you can find a carrier willing to issue a policy at a price that's less than your COBRA coverage, you may want to choose this option. When your COBRA benefits stop, you may also want to shop for your own policy rather than opt for a costly conversion policy from your employer (assuming you're not eligible for Medicare).

Your shopping trip won't be easy, however. There are few sellers, and the ones that do offer coverage make you pass strict health requirements before they issue a policy. Virtually no commercial carriers and only a handful of Blue Cross Blue Shield plans sell policies to anyone who has had heart disease, internal cancer, diabetes, a stroke, adrenal disorders, epilepsy, or ulcerative colitis. Treatment for alcohol and substance abuse, depression, or even visits to a marriage counselor can disqualify you. Check with your state insurance department to find out if your state offers an insurer of last resort. It may be your local Blue Cross Blue Shield plan, and it may be that the plan you're offered will be coverage from an HMO. That's the case in New York, for example.

If you have less serious medical problems, you may get coverage, but on unfavorable terms. Conditions that usually affect one part of the body are candidates for *exclusion riders.* This means a carrier offers a policy but excludes coverage for those conditions or the affected body part either for a short period or for as long as the policy is in force. For example, if you have had a recent knee operation, glaucoma, migraine headaches, varicose veins, or arthritis, your policy will probably carry an exclusion rider. If you have a medical condition that affects your general health—you're significantly overweight or have mild high blood pressure—you may get coverage but at a price 15 to 100 percent higher than the standard premium.

Pay particular attention to a policy's renewability clause. Few companies guarantee to renew your coverage. Most policies are "conditionally renewable," that is, the company can refuse to renew your policy, but only if it does so for all other similar policies in your state. You have some protection, then, because the company can't single you out for cancellation. But you can still lose your coverage eventually. Some companies use conditionally renewable policies as a lever to force insurance regulators to grant them rate increases, and a number of carriers have canceled policies in states where regulators were unwilling to raise rates. Ask whether the company you're considering has canceled any health policies. Past practice may give you a clue to what it will do in the future.

A few policies are "optionally renewable." A company can choose not to renew your insurance whether or not it renews coverage for others who have the same policy. Avoid these policies if you can.

HIGH-RISK POOLS A fourth option is your state's high-risk pool. Twenty-six states have established such pools as the insurer of last resort for people with serious health problems. (See Appendix B for a list of pools and their addresses.) When your COBRA benefits run out, look to the pool if you are not in good health.

To obtain coverage, you must be a state resident—the length of residency varies from 30 days to one year. You must also have received a rejection notice from at least one carrier. (A few states require more.) Some states will accept you automatically if you have certain medical conditions. In those cases, you won't have to submit proof of rejection. If a carrier will insure you only at a premium that exceeds the price of coverage from the pool or if the insurance you're offered carries exclusion riders, you are also eligible for a pool policy in most states. Some risk pools can insure only a certain number of people. If your pool is full, you may have to wait, an unacceptable alternative for most people.

Alaska, Florida, Illinois, Iowa, Minnesota, North Dakota, Washington, Wisconsin, and Wyoming make some type of Medicare-supplement policies available through their pools. Mississippi and Montana offer certain types of supplemental policies for those over 65. Medicare supplements from the pools may be helpful if you are disabled, under age 65, and rely on Medicare but can't find insurance to cover Medicare's gaps.

Pool coverage is similar to that offered by a major-medical policy, although benefits for mental and nervous disorders, organ transplants, and pregnancy may be less comprehensive. You may, however, pay more out of pocket than you would with a major-medical policy. Some plans require high deductibles and greater coinsurance, and have relatively low lifetime benefit maximums. Deductibles can be as high as $10,000 and lifetime maximums as low as $250,000. Most pools also require policyholders to satisfy a preexisting-conditions requirement. Policies usually won't pay benefits for any medical problem you've had for six months before you applied for coverage, and they will exclude them from coverage for a certain period, generally three, six, or 12 months, depending on the plan.

Premiums are very high, which is not surprising, since policyholders will almost certainly file claims. A 62-year-old man living in Chicago would pay $10,740 a year for a policy with a $500 deductible from the Illinois pool.

IF YOU RETIRE AT AGE 65

If you are 65 and your employer offers you health insurance, you have to decide whether to take that coverage and/or buy a Medicare-supplement policy. Consider your spouse's coverage, as well. He or she may have no insurance from your employer, in which case you have to buy him or her a Medicare-supplement policy, assuming your spouse is eligible for Medicare.

Employers use three basic approaches in fashioning health coverage for their retirees:

CARVE-OUT COORDINATION OF BENEFITS This is the most common approach. You receive the same benefits as active employees. The insurer calculates the portion of the claim the policy covers if Medicare were not in the picture. It then adds the amount the active employee would pay under this arrangement to the amount Medicare pays for you. The insurer subtracts this total from the amount of the claim and pays the difference.

Example: You incur $1,100 in medical expenses. Medicare's allowed charge is $750, of which it pays 80 percent, or $600. Your policy has a $100 deductible, which the carrier subtracts from the amount of the claim, leaving $1,000 that you are responsible for paying. Under the terms of the policy for active workers, the carrier pays 80 percent of $1,000, or $800. The plan then subtracts Medicare's $600 payment, leaving $200 to be paid by the plan. Thus, Medicare pays $600, the insurance company $200, and you $300.

Under the carve-out method, your total benefit—from the employer plan plus Medicare—is the same as it was before you retired, assuming, of course, the plan is the same.

STANDARD COORDINATION OF BENEFITS WITH MEDICARE This is the most generous method, and fewer employers are using it. The insurer determines the portion of your expenses eligible for payment, subtracts the deductible, then pays 80 percent of the remainder. But if that amount plus Medicare's payment is greater than the total claim, the insurance company reduces what it pays to you. You cannot profit from an illness. *Example:* Let's return to the $1,100 claim on which Medicare pays $600. Five hundred dollars remains unpaid. In calculating what you should receive, the insurance company subtracts the $100 deductible from the $1,100 claim, leaving $1,000 on which it bases its payment. The company then pays 80 percent, or

HEALTH INSURANCE FROM YOUR EMPLOYER   151

$800. (In this example, we assume that the $1,000 is the company's "usual and customary" reimbursement level for the particular procedure.) The $800 plus the $600 Medicare payment exceeds the amount of the claim, so the insurance company pays only the $400 that remains after Medicare pays its share. In this example, you pay only the $100 deductible, if you haven't already paid it for some other claim. If you have paid it, you have no out-of-pocket expenses.

EXCLUSION COORDINATION OF BENEFITS This method recognizes only the part of a claim Medicare does not reimburse. The deductible, if it has not been paid, is subtracted from the portion of the claim Medicare doesn't cover; the insurer pays 80 percent of what's left. *Example:* Medicare pays $600 of the $1,100 claim, leaving $500 unpaid. The insurer subtracts the $100 deductible, leaving $400, of which it pays 80 percent, or $320. The insurer's payment of $320 plus Medicare's contribution of $600 equals $920. That leaves $180 for you to pay, along with any deductible that hasn't been satisfied.

OTHER APPROACHES

Your employer may simply set aside a sum of money for you to spend on health care. These accounts can range in size from a few hundred dollars to $20,000, depending on whether your employer intends for the account to supplement other health insurance or provide major coverage. If you are offered such an account, you should also buy a good supplemental policy unless your employer sets up an extraordinarily large account, which is rare. Some companies offer retirees regular Medicare-supplement policies similar to those you can buy on your own (see Chapter 10). Still others offer policies that pay only for hospital-related charges, which is limited coverage indeed.

MANAGED-CARE OPTIONS Some employers are offering their retirees an HMO arrangement in addition to the traditional indemnity-insurance options and sometimes in place of indemnity coverage. You may have no choice but to join an HMO if you want your employer to pick up part of the cost of your health insurance. With an HMO, you give up some freedom to pick and choose your health-care providers, and there are lingering questions about the quality of care seniors receive. But in return, you may find your monthly costs for premiums as well as out-of-pocket costs are lower in an HMO. Beware, however, that the economics of government payments to the HMOs are changing, and an HMO that's attractive today may not be attractive tomorrow, when it increases its premiums and stops offering extra benefits like eyeglasses, dental care, and coverage for prescription drugs, which most Medicare supplements don't provide. Chapter 11 discusses managed-care options in more detail.

Many employers offer prescription-drug coverage if retirees use a managed program. This often takes the form of a mail-order pharmacy where a retiree sends away for a supply of medication. Chapter 11 discusses the rules and limitations of such programs in more detail. If you don't have to use a mail-order arrangement, you probably will be required to fill your prescriptions at certain pharmacies that offer discounts to both employers and employees.

Drug benefits are often key in deciding which options you should choose for your health benefits. Even though you don't use many drugs now, you have no way of knowing whether you'll need more five or 10 years from now. If the drug coverage is reasonably generous and the premium relatively low, the benefit, although "managed" in some way, may tip the balance in favor of your employer's coverage.

EMPLOYERS' SPENDING CAPS Keep in mind that many employers aren't going to continue shelling out for retiree coverage indefinitely. In 1996, 39 percent of large employers had placed a dollar "cap" on the amount of money they spent for health benefits. It's a safe bet that more employers will do the same. There are several ways employers impose caps. For example, an employer may decide to spend no more than twice what was spent in 1990. Some may say that their per-person subsidy will not exceed a set amount, such as $2,000. Others may relate the amount of the cap to years of service. No matter the method, the bottom line is the same: Once the cap is reached, you'll pay more out of pocket for your coverage. Let's say, for example, that your employer will pay 90 percent of the cost of the coverage until a cap of $1,800 is reached. If the cost of providing health-care coverage increases to $2,500 in 10 years, you may pay 25 percent of the cost instead of 10 percent. If it rises to $4,400 in 20 years, your share could increase to 58 percent.

Finding out if your employer has capped what it will spend for your health care is crucial. If a cap is in place, be sure you understand how it works and how much of the cost of your coverage you may have to assume later on. Remember, income in retirement often shrinks as you age. If you find that 20 years from now you'll be assuming a large share of the cost, you may want to consider other options.

COMPARING YOUR EMPLOYER'S PLAN WITH OTHER POLICIES Your out-of-pocket medical expenses are lowest if your former employer uses the standard coordination-of-benefits approach; they are highest under a carve-out arrangement.

If your employer uses the standard coordination-of-benefits approach and pays the entire cost of your coverage, an additional Medicare-supplement policy is a waste of money. The same is true if your employer uses either the carve-out or the exclusion approach and pays the entire premium. Under these plans, you have small out-of-pocket expenses but pay nothing for the coverage. If you buy a generous supplemental policy, you will spend $1,500 or more a year on premiums. Plans with prescription-drug coverage cost even more. Of course, if your employer terminates its health plan or goes out of business, your good coverage could evaporate. In that case, you would have to buy a Medicare-supplement anyway.

If you still want a supplement, consider a less-expensive barebones policy that covers only the 20-percent Medicare copayment. Look for Medicare-supplement Plan A when you do your shopping for a policy (see Chapter 10). If your employer uses the carve-out or exclusion approach and requires that you pay most of the premium, you may be better off buying a Medicare-supplement policy that pays most of your bills and forgoing your employer's coverage. The premium may be less than what your employer would charge.

Example: Let's return again to our hypothetical claim of $1,100. As noted, Medicare's allowed charge is $750, of which Medicare pays 80 percent, or $600, assuming the $100 deductible has already been paid. You are responsible for the 20 percent copayment, or $150. But your physician refuses to accept assignment, does not take Medicare's $600 as full payment, and instead bills you for the remaining $350, which is the total charge minus the allowed charge ($1,100 minus $750 equals $350). Besides the $150 copayment, you also pay $350 of excess charges, for a total of $500. If you have neither coverage from your employer nor a supplemental policy, your out-of-pocket expenses are $500, again assuming you've already paid the annual deductible. If you have not paid the deductible, Medicare will pay only $500, and you'll have to come up with $600.

If you have insurance from your employer, who has used one of the three approaches outlined in this chapter, you pay, in addition to the deductible, $0, $180, or $300, depending on the plan. If you have no employer-provided coverage but carry a Medicare-supplement policy, the amount you pay depends on the policy you bought. All Medicare-supplement policies must cover the 20-percent copayment. But they don't all cover the Part B deductible or excess physicians' charges from doctors who don't accept Medicare payment as payment in full. If your supplemental policy pays just the coinsurance, your out-of-pocket expenses are $350. If it covers excess charges, either 80 percent or all of the $350 is paid, depending on the type of supplement you buy. Your deductible would also be paid if your supplement covers it.

If the premium for your employer's coverage is about the same as you would pay for a Medicare-supplement policy that covers excess physicians' fees, work through a few hypothetical claims to see which policy pays the most.

In making your decision, consider coverage for extras such as prescription drugs or preventive care. Sometimes, employer-provided policies cover these; sometimes, Medicare-supplemental policies do. If your employer's plan pays for prescriptions, you may be asked to use a mail-order drug company and pay a small copayment ranging from $2 to $10 but sometimes more. This coverage could be valuable if you regularly use medication. If the basic coverage of two competing policies is equal, coverage for these extras might tip the balance in favor of one policy or another. In a few instances, you might want both.

If your employer's plan is generally inferior but covers prescription drugs that you need to take on a regular basis, you may want to keep the plan and buy a 20-percent supplemental policy. Likewise, check policy exclusions. If you have a preexisting health condition for which you might need immediate coverage, you are probably better off staying with your employer's coverage.

Remember, if you have just turned 65 and you buy a Medicare-supplement policy, the insurance company cannot ask you any questions about your health. You have a six-month period during which insurance companies cannot "underwrite" you (see Chapter 10).

10

I·N·S·U·R·A·N·C·E

TO SUPPLEMENT MEDICARE

FROM THE BEGINNING, MEDICARE WAS NEVER meant to cover the entire health-care bill for the elderly. Initially, the gaps left by Medicare coverage were small—as were the premiums for supplemental policies. But the gaps widened as health-care costs escalated, and now Medicare-supplement insurance has become a major expense for older Americans. Fifty-four percent of all beneficiaries have incomes less than $15,000 a year, and beneficiaries pay on average $2,600 out of pocket for deductibles, premiums, and coinsurance. Eleven percent spend more than $100 each month for perscription drugs.

Complicating the shopping picture for seniors are the new Medicare + Choice options, which we will discuss in Chapter 11. As we point out in that chapter, some of those options are risky and fraught with hidden costs, and you are best to avoid them. For most people, Consumers Union recommends remaining with traditional Medicare coverage along with traditional Medicare-supplement insurance, often referred to as a Medigap policy, if you can afford the continually rising premiums. This chapter will walk you through the particulars of buying this insurance. For further help, you can also contact your state insurance-counseling program, if there is one (see Appendix C). Counselors can help you sort out the insurance coverage you already have, tell you what you need, and advise you whether the policy you are considering is right for you.

ASSESSING YOUR NEEDS

When you review your health-insurance needs in preparation for retirement, first see if you can continue coverage under your employer's health plan (or your spouse's if he or she is still working). If that insurance covers Medicare's gaps and if the employer picks up most of the bill, you probably don't need another policy. But if coverage from an employer is inadequate or you must pay for it yourself and the cost is greater than coverage purchased on your own, you must buy your supplement from private insurance carriers.

Of course, if your income is low enough to qualify you for Medicaid, you don't need a policy. Similarly, if your income is moderate to low but not low enough for Medicaid, or if you take multiple prescription drugs, consider joining an HMO (health-maintenance organization), which we discuss in Chapter 11. On page 141, we describe two programs that help low-income retirees pay their premiums for Medicare-supplement policies and some of Medicare coinsurance, as well.

In beginning your search for a supplement, you must first understand what Medicare pays and what gaps remain in your coverage. Once you know what Medicare leaves uncovered, familiarize yourself with the coverage supplied by each policy.

THE 10 STANDARDIZED PLANS

In 1990, Congress passed legislation that put an end to much of the confusion about Medicare-supplement insurance. It asked the National Association of Insurance Commissioners (NAIC), an organization composed of state insurance regulators, to create 10 standardized Medicare-supplement policies. The Balanced Budget Act of 1997 authorized carriers to sell two additional options with very high deductibles. Insurers can offer only the prescribed plans and the two new options.

The plans are designated by the letters A through J and offer different combinations of benefits. The two new options are known as high-deductible F and high-deductible J. Each plan is the same from insurer to insurer. For example, one company's Plan C is identical to another's Plan C. Therefore, the main differences among policies are price and the quality of the service provided by the insurance company.

Not all 10 policies may be approved for sale in your state, however, and not every insurance company offers every plan. Once you decide which plan suits your needs, seek out the companies that sell that particular plan. If the plan of your choice is not offered in your state (your state insurance department can tell you this), then choose the one that is available and comes closest to meeting your requirements.

THE PLANS AND THEIR BENEFITS

The following is a guide to the types of coverage provided by each Medicare-supplement plan (also see *Table 13*):

PLAN A Every insurer must offer Plan A, which provides certain core, or basic, benefits. These include:

• Coverage for Part A coinsurance—the daily amount you must pay for a hospital stay if you're hospitalized from 61 to 90 days. In 1998, Part A coinsurance is $191 a day.

• Coverage for Part A coinsurance—the daily amount you must pay for a hospital stay that lasts from 91 to 150 days. In 1998, that amount is $382.

• Coverage for an extra 365 days of hospital care after you have exhausted all of your Medicare benefits.

• Coverage for the cost of the first three pints of blood you may need as an inpatient in a hospital. In other words, policies will cover the Part A blood deductible.

• Coverage for Part B coinsurance—20 percent of Medicare's allowable charge.

PLAN B Includes all the benefits of Plan A plus:

• Coinsurance coverage for a stay in a skilled-nursing facility. Medicare requires beneficiaries needing skilled-nursing care to pay coinsurance for stays that last from 21 to 100 days. In 1998, the amount of the coinsurance was $95.50. After that, neither Medicare nor Medigap insurance pays any part of the bill.

• Part A hospital deductible. This was $764 in 1998.

PLAN C Includes all the benefits of Plan A plus:

• Coinsurance coverage for a stay in skilled-nursing facility.

• Part A hospital deductible.

• Emergency medical care in foreign countries.

• Part B deductible—$100 in 1998.

PLAN D Includes all the benefits of Plan A plus:

• Coinsurance coverage for a stay in a skilled-nursing facility.

TABLE 13 •   WHAT MEDICARE SUPPLEMENT
POLICIES COVER

	Plan type									
	A	**B**	**C**	**D**	**E**	**F**	**G**	**H**	**I**	**J**
PART A HOSPITAL COINSURANCE, DAYS 61-90 $191 *per day,* 1998	✓	✓	✓	✓	✓	✓	✓	✓	✓	✓
PART A HOSPITAL COINSURANCE, DAYS 91-150 $382 *per day,* 1998	✓	✓	✓	✓	✓	✓	✓	✓	✓	✓
ALL CHARGES FOR EXTRA 365 DAYS IN HOSPITAL	✓	✓	✓	✓	✓	✓	✓	✓	✓	✓
PART A BLOOD DEDUCTIBLE, 3 PINTS	✓	✓	✓	✓	✓	✓	✓	✓	✓	✓
PART B BLOOD DEDUCTIBLE, 3 PINTS	✓	✓	✓	✓	✓	✓	✓	✓	✓	✓
PART B COINSURANCE *20% of allowable charges*	✓	✓	✓	✓	✓	✓	✓	✓	✓	✓
SKILLED-NURSING FACILITY COINSURANCE, DAYS 21-100 $95.90, 1998	—	✓	✓	✓	✓	✓	✓	✓	✓	✓
PART A DEDUCTIBLE $763 *per year,* 1998	—	✓	✓	✓	✓	✓	✓	✓	✓	✓
EMERGENCY CARE IN FOREIGN COUNTRIES	—	—	✓	✓	✓	✓	✓	✓	✓	✓
PART B DEDUCTIBLE $100 *per year*	—	—	✓	—	—	✓	—	—	—	✓
PART B EXCESS CHARGES	—	—	—	—	—	[1]	[2]	—	[1]	[1]
AT-HOME CARE NEEDED AFTER AN INJURY, ILLNESS, OR SURGERY	—	—	—	✓	—	—	✓	—	✓	✓
PRESCRIPTION DRUGS	—	—	—	—	—	—	—	[3]	[3]	[4]
PREVENTIVE MEDICAL CARE	—	—	—	—	✓	—	—	—	—	✓

[1] *Pays 100 percent of difference between doctor's bill and amount Medicare pays.*
[2] *Pays 80 percent of difference between doctor's bill and amount Medicare pays.*
[3] *$1,250 maximum yearly benefit; $250 deductible; 50-percent coinsurance.*
[4] *$3,000 maximum yearly benefit; $250 deductible; 50-percent coinsurance.*

- Part A hospital deductible.
- Emergency medical care in foreign countries.
- Coverage for at-home care following an injury, illness, or surgery. This benefit covers assistance with activities of daily living, such as eating, bathing, and dressing. *Note:* The at-home-care coverage is limited to a short period. For example, the benefit is limited to $1,600 per year, and your physician must certify that visits by a licensed home health aide, homemaker, or personal-care worker are necessary because of a condition for which Medicare has already approved a home-health-care treatment plan for you. The benefit can be used for up to eight weeks after Medicare's home health benefit ends.

PLAN E Includes all the benefits of Plan A plus:
- Coinsurance coverage for a stay in a skilled-nursing facility.
- Part A hospital deductible.
- Emergency medical care in foreign countries.
- Preventive medical care not covered by Medicare. This benefit covers the cost of an annual physical, fecal occult blood tests, mammograms, thyroid and diabetes screening, a pure-tone hearing test, and cholesterol screening every five years.

PLAN F Includes all the benefits of Plan A plus:
- Coinsurance coverage for a stay in a skilled-nursing facility.
- Part A hospital deductible.
- Part B deductible.
- Emergency medical care in foreign countries.
- One hundred percent of Medicare Part B excess charges. An excess charge is the difference between Medicare's approved amount or allowed charge (see Chapter 8) and the amount the physician actually bills.

Plan F offers a high-deductible option. You must pay the first $1,500 of your medical expenses yourself before the policy pays any benefits.

PLAN G Includes all the benefits of Plan A plus:
- Coinsurance coverage for a stay in a skilled-nursing facility.
- Part A hospital deductible.
- Emergency medical care in foreign countries.
- Coverage for at-home care following an injury, illness, or surgery.
- Eighty percent of Medicare Part B excess charges.

PLAN H Includes all the benefits of Plan A plus:
- Coinsurance coverage for a stay in a skilled-nursing facility.
- Part A hospital deductible.

- Emergency medical care in foreign countries.
- Coverage for at-home care following an injury, illness, or surgery.
- Fifty percent of the cost of prescription drugs up to an annual maximum benefit of $1,250 after the policyholder satisfies a $250 annual deductible. This is the basic prescription-drug benefit.

PLAN I Includes all the benefits of Plan A plus:

- Coinsurance coverage for a stay in a skilled-nursing facility.
- Part A hospital deductible.
- Emergency medical care in foreign countries.
- Coverage for at-home care following an injury, illness, or surgery.
- One hundred percent of Part B excess charges.
- The basic prescription-drug benefit.

PLAN J Includes all the benefits of Plan A plus:

- Coinsurance coverage for a stay in a skilled-nursing facility.
- Part A hospital deductible.
- Part B deductible.
- Emergency medical care in foreign countries.
- Coverage for at-home care following an injury, illness, or surgery.
- Preventive medical care.
- One hundred percent of Part B excess charges.
- Fifty percent of the cost of prescription drugs up to an annual maximum benefit of $3,000 after the policyholder meets an annual $250 deductible. This is the extended drug benefit.

Plan J offers a high-deductible option. You pay the first $1,500 of your medical expenses before the plan pays any benefits. The prescription-drug deductible must be met, as well.

THE COST

What you pay for a supplemental policy largely depends on how much coverage you want. The more coverage, the more it costs. Plan A, with only the most basic benefits, could cost a 65-year-old as little as $359 or as much as $1,600 a year, depending on the company and where the policyholder lives (premiums are higher in areas where medical care is very expensive). Plan J, on the other hand, which offers the most comprehensive benefits, could cost more than $3,000 a year. Companies expect that the premium for the two high-deductible options will be about 30 percent less. *Table 14* shows the price ranges for the 10 standardized plans obtained in 1998 from a CONSUMER REPORTS survey of the industry.

What you pay when you first buy a policy and what you pay over time depends on the kind of pricing scheme the insurance company uses. The 1990 reforms of the Medicare-supplement market had an unintended effect. Many companies changed the way they price policies so they can bait consumers with low premiums at the outset and trap them with very high increases later on.

In 1989, most carriers used either "community rates" or "issue-age rates" to price their policies. With community rates, all policyholders, young and old, pay the same premium. With issue-age rates, premiums vary depending on the age of the buyer. But in either case, the annual premium will go up only to reflect increases in the cost of medical services; it will not rise because you get older. Both community and issue-age rates protect policyholders from steep annual increases.

But now most companies use what's called "attained-age" pricing, a less-benign strategy that allows them to gain a competitive advantage by selling cheap policies to 65-year-olds when they first buy a Medicare-supplement policy. With attained-age pricing, the initial premiums, especially for those between 65 and 69, are usually lower than for issue-age or community-rated policies. But there's a catch: Premiums will rise steeply as you get older. Neither insurers nor their

TABLE 14 • COMPARISON OF MEDICARE
SUPPLEMENT POLICIES

▶ *Comparison of Medicare supplement policies for a 65-year-old from 1998 CONSUMER REPORTS survey of the industry*

Medicare plan	Price range
PLAN A	$359 TO $1,601
PLAN B	$566 TO $1,758
PLAN C	$690 TO $2,174
PLAN D	$619 TO $1,899
PLAN E	$613 TO $1,899
PLAN F	$776 TO $2,435
PLAN G	$672 TO $2,070
PLAN H	$1,004 TO $6,955
PLAN I	$1,135 TO $6,888
PLAN J	$1,235 TO $3,333

agents are required to tell consumers how expensive their policies may become. If you buy one of these policies, press the agent and company as hard as you can to find out about future price increases.

To take one example: In 1998, AARP's community-rated policy, underwritten by United Healthcare, costs a 65-year-old living in Chicago $783 for Plan A. A 75-year-old would pay the same. Bankers Life and Casualty, on the other hand, charges the 65-year-old in Chicago $752 and a 75-year-old $998. In 10 years, the 65-year-old who bought the Bankers policy would experience a price increase each year (or every couple of years) as he gets older in addition to increases for the rising cost of medical care. The person with the AARP policy would experience increases only for inflation in medical services and, in the end, may pay less than if he had bought the policy from Bankers.

AARP is one of the few sources of community-rated policies, although you might find a Blue Cross plan offering them in certain areas. Connecticut, Maine, Massachusetts, Minnesota, New York, and Washington require companies to sell community-rated policies. Florida and Georgia require companies to sell issue-age policies.

What you'll pay also depends on how thoroughly the insurance company underwrites—that is, how strictly it scrutinizes the health of prospective policyholders. A carrier that underwrites stringently is able to charge less because it accepts only the healthiest people as customers. A company with a cheap policy may turn out to be tough when it comes to accepting people with certain health conditions.

WHAT ABOUT YOUR HEALTH?

When companies "underwrite," they generally ask if you have had certain health problems, such as internal cancer, heart or vascular surgery, or Alzheimer's disease. A "yes" answer to any question about your health invites further scrutiny and most likely triggers a rejection. Fairly common conditions, such as prospective surgeries or cataracts, could also mean a rejection. If you apply for the plans with drug coverage, a company will probably be very picky. For example, it may not sell you a policy if you use prescription drugs at all. In 1998, all AARP policies, with the exception of the plans with drug coverage, were available to anyone regardless of their health. In insurance parlance, those policies are known as "guaranteed-issue" policies. You might find a Blue Cross plan in your state also selling guaranteed-issue policies, or your state may even require companies to offer them. A few do. However, if you are just becoming eligible for Medicare and are entering the Medicare-supplement market for the first time, the six-month rule discussed below applies, and you will be able to sign up for any of the standardized plans. If you decide instead to sign up for one of the new Medicare + Choice options explained in Chapter 11, and then decide you don't like it, there are other rules. (See pages 187-188.)

THE SIX-MONTH RULE

A federal rule prohibits insurance companies from checking on the health of applicants 65 and older during the first six months after they sign up for Medicare Part B. In other words, they must sell you a guaranteed-issue policy. This rule is helpful if you have a chronic health condition. In that case, you should buy your Medicare-supplement policy as soon as you sign up for Part B. Don't let this six-month window slip by. If you wait too long, you run the risk of not being able to buy a policy because your health condition is unacceptable to some carriers. If you do get coverage after the six-month window, you may end up paying a far higher premium because insurance companies try to compensate for the greater risk you present to them. During the six-month window, companies are not allowed to charge you a higher premium. During the so-called open window, companies that offer prescription-drug plans must also issue policies to anyone regardless of their health status or the number of medications they take. Companies can still impose a preexisting-conditions limitation for six months. Under the Health Insurance Portability and Accountability Act, however, an insurer can't make you fulfill a preexisting-conditions limitation if you take a Medicare-supplement policy within 63 days of leaving your previous coverage. (See page 147.)

If you are 65, still working, and wait to apply for Part B, you can remain under your employer's plan and still be eligible for the open window. When you stop working or are no longer covered by your employer, you can apply for Part B during the seven-month period that begins with the month you are no longer working. When you do, you are still eligible for the six-month open-enrollment window and can buy a policy without meeting the insurer's underwriting requirements. If your employer does offer coverage and you continue to work, you may want to delay signing up for Medicare Part B. If you sign up and then don't buy a supplemental policy within the next six months, you could be out of luck.

If you work for a firm with more than 20 employees, your employer's coverage will be primary. It's probably not worth the trouble to get Medicare to pay for small amounts not covered by your employer's insurance. That is especially true if your health coverage is provided through a managed-care plan, for which the copayments are likely to be small and which may offer prescription-drug coverage.

The same holds true if you are over 65 and retired and are covered under your spouse's employer's insurance. When you and your spouse are no longer covered by that plan and apply for Part B, you are still eligible for the six-month window.

If you work for a company with fewer than 20 employees and continue to stay on the job, Medicare becomes your primary insurance, and your employer can provide you with a supplemental policy. But many small firms don't, and most likely, you'll have to buy one on your own. Be sure to do so before the six-month window closes.

If you are over 65 and retired but so far have chosen not to enroll in Part B, you can still do so subject to the requirements described previously. When you do enroll, your six-month window begins.

SHOPPING FOR A POLICY

As you begin your shopping trip, we suggest you contact your state insurance department (see Appendix D) and find out what plans are available in your state. Also ask the department for a list of the companies licensed to sell Medicare-supplement insurance. Once you have this information, here are some points to keep in mind:

PART B EXCESS CHARGES At one point, most consumers needed protection from balance billing—charges by doctors who did not take assignment and billed more than Medicare's allowable charge. However, in recent years Congress has limited the extra charges doctors can bill to no more than 15 percent above the allowed amount. Most doctors have found it's not worth their while to balance bill. In fact, about 80 percent of all doctors take assignment; that is, they take Medicare's allowed amount as payment in full. But if the doctors you see most often don't take assignment, then you may want to consider a plan that covers excess charges.

Four plans—F, G, I, and J—cover some or all excess charges. Plans I and J cover 100 percent of them plus prescription drugs. They are likely to be the most expensive plans, and if you already use prescription drugs, companies may not be eager to sell you this coverage (except during the six-month window). Or you may not want prescription- drug benefits. In that case, you can choose only Plan F or Plan G if you just want coverage for excess charges. High-deductible Plan F and high-deductible Plan J also cover excess charges, but the steep deductible may make those options unattractive.

THE FEWEST FRILLS Plans B, C, and D cover most of the basics with the fewest frills. Unless you have a good reason to buy coverage for excess charges, you'll save money if you skip Plan F and its higher-priced cousins—Plans G, I, and J. Though you may not now have high prescription-drug costs, the older you get, the more likely you will have to take one or more expensive medications permanently for chronic conditions or even for prevention. Plan C is the most widely available plan, but Plan B might be a better choice if you can find it. It covers most of the important gaps and is somewhat cheaper. In 1998, the average annual premium for Plan B was $1,252, 28 percent less than the average premium of $1,466 for Plan C. Plan D may also be a better value than Plan C, but it, too, may be hard to find. Unlike Plan C, it doesn't cover the $100 deductible for Part B services (see below). Plan D covers some at-home recovery services that can be useful.

PART B DEDUCTIBLE Buying coverage that pays the first $100 of any physician or hospital outpatient charge is simply dollar trading, since you may pay $100 in extra premiums for the coverage. However, one of the plans that covers excess physicians' charges also includes coverage for the Part B deductible. If your choice comes down to Plan F because you want coverage for excess physicians' charges and you can afford that plan, you will get coverage for the Part B deductible, anyway.

THE HIGH-DEDUCTIBLE PLANS In an attempt to shift a greater portion of the cost of medical care to beneficiaries, Congress created the two high-deductible plans. If you take either one of them, you'll have to pay $1,500 out-of-pocket before you'll have any coverage from the policy. That means you'll have to pay the Part A and Part B deductibles and coinsurance yourself until you reach the $1,500 limit. For most beneficiaries this is large financial burden. We don't recommend you assume it. Policies were not available when this book went to press, so it's not possible for us to say whether the lower premiums they may carry are worth the increased out-of-pocket costs.

• At-home care following an injury, illness, or surgery. This benefit is somewhat limited. For that reason, it may not be high on your list of needed coverages. Furthermore, if you already own a long-term-care policy that has such a benefit, you don't need to pay another premium for similar coverage.

• Preventive medical care. In 1997, Congress authorized Medicare to cover some preventive services, including yearly mammograms, colon-cancer screening, bone-mass measurement, flu shots, and diabetes-glucose monitoring. Only two plans offer preventive-care benefits—Plan E and Plan J. Plan E is usually hard to find, and Plan J, which covers drugs, is usually too expensive for most people or unavailable if you already take a lot of prescription drugs.

• Emergency care in foreign countries. All policies except Plan A include coverage for emergency care while you're in a foreign country. You may wonder why you need this coverage if you rarely or never travel abroad, but you have little choice in the matter. Insurance companies claim that this benefit adds only a negligible amount to the premium, and the coverage can protect you if you're on a cruise ship.

• Prescription drugs. Only three plans—H, I, and J—cover prescription drugs. In theory, this is a good benefit to have, especially if you already take maintenance drugs. However, as we've pointed out before, you may not be able to obtain a policy that offers drug coverage if you currently take prescription drugs on a regular basis. Furthermore, you'll have to meet a high deductible ($250) before the policy begins to pay, and these policies are usually very expensive. Before committing yourself to a high annual premium for prescription-drug coverage, total the annual cost of your drugs. Because of the 50-percent coinsurance and the deductible, you'll have to incur drug costs of at least $2,750 a year to make it worthwhile to buy Plans H and I. To get the $3,000 worth of benefits for Plan J, you'll need to spend at least $6,250 a year on prescription drugs. If your drug bills are significantly below those amounts, the coverage probably isn't worth the extra premium, although you may need such coverage in the future. You have to weigh the value of paying more now against the likelihood you may use the benefit later. If you take a lot of drugs, you might be better off at an HMO, which may offer more coverage at a lower price. (See Chapter 11.) Furthermore, the HMO has to take everyone who applies. It can't turn you down just because you take a lot of medications. HMOs, however, have other drawbacks, which we also discuss in Chapter 11.

• Preexisting-condition clauses. These impose a waiting period before the policy covers you for medical conditions you have at the time the policy is written. Policies specify how long you must have had such a condition—typically three or six months—for the waiting period to apply, and then state how long you must wait before coverage begins for that condition. In most policies, the waiting period is six months, but it may be shorter. A few companies offer coverage from day one for any health condition. If you have been covered by one Medicare supplement policy and switch to a new one, the new carrier cannot make you satisfy another preexisting-conditions requirement.

Keep in mind that if you are buying a Medicare supplement policy after you no longer have health-insurance coverage from your employer and you meet the requirements of the Health Insurance Portability and Accountability Act (see Chapter 9), the insurance company selling the supplemental policy can't make you satisfy another preexisting-conditions requirement. Remember, though, you have to sign up for the new policy within 63 days after your previous coverage ends. If you don't, you lose the protections of the act and must satisfy the preexisting-conditions requirements the new insurer demands.

• Automatic claims handling. A company that offers this service receives, directly from Medicare, the claims information that appears on a policyholder's Explanation of Medicare Benefits (EOMB). It then pays policyholders whatever benefits are due. Policyholders don't have to wait for their EOMBs and then submit them to the insurance carrier. This shortcut is important and could tip the balance in favor of one company's plan over another, although many companies now offer it.

• Renewability. All policies sold now must be guaranteed renewable. This means the company can't cancel your coverage as long as you continue to pay the premiums. Very old policies, however, can be conditionally renewable; a company may be able to cancel your coverage but must do so for all those who had purchased similar policies.

If your policy is issued through a group, you also have some protection if the group terminates its master contract with the insurer or if you leave the group. You have the right to buy an individual policy with substantially the same benefits and premiums as the group policy.

SWITCHING POLICIES

If you are over 65 and already own a Medicare-supplement policy that provides you with adequate coverage, don't buy one of the standardized policies; you probably don't want one of the new Medicare + Choice options, either. As we note in Chapter 11, those options can be risky, and little is known about how they will really work. You may also find agents trying to sell you a new supplement, perhaps at a lower price than you're now paying. It's tempting to switch for a better price. But premiums for most Medicare-supplement policies rise every year, and today's bargain may be next year's costliest contract. If your health has changed significantly, you may not qualify for a new policy or perhaps not the one you want. If you do decide to switch, don't cancel your old policy until you're sure the new company will accept you.

Be sure you understand the rules for switching from one of the Medicare + Choice options back to a Medicare supplement. We discuss them on page 187.

SUPPLEMENTAL POLICIES AND THE DISABLED

If you have been disabled for 24 months and are receiving Social Security disability benefits, you are eligible for Medicare. Unfortunately, you will have a hard time finding a supplemental policy to fill in Medicare's gaps because most companies sell such policies only to those who've turned 65. Contact several companies to see if they will sell a supplement to someone in your situation. If you live in one of the states that has a high-risk pool for people with health problems, contact the pool to see if it offers a Medicare-supplement policy. Some do (see Appendix B). The following companies have told us they sell policies to the disabled: Aid Association for Lutherans; Anthem Blue Cross Blue Shield of Connecticut; Anthem Blue Cross of Indiana; Anthem Blue Cross of Kentucky; Bankers Life and Casualty; Blue Cross Blue Shield plans in Rhode Island, Oklahoma, Nebraska, Maine, Michigan, Louisiana, and New Hampshire; Capital Blue Cross; Central States Life and Health; Continental Life; Equitable Life and Casualty; Federal Home Life; Finger Lakes Blue Cross Blue Shield; First United American; Harvest Life; Highmark Blue Cross Blue Shield; Security Life; Sierra Health; Standard Life and Accident; Trigon Blue Cross Blue Shield; United American; AARP/United Healthcare; and World Insurance. Blue

Cross Blue Shield of Tennessee and Blue Cross Blue Shield of Illinois will sell policies to the disabled only if they were currently insured with them at the time of their disability. Companies may not sell policies in all states, only in those that require them to do so. Nor do they have to offer a large selection of the standardized plans. We found that these companies are most likely to offer Plans A and B, the ones with the most limited benefits. HMOs have to accept disabled people, and coverage from one of them may be a disabled person's only option.

MEDICARE SELECT

Some carriers, notably AARP/United Healthcare and many Blue Cross Blue Shield plans, offer Medicare Select plans in certain states. These are supplemental policies that restrict the health-care providers, primarily hospitals, you can use. In some states, like California, not all the Blue Cross doctors and hospitals are part of the select network. Because the insurance company negotiates discounts with providers, it can pass some of the savings on to you in the form of lower premiums. Medicare Select policies are, on average, 19 percent cheaper than traditional supplements.

If you find insurance companies offering Medicare Select policies in your state, you might want to consider them if your family doctor and the specialists he or she regularly refers to have privileges at one or more of the hospitals in the network. But to the extent that policies limit your choice of hospitals, they also limit your choice of specialists. With Medicare Select, you'll have freedom to control your own health care—an option not found in an HMO—and pay lower premiums than you would with a traditional policy. Such a policy may be a good compromise between an HMO and a regular supplement. Your state insurance department listed in Appendix D can tell you which companies sell this product.

HOSPITAL-INDEMNITY AND
DREAD-DISEASE POLICIES

Hospital-indemnity policies pay a fixed amount each day you're in the hospital. Dread-disease policies pay benefits only if you contract cancer or some other specified illness.

Such policies are among the worst buys in health insurance. These policies tend to cost you more in premiums than they'll ever pay in benefits, because the chances of meeting the criteria for the limited benefits are pretty small. Policies are sold to buyers through enticing but often misleading advertising: "Cash benefits of $2,250 a month, $525 a week, $75 a day. . . . You cannot be turned down. . . . No salesman will call," reads a flyer for one policy.

How does a hospital-indemnity policy work? You get a fixed dollar amount for each day you spend in the hospital. This policy has no complicated deductibles or coinsurance. The trouble is, the fixed benefit is skimpy to start with and grows less valuable each year.

Plans usually offer daily benefits of $30, $50, or $75; sometimes more. But with the cost of a day in the hospital averaging around $900 in 1998, such policies barely dent your bill. Furthermore, to collect the high benefits touted by some of the ads, you'll need to be hospitalized for as long as a month—an unlikely prospect, since the average hospital stay is only about seven days. Finally, the benefit is fixed. In time, inflation in hospital and medical costs inevitably shrinks its value. Dread-disease policies offer similarly inadequate benefits.

Although the premiums for these coverages are low, running anywhere from $200 to around $500 a year, these policies are generally superfluous. Since Medicare pays virtually all of your hospital bill, there's no need for an additional policy that pays for the same service. If you choose a supplement that covers the Part A deductible, you certainly don't need a hospital-indemnity policy that also pays the deductible. You're better off taking the few hundred dollars you would spend on hospital-indemnity premiums and buying a good Medicare supplement, and perhaps putting the money toward a long-term-care policy that offers inflation protection. Some companies tout these policies as a way to pay for extra expenses that often accompany a serious illness—parking fees, meals, hotel bills, and so on. In other words, people are using this type of insurance to pay for non-health-related incidentals. It's an inefficient way to buy health insurance, and you're gambling that you or a family member is unlucky enough to get one of the named illnesses in the policy.

How to compare policies

We suggest you compare policies sold by at least three companies. In 1998, CONSUMER REPORTS found big price differences for the same plan sold by different carriers in the same city—as much as 60 percent between the most expensive and least expensive policies in some places. Once you decide on the plan you want, list the annual premium the company is quoting. Note the preexisting-conditions requirements and whether the company offers automatic claims handling. If two policies are similarly priced but one has a more liberal preexisting-conditions clause and the company also offers automatic claims handling, then that is the policy to buy.

N · E · W
MEDICARE + CHOICE
O·P·T·I·O·N·S

IN 1997, CONGRESS CHANGED THE RULES of the game for Medicare, already an incredibly complicated program. In past years, confusion surrounding the program was exacerbated by the flim-flam and abusive presentations by sellers of Medicare-supplement policies who preyed on the elderly. Congress cleaned up the marketplace in the early 1990s by authorizing standardized supplement policies (see pages 156-157). But now, by introducing more choice with non-standard benefits, the Balanced Budget Act of 1997 moves the marketplace away from consistency and standardization accomplished by earlier reforms and makes the choices faced by current and future Medicare beneficiaries far more difficult.

Spurred on by certain interest groups, Congress is trying to remake Medicare into a "defined-contribution" plan instead of a health-insurance plan with a predetermined set of benefits available to everyone. Under a defined-contribution plan, Medicare will make a fixed payment to insurance companies, which are allowed to add a range of extra benefits and charge a hefty premium. Over time, Medicare's contribution is unlikely to grow sufficiently to keep pace with continuing increases in medical costs, while premiums are likely to increase substantially. If that happens, more and more of the cost of care will be shifted to beneficiaries, some of whom will be unable to shoulder the burden.

The new Medicare + Choice options are a first step toward a defined-contribution plan. Knowing what these options are, how they work, and how they interact with Medicare and Medicare-supplement insurance is crucial for anyone preparing for retirement. Future medical expenses should be a consideration as you go about retirement planning. As we went to press, much was still unknown about some of the options. Nevertheless, we sketch out how these options will work and how they stack up with one another. We outline the different choices and tell you how to make decisions.

THE OPTIONS YOU WILL HAVE One of your options, of course, will be to elect traditional Medicare and a traditional Medicare supplement. In the section that follows, we also present information on that option, but for a more in-depth discussion, see Chapters 8 and 10. With all of the options, you will still have to pay Part B premiums, which we note in *Worksheet 7*, "Health insurance annual fees" in the back of the book, are continually rising. The premiums noted in the following section are specific to the various options.

TRADITIONAL MEDICARE AND MEDIGAP POLICIES With these, you go to a doctor of your choice. The doctor bills Medicare. Medicare pays the doctor and sends you an explanation of benefits detailing what it paid. The supplemental policy pays some of what Medicare doesn't; you pay any remaining charges.

Plan C is best for most people. Plans H, I, and J offer prescription-drug coverage. They have deductibles of $250 and annual limits on how much the plan will pay. There are now two new plans, high-deductible F and high-deductible J, which require you to pay $1,500 before the policies will pay any benefits.

Out-of-pocket expenses:	Premiums: Can be high-range, from $359 for Plan A to $4,419 for Plan J. Coinsurance: None—usually paid by supplemental policy. Deductibles: Usually none—paid by supplemental policy.
Physician oversight:	None. Deductibles are high for the new F and J variations.
Approval for services:	None. Can use any physician or hospital, but a Medicare Select policy requires the use of certain network

	hospitals.
Billing protections:	Yes—doctors who do not accept assignment can charge you no more than 15 percent above Medicare's approved amount.
Biggest advantage:	Freedom to choose doctors and hospitals.
Biggest disadvantages:	Lack of coverage for prescription drugs on most plans. Plans offering drug coverage may not be available to sick people. Premiums rising rapidly. Large out-of-pocket costs for the new high-deductible plans.
Recommendation:	The best choice for those who put a high value on choosing any doctor or hospital they want, and who can afford the premiums for a good supplement.

HMOs You enroll in an HMO that contracts with Medicare, which in turn pays the plan a set amount each month to provide all of your Medicare benefits. Sometimes, the money is sufficient to provide extra benefits not offered by Medicare. You must use providers in the HMO network unless your HMO offers a point-of-service option (POS) that you have elected. If you go outside the HMO's network, the HMO is not required to pay for your care.

Out-of-pocket expenses:	Premiums: Low—between $0 and $2,900 a year. Coinsurance: Low—$5 to $25 for most services. Deductibles: None.
Physician oversight:	Required oversight of care by HMO but no assurance you're getting the correct treatment. You may appeal decisions.
Approval for services:	Usually must go through primary-care physician unless POS option chosen.
Billing protections:	Yes. With the exception of small copayments per visit or service, HMO doctors are not allowed to charge extra

for Medicare services.

Biggest advantages:	Low monthly premiums and coverage for prescription drugs.
Biggest disadvantages:	Extra coverage and free prescription coverage may disappear, and premiums could rise. Many services, including skilled-nursing and home care, may be tightly controlled. You may experience treatment delays.
Recommendation:	HMOs are good for people who need prescription-drug coverage or who can't afford the premiums for a Medicare supplement policy.

PROVIDER-SPONSORED ORGANIZATIONS (PSO) Also known as PSOs, provider-sponsored organizations are a group of doctors or hospitals that form a legal entity and contract with Medicare to provide Part A and Part B services. The organization, which operates under a state license or a waiver from the federal government, bears all the risk for your care. As in an HMO, you agree to get your care from network providers or those the organization may contract with. If you go outside the network, the PSO is not required to pay for your care unless it offers a point-of-service option, and you take it.

Out-of-pocket expenses:	Premiums: Low—likely to be similar to HMOs. Coinsurance: Low—likely to be similar to HMOs. Deductibles: None.
Physician oversight:	Required oversight of care by PSO but no assurance that you're getting the correct treatment or diagnosis. You may appeal decisions, same as in an HMO.
Approval for services:	Usually must go through primary-care physician.
Billing protections:	Yes. With the exception of copayments for visits and services, doctors can't charge extra for services provided by the PSO.

Biggest advantages:	Premiums and copayments may be low. May offer coverage for prescription drugs. If your doctor becomes part of a PSO, you will have continuity of care.
Biggest disadvantages:	Some services may be tightly controlled; may have limited number of network providers. May be hard to access certain specialists. Regulations may be weak, leading to problems with solvency or capitalization. Disruptions in care could occur if plan is sold.
Recommendation:	Those wanting low premiums and low out-of-pocket expenses might find a PSO attractive. So might people wanting certain doctors who happen to be part of the PSO.

PRIVATE FEE-FOR-SERVICE PLANS With these, you buy a policy from an insurance company that has contracted with Medicare to provide all the basic Medicare services. The insurance company can add extra benefits and charge what it wants for them. You have no Medicare benefits other than those paid for by the insurance company; in other words, Medicare won't pay for your care separately. These policies are *not* the same as Medicare-supplement insurance.

Out-of-pocket expenses:	Premiums: Could be very high for some, depending on the company. Coinsurance: Could be very high for some. The plan sets copayments subject to Medicare limits; they may be more or less than Medicare's for any specific service. Plan may impose copayments for extra benefits. Deductibles: Could be very high for some. The plan may set deductibles subject to Medicare's limits. Plan may impose deductibles for extra benefits.

Physician oversight:	None.
Approval for services:	Can go to any doctor or hospital.
Billing protections:	Very few. Providers who contract with the insurance company (or are deemed by Medicare to have a contract) can charge up to 15 percent of the insurer's fee schedule. Providers who don't contract can charge no more than the deductible and coinsurance amounts. You must pay whatever the plan doesn't cover but are entitled to a determination in advance on whether the plan covers a particular treatment.
Biggest advantage:	Freedom to roam the health-care system.
Biggest disadvantages:	Potentially high premiums and very high out-of-pocket expenses. May be hard to understand what insurer is really offering.
Recommendation:	Only the wealthy who can pay high out-of-pocket costs should consider this option.

PRIVATE CONTRACTING WITH PHYSICIANS If the doctor you choose has opted out of Medicare, you can contract directly with that doctor to provide Medicare-covered services. If you do, no Medicare payment will be made for those services, and they will not be covered by supplemental insurance. You sign a private contract, which discloses that the services are covered by Medicare and would be paid if you used another doctor, and you agree to pay all the charges in full. You still may have Medicare payments to cover Medicare services provided by other doctors who have not opted out of Medicare. You can't be forced to sign a contract when you are facing an emergency or an urgent health problem.

Out-of-pocket expenses:	Premiums: Not applicable. Coinsurance: Not applicable. Deductibles: Not applicable; but expenses could be exorbitant, depending on what the

	doctor charges.
Physician oversight:	None.
Approval for services:	None.
Billing protections:	None. Doctors can charge whatever they want.
Biggest advantage:	Freedom to roam the health-care system.
Biggest disadvantages:	Potentially very high out-of-pocket expenses. Doctors must opt out of Medicare for at least two years and sign private contracts with all beneficiaries for the two-year period. If you sign a contract with any of those physicians, you will not have Medicare payment for the services of that doctor as long as he or she is out of Medicare. Arrangements may be subject to billing abuse.
Recommendation:	Only the wealthy who can pay the full cost of their care should consider this option.

MEDICAL SAVINGS ACCOUNTS (MSAS) With these, you buy an insurance policy with a high annual deductible (at least $1,500 but no more than $6,000) that covers the basic Medicare services and possibly extra benefits. You may count toward the deductible only expenses for Medicare-covered services that would have been paid had you stayed in traditional Medicare as well as any extra services covered by the plan. After the deductible is met, the insurance company will pay Part A and Part B benefits, and other services the policy covers. Medicare makes a monthly payment to the insurance company to provide the standard coverage. The difference between the premium it charges and the payment Medicare makes is the amount that will be deposited into your tax-deferred medical savings account each year.

Savings can be used tax-free to pay for tax-qualified medical expenses, which are defined by the IRS. Funds locked in the MSA may accrue from year to year. If the account balance falls below a certain amount because of withdrawals for nonmedical expenses, you're subject to a tax penalty. If you are healthy and never use the money, you can spend it on anything you like at the end of the year, but if you use it for nonmedical purposes, the money withdrawn will be taxed as income.

Out-of-pocket expenses:	Can be high, low, or moderate, depending on company marketing strategy and Medicare payment rates.
Coinsurance:	Doesn't apply until deductible is met; then can be high, low, or moderate.
Deductibles:	Very high.
Taxes:	Withdrawals for nonmedical expenses are subject to income taxes.
Physician oversight:	None.
Approval for services:	MSAs may be indemnity policies or managed-care arrangements. If indemnity, no requirements to go through a primary-care doctor. If managed care, must usually use primary-care physician and get approvals for referrals to specialists. Insurer may have tough "usual, customary, and reasonable" rules for paying bills.
Billing protections:	None.
Biggest advantage:	If MSA is an indemnity policy, have freedom to roam the health-care system.
Biggest disadvantages:	Potentially very high out-of-pocket expenses and no protections against billing abuses by physicians. Savings account will be of limited value if you get sick. Services could be tightly controlled in managed-care arrangements.
Recommendation:	Not recommended. This is a $6,000 gamble against an insurance company that you will stay healthy.

MANAGED-CARE COUSINS

You may find that some managed-care plans offer preferred-provider organizations (PPOs) or point-of-service options (POS). These arrangements provide some freedom to get care outside the HMO. In a PPO, you go to any doctor in the plan's network without first going through a primary-care physician. If you go outside, the plan may require you to pay larger copayments or higher monthly premiums. With a POS, you can go outside the network and pay a higher premium or larger copayments, depending on the rules. PPOs and POS arrangements may look like provider-service organizations (PSOs), which could operate differently. You will have to be very careful to understand what you have and what the plan's rules are.

THE OPTIONS AND PRESCRIPTION DRUGS One of the main reasons you might want to choose a Medicare + Choice option is for prescription-drug coverage. While some of the newer choices, such as the private fee-for-service plans and medical savings accounts, may offer drug coverage, it's hard to say how good those benefits will be. As we went to press, companies had yet to market any of these products. We do, however, know something about the drug benefits offered by HMOs, which vary considerably. We discuss those later in this chapter and tell you how to determine how good a plan's benefit is by using table 15 on pages 182-183. Some careful planning is in order to make sure you choose a plan that provides the greatest value.

For several years, many HMOs lured Medicare beneficiaries into their plans by offering low or no monthly premiums and adding coverage for prescription drugs. However, those freebies are disappearing as HMOs receive less money from Medicare to provide care. Furthermore, the benefit may sound better than it actually is. By the time you consider copayments, the yearly maximum, and any premiums you'll have to pay, the savings is far less than you think. It's easy to underestimate how expensive your drugs will be. HMOs have seen their pharmacy costs rise some 18 to 20 percent each year. Some of the increase is due to price inflation; some results from the use of more drugs. Whatever the reason, those trends are not likely to change, so be prepared to pay more for your prescriptions over time, even in an HMO.

KNOWING THE BASICS Most plans limit the amount they'll pay for prescription drugs. Which plan has the better arrangement depends on three elements: the annual cap, the copayments, and how the price of the drug is charged against your cap.

• The cap. This is the maximum amount the plan will spend for your drugs each year. You may find that some plans have no caps and will pay an unlimited amount, but those managed-care organizations

TABLE 15 • PAYING FOR YOUR MEDICATIONS

▶ *Prescription-drug benefits may tempt you to join an HMO. But that coverage may be less than you think. You must evaluate the benefit and compare it to your current costs. This example shows a calculation from a hypothetical beneficiary who takes three medications.*

Step 1: *Figure current monthly costs*

Calculate your monthly prescription-drug costs.

Medications	Monthly cost
ZOCOR (3-MONTH SUPPLY FOR $162)	$54
ZITHROMAX	31
ALLEGRA	40
TOTAL MONTHLY PRESCRIPTION COST	125
TOTAL CURRENT ANNUAL COST ($125 X 12)	$1,500

Step 2: *Size up the HMO's cap*

For each HMO you are considering, find out its maximum annual benefit, called the cap. In this example, the HMO has a cap of $1,000.

Step 3: *Determine the copayment*

For each HMO, list all the copayments for the drugs you are taking. The example below shows typical copayments you might find; pick the arrangement you're most likely to use.

Medications	Mail order or pharmacy	Brand or generic	Covered in formulary	Copayment
ZOCOR	MAIL ORDER	BRAND	YES	$15/QUARTER
ZITHROMAX	PHARMACY	BRAND	YES	$10/MONTH
ALLEGRA	PHARMACY	BRAND	YES	$10/MONTH
TOTALS				
ZOCOR (4 QUARTERS X $15 PER QUARTER)				$60
ZITHROMAX (12 MONTHS X $10 PER MONTH)				120
ALLEGRA (12 MONTHS X $10 PER MONTH)				120
TOTAL ANNUAL COPAYMENTS				$300

TABLE 15 • PAYING FOR YOUR MEDICATIONS *CONTINUED*

Step 4: *Calculate the saving*

List the annual copayments, any expenses over the cap, and the premium you'll pay. Compare this to your current costs.

ANNUAL COST (FROM STEP I)	$1,500
MINUS TOTAL ANNUAL COPAYMENTS	-300
COST AFTER COPAYMENTS	$1,200
MINUS HMO MAXIMUM ANNUAL BENEFIT (FROM STEP 2)	-1,000
UNCOVERED COST	$200
MONTHLY HMO PREMIUM	$50
MULTIPLY BY 12	X 12
ANNUAL PREMIUM	$600
Total saving	
COST AFTER COPAYMENTS	$1,200
MINUS UNCOVERED COST	-200
MINUS ANNUAL PREMIUM	-600
SAVING	$400

are a dying breed. Even if you find a plan without a cap, that generosity may not last long. Typically, annual caps range from $200 to $4,000. A few plans may allow you to carry over unused amounts from one year to the next. A few plans also have quarterly caps.

• Copayments. These are amounts the HMO asks you to pay toward the cost of the drug. Within the same plan, copayments vary depending on whether you buy a brand name or a generic and on whether you elect to buy through the mail or go to the local pharmacy. Some plans don't require any copayments. Some make their members pay as much as $30 for each prescription for a month's supply of a medication purchased at a participating pharmacy. You may have to pay more for a brand-name drug than a generic, and with some plans you have to pay the difference between the price of a generic and the price of a branded drug. Mail-order programs at a managed-care plan can save you money. A CONSUMER REPORTS study in 1998 found that they can save 30 percent or even more at some plans. HMOs may also have different copayments, depending on whether the drug you need is on their formulary. For formulary particulars, see below.

• How drug price is applied to cap. An HMO subtracts from the cap the price of each drug you take. If you use a lot of medications and exhaust the cap early in the year, you may find yourself with high out-of-pocket expenses. The higher the drug price a plan applies toward the cap, the faster you'll use up the benefit. If two plans have a cap of $1,000 and one HMO applies, say, $50 to the cap and another applies $35, the plan applying the lower amount offers the better deal.

Plans may use three different prices to arrive at an amount to charge against the cap: the retail price of the drug, the average whole-sale price, or a discounted price to the pharmacy, which may be the average wholesale price minus the discount plus a dispensing fee. Obviously, the retail price is the least favorable, since a higher price will quickly eat into the cap. The best arrangement is some discount from the average wholesale price, and many HMOs told CONSUMER REPORTS that they often use the lower amount to charge against the cap. But some will use a higher amount, and it's important to find out which the plan uses. That information may be hard to get, but we recommend persistence. Otherwise, you won't really know which plan offers the best benefit.

OPEN OR CLOSED FORMULARY In 1998, about half of all HMOs had an open formulary. That means that the plan will pay for almost any drug you need, subject, of course, to copayments and caps. In a closed formulary, it will pay only for drugs on its approved list. Plans use closed formularies to help them control the rising cost of medications and to help physicians prescribe drugs more efficaciously. "Open" and "closed" are slippery terms, however. An open formulary may still have some restrictions. A close formulary may still offer beneficiaries some leeway.

It's important to know, before you join, if an HMO formulary carries a particular drug you're taking. But just because it's on the formulary today doesn't mean it will be on it tomorrow. Formularies change constantly. Here again, persistence may be in order, since some plans may not want to tell you about their formularies until after you join.

If a drug is not on the formulary, some plans may pay for a portion of the drug's cost, asking you to pay a set copayment. Or it may have a procedure for allowing your doctor to appeal to the HMO to have it pay for the drug. How easy it is for the doctor to appeal and override formulary restrictions is a useful piece of information. Some HMOs make doctors jump through a lot of hoops to get a nonformulary drug approved. Others leave the decision up to the doctor. If the doctor has to appeal, the plan may want to know such things as the history of your illness, why you can't take the drugs on the formulary, and what sorts of problems you've had with them. HMOs told CONSUMER REPORTS that appeals are approved roughly 75 percent of the time.

POINTS TO KEEP IN MIND ABOUT DRUG BENEFITS

• Know whether drugs you are taking are on the plan's formulary before you sign up. Some HMOs don't let you see the formulary until you become a plan member. Obviously, that's not helpful. If your drug isn't on the formulary and you cannot take a substitute drug on the list, find out how easy it is to override the restrictions or choose another HMO that includes your drug on its list. Keep in mind that formularies are constantly changing. Even if your drug is on the list today, it may not be tomorrow.

• Know how the HMO charges the drugs against your annual cap. This will tell you how long the benefit will last.

• Weigh the pros and cons of filling your prescriptions through the mail or at a local pharmacy. The pharmacy may be more convenient, but the copayments could be higher.

• Do the math. Use the table on pages 182-183 to determine what savings you'll actually realize from the plan.

• Be prepared for change. Nothing is static in managed care, and the drug benefits are the ones most likely to change. A good deal today may not be so good in the future, and you may have to switch plans to get better benefits. Eventually, however, your ability to switch plans will be limited, as we describe on pages 187-188.

MAKING TRADE-OFFS

None of the options is a perfect solution to your medical coverage in retirement. There are pluses and minuses to each. Some have more drawbacks than others, however, as we've noted in the section detailing all of the options. Which option you choose depends on how much risk you want to take now and in the future. Because of continuing inflation in health-care services, the premiums and other costs will continue to rise.

We recommend that most people stay in traditional Medicare and buy a Medicare supplement policy, which we've discussed in Chapter 10. This option carries the least amount of risk, the fewest unknowns, and provides the greatest flexibility. The downside is that premiums for the policies continue to increase, making them unafford-able for some people. The HMO options are attractive mainly for their prescription-drug benefits, but those benefits may be less useful than you think. Provider-sponsored organizations (PSOs) may seem attrac-tive at first, but if the experience of hospital-owned HMOs is an indi-cator, you could find yourself in a financially shaky plan. Many hospi-tal-owned HMOs have lost money—they've priced their plans too low for the claims they've had to pay. When that happens, they must raise premiums or sell their business to another managed-care company, per-haps causing disruption in your care. Approach PSOs with caution. We can't endorse the private fee-for-service option, either, at least not until more is known about them. Nor can we advise you to take a medical savings account or enter into private-contracting arrangements with your doctor unless you are wealthy and willing to assume potentially very large out-of-pocket medical expenses.

Because so many of the new options are managed-care plans, you may be concerned about the quality of medical care you'll receive if you go into one of them. In the past few years, some organizations have tried to rate the quality of HMOs, using data from the National Committee for Quality Assurance. NCQA's so-called HEDIS measures let you know what proportion of an HMO's members receive mammo-grams, immunizations, Pap smears, and so forth. HEDIS stands for Health Plan Employer Data and Information Set. Information about HEDIS measures will eventually be available on the web site of the Health Care Financing Administration (HCFA), which administers Medicare. Look for *Medicare.gov*.

Many of the measures, however, don't get to the heart of the quality issues in medicine: underuse, overuse, and misuse. Nor do they answer the key question: Will HMO A take better care of me than HMO B when I get sick? Measures that purport to tell you how many procedures an HMO has carried out have a major shortcoming, since they don't adjust for a plan's demographics. For instance, one plan might look better than another simply because it has more sick people in it who require more services. Furthermore, no one knows how to interpret what the numbers mean. What is the threshhold for too many endarterectomies, for example?

In short, we don't believe that those measures, which are still in their infancy, are a reliable guide for picking an HMO. However, consumer-satisfaction data that the HCFA will eventually release may be more useful. This data, known as CAHPS, for Consumer Assessment of Health Plans Study, will give you some idea of which plans other Medicare beneficiaries liked best. Again, don't confuse satisfaction with quality medicine. They aren't the same. To obtain CAHPS data, visit the HCFA web site, *www.Medicare.gov.*

Getting quality medical care is not just an issue in managed care but in fee-for-service medicine as well. Even though you choose an option that allows you to float around the medical system, there's no assurance that the care you receive will be top-notch or that the doctor will do the right thing correctly and avoid doing the wrong things.

ENROLLMENT RULES AND LOCK-INS

To be eligible for any of the Medicare + Choice options, you must be entitled to Medicare Part A and enrolled in Medicare Part B. If you decide not to take Part B when you are first eligible, you can still sign up each year for both Part B and the Medicare + Choice options during the three-month general open-enrollment period. If you do, your coverage will be effective July 1 of that year.

Currently, Medicare beneficiaries have lots of freedom to move in and out of health plans and switch from one HMO to another. All you have to do is disenroll from a plan and go back on traditional Medicare the following month. It may, however, be hard to get your Medicare-supplement policy back if your health has gotten worse or you can't afford the premium. The Balanced Budget Act restricts this freedom over the next few years.

If you choose any of the Medicare + Choice options except medical savings accounts, you can move from one to another any time until 2002. If you elect one of the options during the open-enrollment period in the fall of 2001, you will be able to change only once during the first six months of 2002. After that, you may elect a Medicare + Choice option in the November enrollment period in 2002, but you will have only the first three months of 2003 to make a change. In subsequent years, you will have only the first three months of the year to change. If you don't like the arrangement you've chosen, you're stuck for the rest of the year.

The rules are different for medical savings accounts. You are effectively locked in for a year if you select that option. For example, if you choose one in the fall of 1998 and don't change your mind by December 15, you are effectively locked into that plan until December 31, 1999.

There are still different rules governing Medicare-supplement policies. Let's say when you are first eligible for Medicare, you enroll in one of the Medicare + Choice options. You don't like it and get out within 12 months. The law says you can go back to traditional Medicare and any Medicare supplement being sold. Even if your health takes a turn for the worse, an insurance carrier must sell you the policy of your choice.

However, if you stay in one of the new options longer than 12 months, the rules are more restrictive. You will be able to return to traditional Medicare and get a supplemental policy only under certain conditions: for example, you move outside the plan's service area, the plan engages in a material marketing misrepresentation, violates the contract, or the insurer becomes insolvent. In those cases, supplemental insurers are required to offer you only Plans A, B, C, and F.

If you have stayed in traditional Medicare and have had a supplemental policy, you can always switch from one policy to another, subject, of course, to the insurer's willingness to accept you and your ability to pay what the insurer charges.

12

I·N·S·U·R·A·N·C·E

FOR LONG-TERM CARE

HALF OF ALL WOMEN AND A THIRD OF ALL men who are now 65 will spend their last years in a nursing home at a cost of some $40,000 a year. Currently, there is no federal entitlement program similar to Medicare that pays long-term-care expenses for the elderly. Some people pay their entire nursing-home bill with their savings. Others begin with their own savings, then turn to Medicaid when their money runs out. Still others rely on Medicaid from the beginning.

Nursing-home patients and their families currently pay about half the $80 billion annual tab for nursing-home care. Medicare pays for about 2 percent of all nursing-home stays, and private-insurance policies pay for about 1 percent. Medicaid, the federal-state program that pays medical expenses for the poor, covers most of the rest. To qualify for Medicaid, patients must make themselves poor by spending down, that is, by using up all of their assets to pay for their nursing-home expenses. Medicaid then steps in and pays the bill.

QUESTIONS TO ASK Given these facts, it's no surprise that many older people are turning to insurance as a way to pay for eventual long-term care. But the decision to buy a policy is one that must be made carefully and judiciously. There are several points to consider beforehand.

WHY DO YOU WANT THE COVERAGE? Insurance companies promote long-term-care insurance as a protection for assets that are built up over a lifetime. In other words, if you are confined to a nursing home, you won't have to tap into your savings so long as you have the policy to cover your expenses. Your money is safe both for you and for your heirs. For many people, this alone is a good reason to buy the coverage.

Another reason for insurance is to protect your assets for your spouse or a dependent member of your family. Or you may simply feel more comfortable having a policy that helps you avoid impoverishment or reliance on government programs or family members in your later years.

Some people also decide to buy a policy as a means of getting into a more desirable nursing home. Many institutions don't like to take Medicaid patients. If you don't have to rely on Medicaid when you first enter, you may have a wider choice of nursing homes. But beware. Some facilities ask residents to leave when they no longer can pay privately and must turn to Medicaid.

CAN YOU AFFORD IT? If you have realistically thought about why you want long-term-care coverage and feel you need the insurance, think about the cost. Ask yourself if you can pay the premium out of your retirement income. For many retirees, the answer is no. Fifty-four percent of all Medicare beneficiaries have incomes of less than $15,000 a year. A 65-year-old could pay about $1,700 each year for a good long-term-care policy with inflation protection. That's more than 10 percent of his or her annual income. Add another $1,200 or so for Medicare-supplement insurance, and decent health and long-term-care insurance comes to about $3,000 a year, or $6,000 for a couple. CONSUMER REPORTS also believes, based on a study of long-term-care insurance in 1997, that premiums for many policies are likely to increase over the years. It's important that your budget be able to accommodate future increases, since it's unwise to drop a policy once you have one.

Of course, if the value of your assets (excluding your house) is $10,000 or less, you probably don't need insurance coverage in most states—you would qualify fairly quickly for Medicaid. If your assets are between $10,000 and $50,000, you probably don't need a policy, either. Your need for long-term-care coverage is marginal at best, especially if those assets produce some of the income you are living on. And you probably can't afford current or future premiums.

If your assets are $50,000 or more and your current income is sufficient to pay the premiums, you might seriously consider buying a long-term-care policy. If your assets far exceed $50,000, you should contact an attorney specializing in estate planning to find other suitable alternatives. *Worksheet 6*, "Long-term-care checklist" in the back of the book, will help you determine what assets you have to protect and whether you are a candidate for insurance.

ARE YOU MARRIED OR SINGLE? Unfortunately, older married women often have far less income to live on once their husbands die, especially if they have not worked outside the home for most of their adult lives. And even though a widow may have less income to pay expensive premiums, her need for long-term care may increase as she gets older. Married men are often cared for at home by their wives, while single women (and men) are more likely to end up in nursing homes, because no one is at home to care for them when they are ill or infirm.

ARE YOU IN GOOD HEALTH? If you have only minor health problems, you should be able to buy a long-term-care policy. But if you have had strokes, heart or respiratory disease, or have limited mobility, a company probably won't insure you. Sometimes, people with specific medical problems can get coverage, but they pay a higher premium to compensate the insurance company for the greater risk they pose.

What Long-Term-Care Policies Cover

After you have evaluated these key questions, take the time to review the policies themselves. Long-term-care insurance is the most complicated of all insurance products sold, so it pays to comparison shop carefully. No two long-term-care policies are exactly alike. Some policies offer comprehensive benefits, paying for services provided in nursing facilities or in various community settings. Others offer coverage only for nursing-home services. And some policies pay only for home care. We don't recommend that you buy this type of insurance. If you decide to purchase a long-term-care policy, these are the main points to consider:

HOW BIG A BENEFIT? The heart of a policy is the daily benefit. Your choice of benefit—somewhere between $20 and $300 a day for nursing-home care—governs the premium you'll pay. The daily benefit for home care, if you choose that option, is typically half the nursing-home benefit. But some policies pay the same amount for home care as for nursing-home care. Some also pay the full daily benefit you select no matter what actual charges you incur. Others pay only actual charges up to the selected benefit. When selecting a benefit, keep in mind that your actual charges may exceed the nursing home's stated rate. Extra charges for drugs, supplies, and special services could boost the bill several hundred dollars each month. So choose a benefit that's at least as high as the average price of nursing homes in your locality. Call several homes to get a feel for their daily rates.

HOW LONG A BENEFIT? Companies offer a selection of benefit periods—one, two, three, four, five, or six years, and lifetime coverage. Not all offer each choice. Because you don't know how long a nursing-home stay will last and because lifetime coverage with an adequate daily benefit is extravagantly expensive, you need to play the odds. Nearly 90 percent of all people who enter a nursing home between the ages of 65 and 94 stay less than four years. Most stay an average of 2½ years. So we consider a four-year benefit a reasonable gamble. Even if you are among the small minority who will require nursing-home care for a longer period, a four-year benefit will at least give you and your family time to prepare for and adjust to the financial consequences of a longer stay.

THE POOL-OF-MONEY OPTION A recent twist in long-term-care policies is the "pool-of-money" approach. For comprehensive policies that include home care, you choose the daily benefit and a benefit period. Then you multiply the annual value of the benefit by the number of years it is to last. The result is a pool of money available to you for either type of care. Say you choose a benefit of $110 a day for a four-year comprehensive policy. The policy will pay a total of $160,000 for home care, nursing-home services, or both. Theoretically, you could trade off benefits for one type of care for another. But in a pool-of-money approach, unlike with a traditional policy, benefits used for one kind of care decrease the amount available for the other. Consider both kinds of policies.

KEEPING UP WITH INFLATION Between 1985 and 1995, nursing-home prices increased an average of 9.7 percent per year, much higher than the rate of increase in the Consumer Price Index. In 1995, for example, with inflation in the general economy at only 2.8 percent, nursing-home prices increased some 8 percent. Because the policy you buy today may be called on to pay benefits 20 or 25 years from now, it's vital your benefits increase with the price of nursing-home care. If nursing-home prices escalate at an 8-percent rate, a nursing home that today costs $110 a day would cost $513 a day 20 years from now. Without inflation coverage, a $110 daily benefit would then be virtually useless.

Policies are typically offered without inflation coverage. Agents don't like to add it, since it raises the premium, sometimes to the point you can't afford the policy. Nevertheless, a policy that doesn't increase with inflation is no bargain and could be of limited use down the road. These are the inflation options agents generally recommend in decreasing order of usefulness:

• Five-percent compounded option. This arrangement, which increases the benefit at a rate of 5 percent a year compounded, comes closest to ensuring that the policy will still provide a meaningful benefit in the future. If you buy a daily benefit of $110, roughly the average cost of nursing-home care today, this option will give you a daily benefit 20 years from now of $292 and thus keep pace with inflation that averaged 5 percent a year. This option, of course, still leaves you short if nursing-home costs increase at a higher pace, but it's the most generous available. The cost of this protection varies by company and by age of the buyer. At age 65, it increases the premium by some 70 percent on average; at age 70, by about 60 percent.

• Five-percent simple option. With this option, 5 percent of the original benefit, not of the previous year's benefit, is added each year. That is, there is no compounding. A $110 daily benefit would increase to $220 in 20 years, leaving you to pay some $72 each day out-of-pocket if nursing-home rates increased 5 percent a year. This option increases the premium for a 65-year-old by about 50 percent on average.

• Extra coverage at the outset. Some agents may paint a realistically grim picture of inflation but suggest you prepare for it by starting out with a daily benefit that's larger than the current daily nursing-home rate. That helps agents close a deal, because the premium will look relatively low compared with the premium for true inflation protection. But it's poor coverage. Agents often recommend this option, particularly for people in their 70s, on the theory that if they enter a nursing facility at all, they're likely to do so in the near future. But a 75-year-old who buys a $130 benefit instead of a $110 benefit will still have a $130 benefit in 10 years. At 5-percent annual inflation, the nursing home would cost $179, leaving a gap of $49 a day, or about $1,500 each month, between the cost of the nursing home and the insurance benefit.

• Increase coverage periodically. Some companies guarantee the right to buy additional coverage every two or three years, or sometimes annually, without passing the company's medical requirements. The amount you can buy may be unlimited; it may be restricted to $10 or $20 increases; or it may be based on some formula related to the

Consumer Price Index. This option has serious drawbacks. You must remember to take advantage of the offer. If you refuse the offer a certain number of times, you lose your right to buy more coverage.

The price of additional coverage is based not only on the coverage but also on your new, higher age, so you will be paying more for those increments over time than you would had you chosen a different option to begin with. One company sells a policy that lets you voluntarily add to the benefit incrementally in a way intended to match the increase in benefits with the "5-percent compounded" option. At the outset, the policy with the incremental option costs a 65-year-old $770 a year, compared with $1,598 for the same benefit with the 5-percent compounded arrangement. Twenty years later, however, the premium for the policy with the "cheaper" inflation protection would be $5,250 a year, while the premium for the "more expensive" option would still be $1,598.

WHEN DO BENEFITS BEGIN? Like most insurance, long-term-care policies have deductibles. They come in the form of "elimination" periods—20, 30, 60, 90, or 100 days—during which you must pay for nursing-home care out of your own pocket. As with other types of insurance, the larger the deductible (or, in this case, the longer the elimination period), the lower the premium.

Don't let a low premium tempt you into choosing an elimination period you can't afford—or may not be able to afford in the future. A policy with a 90-day elimination period might cost $300 a year less than a policy with a 20-day elimination period. After 20 years, you would have saved $6,000 in premiums. But with 5-percent inflation, the 70 additional days of elimination period would cost $20,430.

QUALIFYING FOR BENEFITS

Companies vary significantly in how they determine that you are sufficiently disabled to require long-term care. They measure a disability against a policyholder's ability to perform what industry jargon calls "activities of daily living." There are seven of them—eating, walking, transferring from a bed to a chair, dressing, bathing, using a toilet, and remaining continent. The insurer defines disability by the number of those activities you are unable to perform. Some say you must be unable to perform three out of the seven before you qualify as disabled; others choose six activities and say you must fail to perform two or three of them; still others pare the list to five and say policyholders must be unable to perform two of them. They also note whether you are cognitively impaired and, in a few cases, whether you have a medical condition requiring nursing-home care.

In general, the longer the list of activities and the fewer you have to fail, the easier it is to get benefits. In reviewing a policy, note particularly if bathing is on the list of activities. A disabled person is more likely to need help with bathing than with any other activity. If it's on the list specified in the policy, a policyholder might be able to qualify more easily than with a policy that doesn't include bathing as an essential activity of daily living. Policies also define the inability to perform an activity in different ways. One policy, for example, might consider you disabled if, among other things, someone has to watch over you to make sure you eat. Another might consider you disabled only if you cannot feed yourself at all.

A second way to qualify is to suffer some cognitive impairment. All policies now cover Alzheimer's disease and other types of dementia. But almost all say you must fail certain clinical tests to receive benefits.

A third pathway to benefits is "medical necessity." The policy will pay if you have a medical condition—congestive heart failure, say, or coronary-artery disease—that makes you too frail to care for yourself—even though you may be able to perform all activities when taken individually. On pages 200-201, we note that certain "tax-qualified" policies do not include medical necessity among the recognized reasons for long-term care. If you choose a tax-qualified plan, you may be gaining a minor tax break but giving up an easier pathway to coverage.

WHERE WILL THE POLICY PAY?

All long-term-care policies pay for care in licensed nursing homes. "Assisted-living facilities," which provide less client care than a nursing home, are another matter. Some policies explicitly state they will cover stays in such a facility. Others may or may not cover assisted living as part of an "alternative plan of care." Under such a policy, the insurance company will discuss alternatives to a nursing home with the family but will pay for assisted living only if both parties agree to the alternative. There's no guarantee.

Not all assisted-living facilities that care for elderly people qualify for benefits. Some policies, for example, say that a staff member must be on the premises 24 hours a day, a doctor must be on call, and the facility must be able to supervise medications. A policy may also define a facility by the number of residents, refusing to pay for very small facilities. Companies may require that facilities serve three meals a day or that they cater to special dietary needs.

The daily benefit for assisted-living care is commonly 50 or 60 percent of the nursing-home coverage, but sometimes it is the same as the nursing-home benefit. Occasionally, it might also be the same as the benefit for home care. Although the benefit for assisted living is often smaller than for nursing-home care, some assisted-living facilities cost $3,000 to $4,000 a month, about the same as nursing homes. A flexible policy should cover you for either type of facility. Look for this flexibility when you shop.

WHICH FRILLS ARE USEFUL?

Insurers tack on a number of extraneous benefits, many of them useful more as selling points for insurance agents than as succor for a consumer in need of care. One potentially useful frill is a service offering advice to a policyholder who needs care. Unfortunately, many of the provisions CONSUMER REPORTS examined direct you to an insurance company's in-house service or to a service under contract to the company. Those arrangements are restrictive and may lead you to care that serves the insurer's interest rather than yours. Another potentially useful frill helps pay for alterations to your home—a stair lift, for example—that might help a policyholder stay at home rather than enter a nursing home.

Other frills are nearly universal. These include: a bed-reservation benefit, which reserves your space in the nursing home should you go to the hospital and return; a respite-care benefit, which pays for a substitute caregiver when yours needs a break; and a waiver-of-premium benefit, which pays the insurance premiums once you're in a facility. A few companies waive the premium as soon as a policyholder receives the first payment. But waits of between 60 and 90 days are more typical.

IF YOUR POLICY LAPSES

You should never buy a long-term-care policy unless you intend to keep it for the rest of your life. Unfortunately, it's all too easy for elderly people to allow a policy to lapse inadvertently or because they can no longer afford the premiums. Some companies have begun to add safeguards to make sure the people who want to stay insured do. If you miss a premium, some will send a notice of a missed premium to a third party. Others offer an extra-long grace period—65 days instead of the customary 31, for example. Or the company may offer the right to reinstate the policy after five months if it lapsed because a policyholder was cognitively or functionally impaired. Some policies let policyholders reduce coverage if they can't pay the full premium.

States require companies to offer "nonforfeiture benefits" as an option. This is a promise of a certain value to the policyholder even if the policy lapses. The typical value is the policy's daily benefit provided for a shorter period. If you drop your policy, the company will apply all the premiums you've paid for nursing-home care for as long as the money lasts. This type of benefit adds, on average, 20 percent to the premium. Not many people buy this benefit.

You might find a policy that provides a death benefit refund to the policyholder's estate—the total of any premiums paid minus any benefits the company paid on the policyholder's behalf. This benefit is usually payable only if the policyholder dies before a certain age, typically 65 or 70.

HOW'S YOUR HEALTH?

Insurance companies are strict underwriters. That means they carefully scrutinize your health before they'll issue a policy, in an attempt to weed out people with conditions likely to send them to a nursing home. That includes diabetics, those showing signs of Alzheimer's disease, and individuals with cardiovascular disorders that might predispose them to strokes. Companies have long lists of conditions and long lists of medications that make people unacceptable—conditions like Parkinson's disease, osteoporosis, and chronic pancreatitis, and medicines like Haldol (prescribed for psychotic disorders).

But that doesn't mean that all insurers look at conditions the same way. A condition that's unacceptable to one might be acceptable to another. To gauge this variation, CONSUMER REPORTS asked insurers whether they would cover people with certain health conditions. Almost all said they would not insure a 60-year-old man who showed signs of confusion and disorientation. Most would accept a 65-year-old woman complaining of blurred vision and diagnosed with glaucoma. What about a 68-year-old man with hypertension who had undergone carotid-artery surgery? Here, there was no consensus. Some would deny coverage; others would cover him at higher rates. And one company would insure him only if he had a healthy spouse who could act as a caregiver.

Several companies now sort applicants into various classes and charge them rates commensurate with the risk they represent. The names companies attach to their underwriting classes often add confusion. One company uses the term "standard" to mean its worst class. Another uses the term to mean the middle of five rate classifications. Watch for these "word games" as you do your shopping.

The underwriting process can take a month or two. Applicants answer questions about their health and sometimes furnish a physician's statement detailing health history. Companies usually interview older applicants by phone, looking for signs of cognitive impairment. Occasionally, they conduct face-to-face interviews. Some companies also look for lifestyle clues that suggest likely candidates for a nursing home. A company may say that anyone needing assistance with housekeeping, shopping, and household finances is not acceptable. You may be asked to describe in your own handwriting what you do in a typical day. The theory is that if you are active and get out and about, you're not likely to go to a nursing home any time soon and cost the company a lot of money.

You might hear agents and others talk about preexisting-conditions clauses. These have little practical meaning in long-term-care insurance. The wording in a policy may exclude nursing-home payments for six months for conditions you have when the policy is written. But despite the wording, an insurer probably won't sell you the policy if it suspects you might actually enter a nursing home within six months. Some carriers may issue a policy after you have sufficiently recovered from some illness. Or they may limit the amount of coverage you can buy if you have certain health conditions.

CARE IN YOUR OWN HOME

A few years ago, Sally B., an 85-year-old Virginian, began to need more help. She was afraid of falling and could no longer drive or keep appointments. Soon she needed someone to prepare meals. She became disoriented. Her family arranged for home care, for a housekeeper, and for a driver twice a week. A year later, an aide was coming to fix dinner and stay through the night. There were weekend cooks and daily housekeepers who helped her dress and get around. At the start, the family was paying helpers $1,325 a month. But as time passed and more assistance became necessary, the cost climbed to $8,300 a month.

Sally B. eventually entered a nursing home, where she gets the round-the-clock supervision she needs. By that time, her family had bills of more than $34,000 for her most recent six months of home care. If she had stayed at home for a full year, the cost would easily have exceeded $70,000—some $19,000 more than the annual cost of her nursing home. Sally carried long-term-care insurance that she had bought years ago. The policy's home-care benefit paid $25 a day. Her family collected only $1,603 toward the $34,000 cost of the last six months of care.

Full home care 24 hours a day is just "not reasonable," says Ann Morris, executive director of the IVNA Home Health Care in Richmond, Va. "That's the illusion of home care. People don't realize how expensive 24-hour home care really is." The illusion sells a lot of coverage. Agents know people fear nursing homes, and not without reason. They play off that fear, often pushing home-care coverage as an alternative, knowing full well that the benefit won't help much if someone really needs care every day, 24 hours a day. With home health aides costing around $13 an hour, a typical $55 daily benefit would buy only about four hours of care a day. When it comes to qualifying, the factors used to determine eligibility for nursing-home care usually apply. Chances are, then, that to qualify, one will have to be frail enough to need more than the four hours a day of care the benefit will buy.

The home-care benefit differs from policy to policy. Policies usually will pay home-care benefits for skilled-nursing care, therapists, and aides who assist with dressing, bathing, and other activities of daily living. Most will cover adult day-care services. A few policies pay for the services of dieticians or for home-delivered meals. A few pay for homemaker services, help with cooking, paying bills, doing the laundry, and cleaning.

Insurance companies generally want you to receive home care from licensed home-health agencies, which provide the most expensive kind of help. To access your benefit by using one of these agencies, you may find your benefit won't stretch very far, as it might if you had free choice of providers. Some policies offer benefits for informal caregivers, but keep in mind these benefits are not identical. A company, for instance, may say that informal caregivers are people who already live with you. Another may allow friends and neighbors to assume that role. The daily benefit for informal care may be only one-half the daily home-care benefit. So informal caregivers would get $27.50 a day based on a $55 daily benefit for home care.

Home-care coverage with a benefit paying half the nursing home amount adds about 30 percent to the price of a policy. Some carriers offer home-care coverage that equals the nursing-home benefit. That can boost the price another 20 percent.

Because home-care coverage adds substantially to your premium, we recommend that you carefully consider whether you need it. It may make sense to buy home-care coverage for a husband who is likely to have his wife around to care for him. A woman who is likely to be alone with no family or friends to keep an eye on their care may not need the coverage. As attractive as home care may sound, consider it only if you have a good support network of family and friends nearby. No matter how good the benefit, you'll need people around to watch the home-health aides and chore workers who come in; you may need volunteer help when the paid help has left for the day; and you'll need someone to judge when home care is no longer enough.

TAX-QUALIFIED POLICIES

Under the provisions of the Health Insurance Portability and Accountability Act of 1996, a portion of your premiums for a new class of "qualified" long-term-care insurance plans are tax-deductible as medical expenses, as are a portion of your premiums for certain policies bought before 1997. For 1998, the amount of the premium that can be deducted is $210 per year for people age 40 or younger; $380 for those age 41 to 50; $770 for people age 51 to 60; $2,050 for people age 61 to 70; and $2,570 for those 71 or older. The limits are adjusted each year for inflation.

The deduction, however, may not amount to much in tax savings. Medical expenses, which include the amount of the minimum you can deduct, are generally deductible only as an itemized deduction to the extent that the total of all such expenses exceeds 7.5 percent of adjusted gross income. So a person with, say, $60,000 in adjusted gross income can deduct from income (not from taxes) only those expenses above $4,500 for the year. However, a few people who are self-employed may claim a portion of the deduction as an adjustment to income.

If you think counting the premium as a medical expense would result in worthwhile tax savings, and you itemize deductions, you might consider a qualified plan. But they are far more restrictive than many nonqualified plans. Before you can receive benefits, a licensed health-care provider must certify that for a period of at least 90 days, you are unable to perform at least two of six specified "activities of daily living." You can also qualify if you suffer cognitive impairment that requires "substantial supervision." You cannot, however, receive benefits for a nursing-home stay resulting from "medical necessity"—a common benefit trigger in nonqualified plans.

The benefits of a qualified plan are not taxable, but it's unclear whether that's true for benefits from a nonqualified plan. The Treasury Department has yet to rule on the issue and may not do so for some time. The insurance industry lobbied hard for these tax incentives. Not only are they selling points (if not very convincing ones), but the limitations dictated by law will save insurers money in benefits that should have gone to policyholders in need of care.

PARTNERSHIP POLICIES

We recommend that you compromise on a policy that will pay benefits for four years, since only 10 percent of nursing-home residents stay longer and since lifetime benefits are extremely expensive. But your efforts to insure against financial ruin can be thwarted if you stay after your benefits run out and you are forced to go on Medicaid. In four states—California, Connecticut, Indiana, and New York—you can buy a special policy that guarantees to protect some or all of your assets from a Medicaid spenddown, so you don't need lifetime coverage. The policies are sold by private insurers in a partnership with each state's Medicaid program and are intended to help people with assets of between $30,000 and $100,000, the nonpoor who are most likely to lose everything should they be forced onto Medicaid.

Here's how those "partnership" policies work: In California, Connecticut, and Indiana, you buy a policy that pays benefits equal to the amount of assets you want to protect. If you want to shelter, say,

$100,000 in assets, you buy a policy that comes close to paying out benefits of $100,000; after the insurance company has paid out the policy limits, you become eligible for Medicaid, while retaining $100,000 in assets. In New York, asset protection is even more generous. Buy a policy with three years of coverage, and you can become eligible for Medicaid after that period (or after six years of home care) without spending down any assets.

Partnership policies protect only assets, not income. To become eligible for Medicaid after benefits are exhausted, you must still spend all your income on care, apart from any allowance for a spouse or for personal needs. The same is true for nonpartnership policies. Contrary to what agents may tell you, no policy protects income once benefits are used up and you go on Medicaid.

Some of the partnership policies are better than the more traditional offerings, and several have features we consider paramount, such as built-in 5-percent compounded inflation coverage, so benefits automatically keep up with inflation. Some also have guaranteed coverage for some types of assisted living, which, as we note, you would want in a policy. Partnership policies do have one drawback: If you move to another state, you retain the policy's coverage but not the feature that protects your assets from a Medicaid spenddown after the benefits are exhausted.

Agents don't particularly like to sell partnership policies, and you may hear them disparage the coverage. Keep a lookout for agents who compare the premium for a partnership plan with inflation coverage to the premium for a nonpartnership plan without inflation coverage or without some other important option. They are doing that to make one policy look a lot cheaper than another.

If you live in one of the four states offering these plans, seriously consider them unless you know for sure you are planning to retire outside of the state.

CHOOSING A POLICY

Worksheet 6 in the back of the book can help you keep track of some of the major points as you search for a good policy. Also keep in mind the following points:

• It makes little sense to buy long-term-care insurance before age 55. Between the ages of 55 and 65, consider insurance only if you have a medical condition, such as diabetes, that could get worse and eventually put you in a nursing home. Before retirement, you may want to consider a group policy offered through your employer, because it's likely to be relatively inexpensive and because you may not need to pass a medical test. But do consider insurance by age 65. It gets much more expensive as you grow older. A 65-year-old, on average, will pay about $1,700 a year for a policy; a 75-year-old, $3,900.

• A cheap policy is not necessarily a good policy, nor will a cheap policy necessarily remain cheap in the future. CONSUMER REPORTS asked state insurance departments about rate increases or decreases that insurers have requested for their long-term-care policies. States reported numerous rate increases. Increases of 25 percent were not uncommon, and a few policies had multiple increases totaling 100 percent or more. Companies are unwilling to guarantee rates far into the future. That's because insurers still have too little data to accurately predict how many people will file claims, how large those claims will be, and how many people will let the policy lapse. (If people drop their policies, the company generally keeps premiums it has already collected, without ever needing to pay future claims from those policyholders.)

A company with a low premium may assume that many buyers will allow the policy to lapse before collecting a benefit. If the assumption turns out to be incorrect, the company may have to raise rates. Fewer people are dropping their policies than companies have anticipated. That bodes poorly for future price stability. CONSUMER REPORTS believes that some insurers will be forced into significant price increases. Be sure your budget will accommodate increases of at least 50 percent. Look at the October 1997 issue of CONSUMER REPORTS for Ratings of long-term-care policies. That issues notes which policies might be at risk for future rate increases.

• Think carefully about home-care coverage. Many people in need of care would be much happier staying at home. Unfortunately, that's usually feasible only if family or close friends are available to lend support. If you can't count on a volunteer support network in addition to the professional help insurance will pay for, it may not make sense to pay for home-care coverage. Instead, put your money into the best nursing-home coverage you can afford.

• Buy an adequate benefit period. The longer the policy pays, the more it costs. A four-year benefit is a reasonable compromise.

• Judge the benefit triggers. You don't want a company that will make you jump through hoops to collect a benefit. Try to get a policy that lists bathing among the activities of daily living.

• Update an old policy. Product obsolescence comes fast and furious to long-term-care policies. Policies considered state-of-the-art in the early 1990s are inferior today. An older plan might be very restrictive—it might require a hospital stay before paying benefits for nursing-home care, for example. Or it might not cover assisted living. Hang on to what you have. Chances are that the premium is low compared with the benefits. See if you can update coverage to bring the benefit in line with today's costs and to add inflation protection for the future. See if your insurance company offers future purchase options. If it does, take them.

M·E·D·I·C·A·I·D

AND LONG-TERM CARE

MEDICAID IS A GOVERNMENT PROGRAM that pays medical bills for people who are poor. Even though you probably don't consider yourself poor and may even have substantial assets and income when you retire, you may nevertheless qualify for Medicaid if you or your spouse eventually needs nursing or custodial care. At that point in your life, Medicaid is not a poverty program; it is a lifeline for survival.

Medicaid covers a variety of medical services, including services needed by people with long-term or chronic impairments. All states cover care provided in a nursing facility or at home. In some states, Medicaid also pays for care in adult day-care centers as well as for non-medical personal care that helps with such activities as bathing, dressing, preparing meals, and eating. This kind of care can be given in your home, but the home-care agency that provides your home attendant must be licensed or certified by Medicaid in order for Medicaid to pay the bills. Most states provide home and community-based care under a special "waiver" program from the federal government. Others, such as New York, offer this care as part of their regular Medicaid program. When home care is provided under a waiver arrangement, you may find it difficult to get services. States limit the number of people they'll allow to receive Medicaid money for such services. Sometimes, people waiting for home care end up in nursing homes unnecessarily, because that's where the state will pay for their care.

The federal and state governments share the cost for Medicaid. (In a few states, local governments also participate in the cost.) The federal government pays at least 50 percent of each state's Medicaid budget, and states (and local governments) fund the rest, usually out of general tax revenues. States administer the program within broad federal guidelines. In all states, people receiving Aid to Families with Dependent Children (AFDC) or Supplemental Security Income (SSI) from the Social Security Administration are eligible for Medicaid, usually on an automatic basis. Those people are considered "categorically" needy. Most states also cover the "medically needy"—people who have some income but are still considered poor. If you are not poor but eventually need Medicaid's help to pay for long-term nursing care, you'll most likely be eligible under the medically needy program in your state. In 19 states that don't have a program for the medically needy, you cannot qualify for Medicaid nursing-home assistance at all in 1998 if your income exceeds $1,482 a month, even if your income doesn't cover the cost of a nursing home. In those "income cap" states, people with income slightly above the cap can set up a special type of irrevocable trust, sometimes called a Miller trust, to receive and disburse the income. Medicaid ignores the income placed in the trust in figuring your eligibility, but counts it when determining how much you must pay to the nursing home. The trustee then pays out most of your income to the nursing home, and Medicaid pays the remainder of the monthly bill. Eligibility requirements vary from state to state, and it's more difficult to qualify for benefits in some states than in others. In each state, though, you must meet an income-and-asset test, which means you must have neither income nor assets that exceed a prescribed amount.

Spending Down

Many people who enter a nursing home begin by paying the bills themselves. But if their stay is prolonged, they quickly exhaust their resources and are able to meet their states' income-and-asset test. If you start out paying the bills yourself, you may get into a better facility, since many nursing homes refuse to accept Medicaid patients. (Medicaid claims many homes use illegal methods to refuse needy patients.) But if you're in a facility that takes only private-pay residents and you run out of money and need Medicaid funds, the nursing home may ask you to leave, causing serious disruption to you and your family.

The process by which Medicaid comes to pay your nursing-home bills is called a *spenddown.* In essence, you cannot get assistance from Medicaid until virtually all of your assets are depleted. You may keep only the house in which your dependent or disabled children or your spouse resides, the furniture, a car, a burial plot, burial funds, and a small amount of cash. Once you are eligible for Medicaid, you must spend nearly all your income—from Social Security, pensions, interest, dividends, and so on—on nursing-home care before Medicaid helps. When you have spent enough of your assets on care to reach your state's Medicaid limits and your income is not too high, Medicaid begins to pay your bills. *Table 16* shows what assets and income your state lets you keep. Most states let you keep $2,000 of liquid assets, some a little more, and some a little less. And you may keep a small income allowance for "personal needs"—$30 a month in many states. The more assets you have, of course, the longer it takes to spend down.

Example: Imagine you are a widow living alone in New York City. Your annual income is $15,000, or $1,250 a month. You also have $25,000 in CDs. Nursing-home costs in New York City run about $6,000 a month, so your income is insufficient to cover the cost. You must turn to Medicaid for help. But at the time you enter the nursing home, your assets and income exceed New York's Medicaid limits— $600 in annual income and $3,500 in assets for a single person. You enter the nursing home and for a while pay the bills out of your savings. You must spend $20,000 of the $25,000 before Medicaid steps in. (New York allows you to keep $5,000: a $3,500 allowance plus $1,500 for burial expenses.) If you turn over *all* your monthly income to the nursing home (excluding the personal-needs allowance), you have to withdraw $4,750 from your savings each month to cover the $6,000 monthly bill. At that rate, you would spend the $20,000 "excess" assets in a little more than four months. After that, you are eligible for Medicaid. Once you qualify for coverage, Medicaid requires you to spend virtually all your monthly income for your nursing care. You can keep $50 of your $1,250 monthly income for personal needs and deduct medical expenses, including health-insurance premiums if there are any. The rest must go to the nursing home. You keep the $50 personal-needs allowance and contribute $1,200 toward your care; the state of New York pays the rest of the monthly bill—$4,800 a month.

TABLE 16 · WHAT YOUR STATE LETS YOU KEEP
BEFORE MEDICAID WILL PAY

▶ *The table below gives the minimum assets and income each state allows nursing-home residents and their spouses to keep. These amounts change each year. States marked with an * are "income cap" states. If your income is higher than $1,482 a month, you cannot qualify for Medicaid even after spending down all assets unless you set up a Miller trust.*

State	Assets allowed resident	Spouse's minimum asset allowance	Resident's monthly needs allowance	Spouse's monthly income allowance
ALABAMA*	$2,000	$25,000	$30	$1,357
ALASKA*	2,000	80,760	75	2,019
ARIZONA*	2,000	16,152	74.10	1,482
ARKANSAS*	2,000	16,152	40	1,357
CALIFORNIA	2,000	80,760	35	2,019
COLORADO*	2,000	80,760	34	1,357
CONNECTICUT	1,600	16,152	50	1,356.25
DELAWARE*	2,000	25,000	42	1,357
DISTRICT OF COLUMBIA	2,600	80,760	70	2,019
FLORIDA*	2,000	80,760	35	1,357
GEORGIA	2,000	80,760	30	2,019
HAWAII	2,000	80,760	30	2,019
IDAHO*	2,000	16,200	30	1,356
ILLINOIS	2,000	80,760	30	2,019
INDIANA	1,500	16,152	30	1,356
IOWA*	2,000	24,000	30	2,019
KANSAS	2,000	16,152	35	1,357
KENTUCKY	2,000	80,760	40	2,019
LOUISIANA*	2,000	80,760	38	2,019
MAINE	2,000	80,760	40	1,357
MARYLAND	2,500	16,152	40	1,357
MASSACHUSETTS	2,000	16,152	60	1,357
MICHIGAN	2,000	16,152	30	1,357
MINNESOTA	3,000	22,828	64	1,357
MISSISSIPPI*	2,000	80,760	44	2,019
MISSOURI	1,000	16,152	30	1,357
MONTANA	2,000	16,152	40	1,356
NEBRASKA	4,000	16,152	40	2,019
NEVADA*	2,000	16,152	35	1,326
NEW HAMPSHIRE	2,500	16,152	40	1,357
NEW JERSEY	2,000	16,152	35	1,357

TABLE 16 • WHAT YOUR STATE LETS YOU KEEP, *CONTINUED*

State	Assets allowed resident	Spouse's minimum asset allowance	Resident's monthly needs allowance	Spouse's monthly income allowance
NEW MEXICO*	$2,000	$31,290	$30	$1,357
NEW YORK	3,500	80,760	50	2,019
NORTH CAROLINA	2,000	16,152	30	1,357
NORTH DAKOTA	3,000	80,760	40	2,019
OHIO	1,500	16,152	40	1,357
OKLAHOMA*	2,000	25,000	30	2,019
OREGON*	2,000	16,152	30	1,356
PENNSYLVANIA	2,400	16,152	30	1,358
RHODE ISLAND	4,000	16,152	40	1,357
SOUTH CAROLINA*	2,000	66,480	30	1,662
SOUTH DAKOTA*	2,000	20,000	30	1,357
TENNESSEE	2,000	16,152	30	1,356
TEXAS*	2,000	16,152	30	2,019
UTAH	2,000	16,152	45	1,357
VERMONT	2,000	80,760	45	2,019
VIRGINIA	2,000	16,152	30	1,327
WASHINGTON	2,000	80,760	41.62	1,357
WEST VIRGINIA	2,000	16,152	30	1,357
WISCONSIN	2,000	50,000	40	2,019
WYOMING*	2,000	80,760	30	2,019

IMPOVERISHING YOUR SPOUSE

For many families, a spenddown once meant poverty for the spouse who remained at home, since all the family's assets went toward nursing-home care for the other spouse. However, Congress has made it a little easier for spouses to maintain a more comfortable standard of living. (This also means that a spenddown occurs sooner, since more of the family's assets are sheltered.)

Federal law provides a formula to determine how much of a couple's assets the spouse living at home can keep. States can adjust the result upward to favor the applicant, up to a federally imposed ceiling. A couple's home, household goods, a car, and personal effects are not counted as assets. Both the asset and income limits are adjusted for inflation and change each year. If your family members would suffer financial hardship because of the limits, they can petition the state to allow them to keep more money.

Let's see how these provisions work in New York, a state that has adopted the maximum limits for both income and assets. In 1998, after adjusting for inflation, the asset limit was $80,760 and income limit was $2,019. Suppose a couple's monthly income is $1,000 and their assets total $25,000 when the husband enters a nursing home. After deducting the $50 personal allowance for the husband, $950 of their $1,000 monthly income is left. His wife, who remains at home, can keep all of that, since it is less than $2,019. The husband keeps $5,000 of the couple's $25,000 of assets (plus a $1,500 burial allowance), and the wife keeps the remaining $20,000, since it is less than the state's $80,760 maximum-asset limit. Medicaid then pays all the nursing-home bills, which run around $6,000 a month.

But suppose the couple has a monthly income of $2,500 and $100,000 of assets. After deducting the $50 personal-needs allowance, $2,450 remains. The wife gets to keep only $2,019; $431 goes to the nursing home. Medicaid's share of the monthly nursing-home bill is $5,569. But before it starts to pay at all, Medicaid requires the couple to spend down. As in the previous example, the husband keeps $5,000, which leaves $95,000. His wife can retain $80,760, and they have to spend the remaining $14,240 before Medicaid steps in.

PROTECTING YOUR ASSETS

In states like New York, California, and Florida, which have adopted high income-and-asset limits, middle-income people qualify more quickly for Medicaid than they would in states that have lower limits. In a state that applies the federal formula without any upward adjustment, a couple whose assets, for example, are $100,000 would get to keep one-half that amount, or $50,000, for the spouse at home plus $2,000 for the spouse in the nursing home. The couple would have to spend $48,000 before Medicaid would pay.

In determining your eligibility for Medicaid, a state carefully reviews all the assets available to you and your spouse. Your home, your car, personal property, and a limited amount set aside for burial expenses are not counted in determining your eligibility for Medicaid. Putting an asset in your spouse's name doesn't protect it from Medicaid, and states consider money held in joint bank accounts as an available asset to pay for nursing-home care.

If you give away assets within 36 months of applying for Medicaid or set up a trust within five years of this date, you may be ineligible for Medicaid. If you transfer assets for less than their fair market value fewer than 36 months before applying or set up a trust in fewer than 60 months before applying, you are usually ineligible for Medicaid coverage for nursing-facility services or for services obtained under a special home and community program (the state waiver program), for a period equaling the value of your assets you transfer divided by the average monthly cost of nursing-home care in your area. The period of ineligibility begins on the first day of the month after you transfer assets. (Depending on the laws of your state, there may be no period of ineligibility for transferring assets if you receive care in your home.)

Let's say a widow in Florida decides she can get by on Social Security and a small pension without dipping into a $60,000 nest egg she had hoped to leave to her three grandchildren. Fearful that a future stay in a nursing home would consume much of her grandchildren's inheritance, she gives each of them $20,000. A year later, she enters a nursing home. Medicaid would not pay for her care immediately, since she had given away assets that could have been used for her care. Instead, it would divide the $60,000 given away by a factor reflecting the monthly cost of nursing-home care in her area ($3,300). The result, 18, is the number of months she would be ineligible for Medicaid, counting from the month of the gift. The woman would not receive any benefits until she had been in a nursing home for six months (18 minus the 12 months since the date of the gift). She could only hope her grandchildren were willing to ante up some of the $20,000 that six months of care would cost.

You can also make some kinds of transfers regardless of the 36-month limitation and not jeopardize your eligibility for Medicaid benefits. For example, you can transfer your home to your spouse; to a minor, disabled, or blind child; or to a sibling who had an equity interest in your home and who has lived there for at least one year before you need nursing-home care. You can also transfer your home to a child of yours who has lived with you for at least the two years before you were institutionalized and who provided care that delayed your nursing-home stay. If you, your spouse, or a dependent relative remain in your home, Medicaid cannot count it as an asset in determining your eligibility for benefits. If you transfer your home to someone other than those named above, it's counted as a transfer that results in a period of ineligibility. If you own your home when you die, Medicaid can put a lien on the property to recover what it paid for your nursing care. However, Medicaid cannot foreclose on the lien until your spouse dies, a disabled child is no longer disabled, or a dependent child turns 21. Transferring your home to a spouse may be a worthwhile move to avoid a Medicaid lien after your death or if you are too sick to return home.

As we explain in Chapter 19, you can try to set up a trust so long as you do it 60 months before applying for Medicaid. The trust must be written in such a way that neither you nor the trustee can tap the principal for your benefit. You may receive only the income from the assets held in the trust. This requires some careful planning. If you set up a trust and the trustee has the power to invade the principal for your benefit, Medicaid considers that you own the trust even though you have no control over the principal, never receive any benefits, and have named other beneficiaries. And if the income from the trust is greater than your state's Medicaid income limit, a trust isn't much help. Medicaid still requires you to use any income that exceeds the state limit before it pays its share of your nursing-home bills.

If you are considering setting up a trust, you should consult a local attorney familiar with your state's Medicaid rules. Your state's social services department will ask for a copy of the trust agreement when you apply for benefits. Officials scrutinize it to see whether it complies with the rules as applied by your state and whether the assets you put into the trust should in fact be counted in determining your eligibility. When you set up a trust, you are also gambling that you'll eventually need nursing-home care. If your principal is tied up in the trust and you live a long time without seeing the inside of a nursing home, you could well find yourself in a financial bind. You'll be unable to tap the trust for more money. If you have substantial assets, buying a good long-term-care insurance policy may be a better strategy.

Another device for protecting your assets is to give them away as gifts at least 36 months before you require a nursing-home level of care. Medicaid usually does not count these assets in determining your eligibility. Obviously, if you give money or property away, you won't have the assets or the income from those assets to live on and may find yourself in the position of having to go to your children or the other recipients of your assets and ask for money. Taking such a serious step requires careful planning and coordination with all your sources of income.

APPLYING FOR MEDICAID

Should the time come to apply for Medicaid benefits, the nursing home will help you or your spouse do so. If it turns out that you qualify, Medicaid pays the benefits to the nursing home directly. For the portion of the bills you must pay, Medicaid may collect directly from you or from a surrogate, usually a relative who handles your personal business. In some cases, Medicaid helps arrange to have your Social Security check sent directly to the nursing home. You don't have to deposit your personal-needs allowance with the nursing facility, but if you do, the nursing home must keep your personal-needs allowance in a special account for you.

Because rules governing Medicaid are complicated and change frequently, nursing-home personnel may not always be aware of all the requirements. Even state officials may not keep track of changes in the rules. So if you or your family has been told by Medicaid or a nursing-home administrator that you're ineligible for benefits because you've set up a trust or transferred assets, seek another opinion.

SPECIAL HEALTH-CARE
D·E·C·I·S·I·O·N·S

IN THE PAST, IF SOMEONE WAS TERMINALLY ill or critically injured, he or she would simply die within a "normal" period of time. But with advances in medical technology, it's possible to keep critically ill and comatose people alive for years. You must consider that possibility when you plan for retirement.

You can keep some control over these life-and-death decisions by making a living will or drawing up a health-care proxy. These documents are sometimes referred to as "advance directives" or "health-care declarations."

LIVING WILLS

A *living will* is a declaration that if you should become terminally ill, you do not want any extraordinary measures taken to prolong your life. (It has nothing to do with the will that disposes of your estate upon your death, nor is it related to living trusts.)

A living will gives guidance to your family and to the medical professionals who will eventually care for you. You can direct them not to use sophisticated and expensive technology to prolong your life if there is no reasonable expectation that you will recover or if the treatment is not likely to do any good. You can specify when your instructions will apply—for example, if you are conscious but

FORM 2·

Living Will

TO MY FAMILY, MY PHYSICIANS, AND ANY COMMITTEE, CON-SERVATOR, OR OTHER LEGAL REPRESENTATIVE APPOINTED FOR ME

I, _____ , make this statement as an expression of my wishes if the time comes when I can no longer take part in decisions for my own future:

If there is no reasonable expectation of my recovery from physical or mental disability, I request that I be allowed to die and not be kept alive by life-sustaining means or heroic measures, and I direct that any such life-sustaining treatments or procedures shall be withheld or withdrawn, as the case may be. I do not fear death as much as I fear the indignity of deterioration, dependence, and hopeless pain. Accordingly, I ask that drugs be mercifully administered to me to alleviate terminal suffering even if they may hasten the moment of death. I also do not wish to receive futile medical treatment, which I define as treatment that will provide no benefit to me and will only prolong my inevitable death or irreversible coma. If the best medical advice you can obtain indicates that my condition is incurable and imminently terminal, or it I am in an irreversible coma, with no reasonable possibility of my ever regaining consciousness regardless of what medical treatment I may receive, I would like you to be guided by this expression of my wishes in authorizing discontinuance of treatment (including not only medical treatment, but also providing me with nourishment or liquids) and permitting me to die, as painlessly as possible.

These directions to my family and physicians and any legal representative who may be appointed for me are written while I am in good health and spirits so that they may be advised of my sincere wishes and considered judgment in this regard. Although this statement may not be legally binding, I ask that it be honored as an expression of my legal right to refuse medical or surgical treatment, and I direct that such persons shall be free from any liability for having carried out my directions.

I hope that you who care for me will feel morally bound to follow the mandates contained in this statement. I recognize that it places a heavy burden of responsibility upon you, and it is with the intention of sharing that responsibility and of mitigating any feelings of guilt that this statement is made.

Signed: _____

Witnessed by: _____

Address: _____

Witnessed by: _____

Address: _____

have irreversible brain damage. You can state which medical procedures you don't want—being resuscitated or put on a mechanical respirator or being a subject for experimental procedures, for example. Your living will can also specify what you *do* want: drugs that help alleviate pain or procedures that keep you alive as long as possible. Although withholding food and water is often a gray area, most states permit you to set forth your wishes about feeding. If you want your doctors to take such a step, you should, however, check with a lawyer in your state before you make such a notation in your living will.

For most people, a written expression of their wishes is essential, and we recommend that you sign one. However, a living will is not an ironclad guarantee that your wishes will be carried out. Because you cannot anticipate every medical situation that could arise, doctors, hospitals, and family members may still have to make their own decisions. Nevertheless, such a will is an expression of your intent, and courts often look at intent in deciding right-to-die cases. The health-care proxy discussed later in this chapter helps overcome the shortcomings of living wills.

HOW TO EXECUTE A LIVING WILL Most states have statutes that permit their citizens to execute a living will, and all states recognize living wills and have forms for them. Although there is no standard form that can be used in all states, a validly executed form from one state may be accepted in another state. Choice in Dying, Inc. (1035 30th St., N.W., Washington, DC 20007, 202 338-9790 or 475 Riverside Dr., Room 1852, New York, NY 10115, 212 870-2003) has copies of forms that are used in various states. Be sure to date the living will and have it witnessed by two people who are not family members and who do not stand to inherit your estate. (Some states also require the signatures to be notarized.)

You should give copies of your living will to your spouse and other family members and to your primary-care doctor. You should also keep a copy among your personal papers but *not* in your safe-deposit box, because no one except you may have access to it. After you have written a living will, you can revoke or amend it as your thinking changes. Hospitals and hospices that are certified by Medicare and Medicaid must tell patients about their right to execute a living will and note in your medical records whether such a document has been made.

HEALTH-CARE PROXIES

A health-care proxy is similar to the durable power of attorney discussed in Chapter 7. You may even hear it called a "durable power of attorney for health care." Whatever its name, the document gives another person the authority to make health-care decisions for you should you be unable to do so. The powers you delegate can be as comprehensive or as limited as you want. For instance, you can direct your agent to instruct physicians not to resuscitate you, to withhold certain treatments, or to administer pain-relieving medications. You can specify how long you are willing to remain in a coma—for example, six months, 30 days, 15 days—before being removed from life-support systems. You can ask your agent to take you out of the hospital if you wish to die at home. And if you choose to remain on life support until you die, you can also make that desire known through your health-care proxy.

All states presently recognize some kind of appointment of a health-care agent by a form of health-care proxy, although the degree of authority given to the agent can vary from state to state. In addition, some states require specific references to procedures in a living will that is combined with the health-care proxy; for example, many states require a higher standard of evidence to permit an agent to withdraw life support or artificial feeding.

The person you name in your health-care proxy to make health-care decisions for you is usually legally bound to carry out your wishes. Nevertheless, some states have rules that might run contrary to your wishes. For example, in New York, a person acting as an agent can order a doctor not to administer food or drink *only* if he or she has reasonable knowledge of your wishes on the subject that were made clear in conversations or through a living will. To avoid any questions, if you want to give your agent broad powers, you should state in your health-care proxy that you have advised your agent of your wishes.

Generally, your agent will be permitted to authorize withdrawal or withholding of life support, although different states require different degrees of proof of your intentions. In Alaska, the withholding or withdrawal of life support by an agent must be based on a living will. By contrast, an agent appointed in a health-care proxy in New York has very broad authority to start or withdraw treatment. You should consult an attorney who is familiar with your state's rules for guidance on what you can include in your directive.

You can obtain the form of health-care proxy for your state from Choice in Dying, Inc. In any case, it is imperative that you discuss your wishes carefully with the person you choose as your agent. Make sure he or she understands what treatments you want and don't want. The document you sign should be witnessed by two people, but not the person you name to carry out your wishes. In some states, the signatures are also required to be notarized. Give copies of the document to your agent as well as to family members and your primary physician.

You should execute both a living will *and* a health-care proxy. The living will is an expression of your philosophy on dying. The proxy directs someone to carry it out when you are unable to do so.

ANATOMICAL GIFTS

You can donate your body or parts of your body for organ transplants, research, or other medical purposes after your death.

In many states, an organ-donor card is attached to your driver's license. If you wish to make an anatomical gift, simply follow the instructions on your license. Usually this means signing the card and asking two witnesses to sign it. If you change your mind, you can revoke the card by destroying it. If your state does not use the driver's-license procedure, you can obtain a Uniform Donor Card from United Network for Organ Sharing (P.O. Box 13770, Richmond, VA 23225-8770 (800 243-6667)) or from one of the organizations listed in Appendix E. Once you have signed either card, carry it at all times. Also make sure that your doctor and the family members who will first learn of your death know that you have signed an organ-donor card. If you die unexpectedly, they then should be able to arrange for the organs you have donated to be removed at a nearby hospital or preservation laboratory.

You can also wear a metal tag engraved with the words "Organ Donor." In addition, you can make your desires known by registering at any of the several central organ-donor registries, which coordinate anatomical gifts and keep records of potential donors (see Appendix E). You can also express your desire to make an anatomical gift when you write your will, but as a practical matter, this isn't a good idea. By the time your will is read, it is usually too late.

FORM 3.

Health Care Proxy

I, _____ , residing at_____ ,
hereby appoint _____ , residing at _____ ,
telephone number _____ , as my health care agent to make any
and all health care decisions for me.

This Health Care Proxy shall take effect in the event I become
unable to make my own health care decisions.

Statement of Wishes and Instructions Regarding
Life-Sustaining Treatment

If I should have an injury, disease, illness, or any other physical or
mental condition which is incurable or irreversible and I am no longer
able to make decisions regarding my medical care, I direct that life-
sustaining treatment and procedures which serve only to prolong artificially the dying process be withheld or withdrawn. I want my care
limited to those measures which will provide me with maximum com-
fort and freedom from pain even if it may shorten my remaining life; I
ask that medication be administered to me to alleviate suffering.

Without limiting the generality of the foregoing statement of
my wishes, if I am (a) in a terminal condition which in the opinion of
my health care agent after consultation with my attending physician is
likely to cause my death in a relatively short time (without the inter-
vention of life-sustaining treatment), or (b) in a state of permanent
unconsciousness, then I direct that all health care be withheld or withdrawn, including, without limitation, nutrition and hydration. I affirm
that I do not make a distinction between nutrition and hydration and
any other kind of treatment and, without limiting the generality of
this Health Care Proxy, I expressly authorize my health care agent, in
his absolute discretion, to direct that nutrition and hydration be withdrawn or withheld from me. It is my intention that these directions be
honored by my family and physicians as a final expression of my right to
refuse medical treatment, and I accept the consequences of such refusal.

General Authority

I direct my health care agent to make health care decisions in
accordance with my wishes and instructions as stated above or as
otherwise known to him with regard to life-sustaining treatment, and,

in the absence of specific knowledge or with regard to health care other than life-sustaining treatment, as he determines, in his absolute discretion. I have placed no limitations on the authority of my health care agent.

Alternate Agent

In the event the person I appoint above is unable, unwilling or unavailable to act as my health care agent, I hereby appoint_____ _____ , residing at _____ , telephone number_____ , as my health care agent and, in the event that he is unable, unwilling or unavailable to act as my health care agent, I appoint _____ , residing at _____ , telephone number_____ , as my health care agent.

I understand that, unless I revoke it, this Health Care Proxy will remain in effect indefinitely or until the date or occurrence of the condition I have stated below:

This Health Care Proxy shall expire: No expiration.

IN WITNESS WHEREOF, I, _____ , have signed this Health Care Proxy this ____ , day of _____ , _____ .

residing at

We declare that _____ , the person who signed this document, is personally known to us and appears to be of sound mind and acting willingly and free from duress. She signed this document in our presence. Neither of us is the person appointed as agent by this document.

residing at

residing at

PART THREE

HOUSING

15

TAPPING THE
E·Q·U·I·T·Y
IN YOUR HOME

YOUR HOME IS PROBABLY YOUR MOST VALUABLE asset. Thanks to the increase in real-estate values in the past decade, your house may now be worth much more than you paid for it, and what's more, you may well own it free and clear. Recognizing that older Americans have a virtual gold mine in their home equity, lenders have fashioned a number of *home-equity conversion* plans that allow homeowners to tap some of that money during their lifetimes.

Don't confuse home-equity conversion arrangements with the widely advertised home-equity loans, which require homeowners to repay the amount borrowed, usually in regular monthly installments. If you fail to repay, the lender can foreclose on the loan, forcing you to sell your house. We don't recommend such loans for people already retired or about to retire. Repaying the loan may prove especially burdensome if you are living on a fixed income.

On the other hand, home equity conversion plans offer advantages if you are cash poor and need extra money to continue living in your home. With these plans, you usually don't have to repay your loan until you move or sell your house. If you die, your estate repays the loan. Home-equity conversion plans, however, do carry some risk. With some arrangements, you might use up all your equity, leaving no financial cushion in your later years, or your lender might default, or the loan payments you receive may not keep up with inflation. So it pays to proceed with caution when considering a home-equity conversion loan.

There are two basic types of home-equity conversion plans— *special-purpose* loans for anything from deferring property taxes to making home repairs, and *reverse mortgages,* which return your equity in the form of monthly payments, a line of credit, or a lump sum that you can use for living expenses.

A third kind of home-equity conversion plan lets you sell your house and lease it back from the buyer (sometimes your children or other relatives) while you continue to live in it. These *sale-leaseback* plans are complicated, and you need a real-estate attorney to arrange one. We discuss only the first two arrangements.

SPECIAL-PURPOSE LOANS TO PAY PROPERTY TAXES

Special-purpose loans used to defer property taxes are available in 22 states (California, Colorado, Florida, Georgia, Illinois, Iowa, Maine, Maryland, Massachusetts, Michigan, Minnesota, New Hampshire, North Dakota, Oregon, South Dakota, Tennessee, Texas, Utah, Virginia, Washington, Wisconsin, and Wyoming) plus the District of Columbia. These programs allow certain homeowners to borrow money from either the state or a local government to pay their property taxes (see Appendix G). Assuming that your house remains your primary residence, the money does not have to be repaid until you die, move, or sell the house. (Moreover, additional deferral may be available if the house passes to your spouse.) With these arrangements, you in effect use the equity in your home to pay your property taxes.

HOW THEY WORK Once you sign up for a program, you decide each year whether you want to defer that year's property taxes. If you do, some states require that you file an application before your taxes are due. The state then sends a check in the amount of your taxes to the local tax collector, or it may send a check made out to both you and the tax collector, and you pay the taxes yourself. Other states require that you first pay the tax and then apply for the loan.

The amount of deferral turns into a loan on which the state or local government charges interest. (You don't have to pay points, loan fees, or other costs associated with mortgage loans.) The loan is secured by a lien against your property. When the property is sold either before or after your death, the state can collect the amount of taxes you have deferred plus accumulated interest, and the amount of the deferral is subtracted from the equity. If you defer the full amount of your taxes each year for several years, it's possible to have little equity left in your home when you move or at your death. In the first case, you'll have little money left to buy another home, and in the second case, your heirs won't receive much money from the sale of your house. On the other hand, if your home continues to appreciate in value, the amount of equity keeps building (although your property taxes are likely to keep increasing, too). States offering these programs usually don't ask you to repay your loans before you sell your home, but you can often do so without prepayment penalties. The loan balance is usually paid from your estate.

ARE YOU ELIGIBLE? In most states, you must be at least 65 to take advantage of a property-tax deferral program. A few states, such as Iowa and Florida, and the District of Columbia have a lower or no age requirement. Many states also have income limitations. A few states allow anyone to qualify regardless of annual income.

To be eligible for property-tax deferral, states usually require that your home be debt-free or nearly so. If you owe a substantial amount on your mortgage or if you've taken a second mortgage or a home-equity loan, you are not eligible to defer your property taxes under most programs. Check Appendix G to see if your state has a property-tax deferral program. If it does, contact the state department of revenue for details.

SPECIAL-PURPOSE LOANS FOR PROPERTY REPAIRS

Using Community Development Block grant funds and other funding sources, state and local governments offer loans to homeowners to replace roofs, porches, plumbing, and heating equipment; install storm windows; or modify a home to accommodate a resident with a physical disability. Such loans, however, can't be used for merely cosmetic improvements. For example, you can't add a family room, but you can widen doorways to accommodate a wheelchair. Often, agencies make loan funds available so older homes can be brought into line with recent local housing codes.

HOW THEY WORK Like property-tax deferral loans, these loans carry a very low interest rate. In some localities, they are interest-free. There are no fees or other costs involved in taking out the loan. You usually don't have to repay the loan until you move, sell your house, or die (then your heirs have to worry about repaying it). So long as you live in your home, you are not required to repay. Some programs even forgive all or part of the loan the longer you remain in your house. However, with some programs, you have to begin repayment as soon as the repairs are completed.

When the time comes for you or your heirs to repay, the money no doubt will come from the sale of the house. It's possible that the improvements you made will increase the value of the house to the point where the loan actually pays for itself. (Of course, that depends on the amount you borrowed.)

Example: If your house is now worth $100,000 and you take out a $10,000 loan and make improvements, your home may immediately increase in value to, say, $108,000. Assuming it appreciates 5 percent each year, after 8 years, the house is worth $160,000. If you then sell the house, the appreciation more than covers the amount you borrowed.

ARE YOU ELIGIBLE? Eligibility requirements can be stiff. Usually, the value of your income cannot exceed a certain amount. For eligibility requirements in your state, check *www.usc.edu/go/hmap/national/national.htm*.

Some jurisdictions require that a residence be in a certain location. In Kentucky, such loan programs are often targeted at rural areas.

Deferred-payment arrangements sometimes go by different names, such as home-repair loans or accessibility loans. Their availability also varies from time to time and from locale to locale. A local agency may have money available to lend only at certain times of the year. To locate a program, call your state's agency on aging (see Appendix A) or community economic development agency.

SHOULD YOU TAKE A DEFERRED-PAYMENT LOAN? If you have trouble paying your property taxes or need to repair your home to make it more energy-efficient, to bring it up to code, or to modify it for a disability, these loans may be just what you need. Their low cost (or no cost) makes them exceptionally attractive. However, once you assume such a loan, it may be difficult, if not impossible, to borrow more money against your home equity. If you think you need more cash than you can get from one of these loans, a reverse mortgage may be a better option even though the costs may be greater. You should also consider how your heirs will repay the loan or how you will repay the money if it turns out your property doesn't appreciate as much as you expect. If you take a loan that requires immediate repayment, make sure your budget can accommodate the payments.

REVERSE MORTGAGES

Reverse mortgages are available in 49 states (all but Texas) plus the District of Columbia and Puerto Rico. With a reverse mortgage, you can withdraw the equity in your house in the form of a tax-free loan and use the money for living expenses. The loan proceeds are paid out in a single lump sum, as a line of credit, as monthly advances, or as any combination of these arrangements. The loan balance increases as you receive payments. In addition, interest is added to the growing balance each month.

In most cases, the mortgage balance need not be repaid until you die, move, or sell the house. If you are away from the house for a long time, in a nursing home, for example, most lenders require that the loan balance be repaid in full.

If you or your heirs fail to repay your reverse mortgage when it comes due, the lender can foreclose on your home just the same as if you defaulted on a traditional mortgage. But the lender cannot require payment from assets other than your home and cannot make claims against your estate or against your heirs to collect the balance.

The amount you can borrow depends on the your age, the number of borrowers, the amount of equity you've built up, the interest rate on the loan, and the type of reverse mortgage you take. Typically, the more equity you have, the lower the interest rate, and the older you are the more you can borrow.

Most reverse mortgages are insured by the Federal Housing Administration (FHA), or backed by the Federal National Mortgage Association—also known as "Fannie Mae." FHA insurance protects you if the lender defaults and is unable to make the required payments, and also protects the lender if the value of your home is less than the balance of your reverse mortgage when it comes due. If that happens, the insurer pays the lender the amount of the shortfall. Insured mortgages are the predominant type of reverse mortgage, and most of them are insured by the FHA.

FHA-INSURED MORTGAGES The FHA program began in 1989 and is expanding. The agency can insure up to 50,000 reverse mortgages originated through September 2000. Through early 1998, approximately 25,500 FHA-insured mortgages had been issued. Borrowers must be age 62 or older to participate in the FHA program. Here's how these mortgages work:

PAYMENT OPTIONS You can receive money from an FHA-insured reverse-mortgage loan in three ways: (1) a payment each month for as long as you (or you or your spouse, if you borrow jointly) live in the home (called a tenure arrangement); (2) a line of credit you may draw on whenever you need cash; or (3) monthly payments for a fixed term of years that you select. You can combine a line of credit with a tenure or a fixed-term arrangement. The FHA lets you switch from one form of payment to another anytime you wish. The costs of switching are minimal.

The line of credit is not fixed. On loans issued after January 4, 1997, the line increases at a rate equal to the interest rate charged on your loan balance. We recommend that you add a line of credit with any payment arrangement. Since the credit line increases over time, that money could come in handy later, when you might need cash to pay medical bills or make repairs to sell your house. With any of the payment options, you are allowed to take a sum off the top of your total loan proceeds. This is called an *initial draw,* and it's not uncommon for borrowers to use this sum to pay off other loans against their property. (The FHA requires that the property be free from other mortgages.)

HOW THESE LOANS WORK To determine the amount you can borrow, the lender must first appraise your home using an independent appraiser. Next, the lender calculates a *maximum-claim amount.* This is the lesser of the house's appraised value or the amount HUD lends for traditional mortgages in different parts of the country. It's possible for the appraised value to far exceed the maximum-claim amount. Under current law, the FHA maximum limits range from $86,317 to $170,362 (higher in Alaska and Hawaii) and may be adjusted annually for increases in housing prices. A proposal has recently been made to raise the limits to $227,150. But as we went to press, Congress had not approved this proposal. If the value of your home exceeds the FHA limit, you might find other types of reverse mortgages more suitable. However, you may still get the most cash from the FHA program, particularly if you select a growing credit line.

If you do apply for a reverse mortgage under the FHA program, the amount you can actually borrow is a portion of the maximum-claim amount and is based on your life expectancy. A 62-year-old can borrow less than an 80-year-old with the same maximum-claim amount. In the case of a couple, the FHA requires a lender to use the age of the younger spouse in figuring the loan amount.

Since reverse mortgages are usually adjustable-rate loans, the interest rate applied to your increasing loan balance is adjusted annually with changes in the Treasury rates. The rate can't increase more than 2 percent each year and no more than 5 percent over the life of the loan. The lender may also offer you a reverse mortgage with the interest rate adjusted monthly. Adjustments under this type of mortgage are subject to a lifetime cap. In either case, the adjustable rate does not affect the amount of payments you receive monthly, but a higher rate causes your loan balance to increase faster. Conversely, a lower rate results in slower growth.

Lenders use two interest rates in preparing a mortgage loan. Currently, the 1-year Treasury rate plus a margin of 2.1 percent (1.2 percent monthly adjustable interest) is used to calculate the interest accruing on the growing balance; the 10-year Treasury rate plus a margin of 2.1 percent (1.2 percent for monthly adjustable interest) is used to figure the payments you receive. For example, if 1-year rates are 5 percent and 10-year rates are 7 percent, your payments would be figured using a rate of 9.1 percent (on an annually adjustable loan), and interest would be accruing on your unpaid balance at a rate of 7.1 percent. In addition, as described below, a monthly insurance premium is added to the 7.1 percent.

When you obtain an FHA-insured reverse mortgage, you must pay an origination fee of 1 to 2 percent of the house's value plus typical closing costs (such as a credit report and appraisal fee). These closing costs usually range from $1,000 to $2,000. You must also pay 2 percent of the maximum claim amount as an initial insurance premium.

The FHA allows you to pay closing costs, the insurance premium, and an origination fee of up to $1,800 out of the loan proceeds. This option minimizes your initial out-of-pocket costs.

Besides the initial costs, you pay additional fees each month. These include a monthly mortgage insurance premium of one-half of 1 percent added to the interest rate charged on the loan balance and a monthly service fee of $30 to $35.

FINDING A LENDER Any lender can write an FHA reverse mortgage, but not all do. To find a lender in your area, contact the nearest Housing and Urban Development field office (see Appendix F). You can also call "HUD User" at 800 245-2691 to obtain a list of lenders participating in the program, or visit their web site at *www.huduser.org*. Free information may also be obtained by calling the American Association for Retired Persons (AARP) Home Equity Center, 601 E. St. NW, Washington, DC at 800 424-3410. Additional information can be obtained by contacting the nonprofit National Center for Home Equity Conversion (NCHEC) at 612 953-4474, or by visiting its website at *www.reverse.org*.

The FHA requires all potential borrowers to receive counseling in a HUD-approved counseling program before they can obtain a mortgage. A counselor (someone other than the lender) must discuss alternatives for getting cash, the financial consequences of taking a mortgage, the tax implications, and the effects of reverse mortgages on eligibility for government benefit programs, such as Medicaid and Supplemental Security Income (SSI).

HOME KEEPER MORTGAGES In 1996, the Federal National Mortgage Association ("Fannie Mae") entered the reverse-mortgage market. Reverse mortgages issued under the Fannie Mae program are similar in many respects to FHA-insured mortgages. However, there are differences.

First, under the Fannie Mae program, the maximum amount you may borrow under the line-of-credit option is fixed. The line will not increase annually. The "maximum-claim amount" under the Fannie Mae program is currently $227,150. This is significantly higher than the current limit under the FHA program, but it does not mean that a mortgage issued under the Fannie Mae program will always pay you more. Check the online calculation at *www.reverse.org* for estimates.

To borrow the maximum amount under the Fannie Mae program, you may have to agree to pay the lender an additional fee equal to a percentage (up to 10 percent) of the value of your home when you finally dispose of it. This can significantly raise your total loan costs—particularly if your home increases in value.

Other fees for mortgages obtained from Fannie Mae lenders include the usual closing costs of $1,500 to $2,000, plus an initial fee of 1 percent of your home's value, plus an origination fee of up to 2 percent of this value.

ARE REVERSE MORTGAGES FOR YOU? Reverse mortgages are complicated financial transactions with serious consequences.

Reverse mortgages will not suit every homeowner. Discuss your plans with a family member or accountant before proceeding. You can also contact the organizations listed earlier in this chapter.

Although reverse mortgages offer financial benefits, they also have their drawbacks. These mortgages don't make sense if you plan to move in a year or two. Consider them only if you plan to stay in your home permanently and can afford to keep paying the taxes and costs of upkeep of your home. If you already have a large mortgage on your home, you will most likely have to pay off that mortgage when you take out a reverse mortgage. If you want to preserve the equity in your home for your children, then reverse mortgages may not be a good option. The lender, not your children, gets most, if not all, of the equity when the house is sold.

Make sure you know the circumstances under which the loan becomes due and payable, particularly if your spouse or other partner wants to remain in the home. Under the FHA program, the loan is due when you die or have not used the house as a primary residence for 12 or more consecutive months. If you go to a nursing home and have no prospects for returning to your home, your relatives or whoever is acting on your behalf has three options for paying off the loan: (1) sell the house; (2) refinance your reverse mortgage balance with a traditional mortgage; or (3) pay the balance out of other assets. Other types of loans have other rules. Many uninsured loans, for example, are payable at the end of a fixed term or when you die, sell the house, or move, if that happens first. The lender can foreclose on the loan and force you to move.

A number of safeguards are built into the FHA program, so if you're seriously thinking of a reverse mortgage, consider an FHA loan. However, remember that any reverse mortgage involves significant costs. You may want to consider alternative sources of raising cash.

If you are still interested in a reverse mortgage, you should compare the costs of various reverse mortgages. Lenders are now required to disclose the total annual loan costs (TALC) of any reverse mortgage. The TALC ordinarily considers all annual costs of the mortgage—interest, origination fees, closing costs, and insurance—and expresses these costs as a single interest rate, which yields the balance due at various future dates. For this purpose, the TALC is calculated assuming the payment of your loan after two years, after your life expectancy, and after a period of 40 percent beyond your life expectancy. The lower the TALC, the better.

You may also want to determine how much of your home equity will be available to your heirs under each of these alternatives.

16

HOUSING
T·A·X
B·R·E·A·K·S

IF YOU OWN YOUR HOME, DECIDING WHETHER
to stay put or move is one of the biggest financial decisions you face
as you plan for retirement. If you do move, the tax consequences of
selling your house and obtaining another can determine your financial well-being in your later years. The Taxpayer Relief Act of 1997
(the "1997 Act") has liberalized the rules for shielding your profits
from taxes. Knowing when and how to use the new law will help
you maximize income from your house and protect your equity from
a painful tax bite.

EXCLUSION

Ordinarily when you sell a home, your profit is taxable at capital-gains
rates. But under rules added to the tax code by the 1997 Act, you can
generally exclude from your income up to $250,000 of your gain from
the sale of your principal residence. If you are married filing jointly, the
exclusion is generally up to $500,000. Any gain in excess of the applic-
able exclusion is taxable at capital-gains rates. Under current law, you
may no longer defer (that is, roll over) this portion of your gain by buying a more expensive home.

The government doesn't treat losses on the sale of a home kindly.
You can't deduct a loss unless part of your home was used for business,

and that part of the loss is then treated like any other business loss.

ARE YOU ELIGIBLE? To qualify for a $250,000 exclusion on the sale of your home, you must satisfy the following three requirements:

- For at least two out of the five years ending on the date of sale, you must have owned the home (the "ownership test");
- For at least two out of the five years ending on such date, you must have used the home as your principal residence (the "use test"); and
- You must not have claimed an exclusion for any other sale occurring after May 6, 1997, and within the two-year period ending on the date of the current sale.

However, even if you do not satisfy the two-year ownership and use tests or you have excluded gain from sale of another residence within the two-year period, you may still be able to claim a reduced exclusion.

A married couple qualifies for a $500,000 exclusion if they satisfy the following four requirements for the sale of their home:

- They file a joint return for the year of sale;
- Either spouse meets the two-year ownership test (above);
- Both spouses meet the two-year use test referred to above; and
- Neither spouse has claimed the exclusion for any other sale occurring after May 6, 1997, and within the two-year period ending on the date of the current sale.

Even if neither spouse satisfies the ownership test or both spouses do not satisfy the use test, they may still be able to claim a reduced exclusion. Similarly, if either spouse has excluded gain from another sale within the two-year period, they may still qualify for a reduced exclusion.

THE TWO-YEAR OWNERSHIP AND USE TESTS

To qualify for a full $250,000 exclusion, you must satisfy the two-year ownership and use tests described in this section and must not have claimed an exclusion for a sale within the past two years.

To satisfy the ownership and use tests, you don't have to live in your house for two continuous years, nor do the two years you own the residence have to be the same two years you live there. As long as you have owned the house for at least 730 days within the five-year period ending on the date of your sale of the house and have lived in it as your principal residence for 730 days within this period, you satisfy these tests.

Example: On October 1, 1996, you moved into a house that your daughter owned in Illinois. You lived there until April 16, 1997, when you bought the house from her. You stayed in the house until December 1, 1998, when you sold it and moved to Florida. Although you lived in the house for more than two years, you can't claim the exclusion, because you didn't own it for two years.

You don't have to be in the house every minute to be treated as living there. Temporary absences for vacations or other seasonal absences don't count against you. You can even rent your house while you are away. But the IRS will not treat you as using a home as your principal residence during lengthy absences. A construction worker, for example, who is away from home on short assignments won't lose the exclusion. But such eligibility might be sacrificed if he or she is on a long-term project that takes six months or more. If you have a similar situation, consult a tax adviser.

While you do not have to be present in a house every day within the five-year period to meet the use test, you must have used the house as your principal residence while you were there. If you live in a rented house or apartment but sell your vacation home when you retire, you do not qualify. To take advantage of the tax break, you must be able to prove that the house you're selling is a house you have lived in as your principal residence. Typically, you must show that for at least two years, you spent more time there than at any other residence.

Example: Since 1985, you have owned a house in Chicago and a vacation condominium in Florida. Since 1992, you have spent nine months of the year in Chicago and three in Florida. If you sell the condo, you won't qualify for the exclusion, because your Chicago house is your principal residence. But if you move to Florida and return to Chicago for a couple of months in the summer, the condo may become your principal residence.

You need not be using a home as your principal residence when you sell it to qualify for the exclusion.

Example: Same facts as in the example above except that on January 2, 1998, you retire and move to the condo. You rarely return to Chicago and in 1999 decide to sell your house there. You sell it in July 1, 1999. You are eligible for the exclusion because, within the five-year period ending on the date of sale, you owned it for two years or more (July 1, 1994–July 1, 1999) and used it as your principal residence for two years or more (July 1, 1994–January 1, 1998).

EXCEPTIONS TO THE OWNERSHIP AND USE TESTS The tax code provides several exceptions to the ownership and use tests.

• The first exception applies if you deferred gain on the sale of a prior home (under the tax rules in effect prior to enactment of the 1997 Act). If you deferred such a gain when you purchased your current home, then for purposes of determining the periods that you owned your current residence and used it as your principal residence, you may include the periods that you owned the prior home and used it as your principal residence.

• The second exception applies if you defer gain from receipt of insurance or condemnation proceeds as a result of the destruction or condemnation of a prior home. Again, if you deferred such a gain when you purchased your current home, then for purposes of applying the ownership and use tests, include periods that you owned the prior home and used it as your principal residence.

• Additional exceptions to the ownership or use tests apply if you acquire a residence from your former spouse. First, if your spouse dies before you sell your residence and you have not remarried on or before the date of such sale, then you are treated as having owned and lived in the residence during any time that your deceased spouse owned and lived there. Similarly, if you acquire an interest in a residence from your spouse during your marriage or from your former spouse "incident to a divorce," then for purposes of applying the ownership test, you are treated as owning the residence for the period your spouse (or former spouse) owned it.

• An important exception to the use test applies to certain tax-payers who are divorced or separated and move out of the family residence. As long as you continue to own an interest in the residence, you are treated as using it during any period during which your spouse (or former spouse) is granted use of it under a court decree of divorce, separate maintenance or support, or under a written separation agreement. Consequently, if the residence is eventually sold, you may still be able to claim an exclusion for your share of the gain even though you have not been physically present in the residence for many years. This represents a significant change from prior law. For purposes of this exception, a decree of divorce includes a final decree. A support decree includes court orders that award alimony on a temporary basis or before the final terms of the divorce or separation are settled.

• Another exception to the use test applies to certain nursing-home residents. You must still actually use your home as your principal residence for at least one year during the five-year period ending on the date of your sale of this residence. But if you are physically or mentally incapable of self-care during this period and live in a nursing home (or other licensed facility), the IRS will treat you as using your home as your principal residence when you are in the nursing home.

Example: You have owned and occupied your principal residence since 1970. In 1994, you suffer a stroke, and on January 1, 1995, you move into a state-licensed nursing home. On December 1, 1998, you sell your residence. You are eligible for the $250,000 exclusion, because within the five-year period ending on the date of sale (from December 1, 1993, until December 1, 1998), you owned the house for two years or more, you occupied the house for at least one year (from December 1, 1993, until January 1, 1995). In addition, your combined residence in your house and in the nursing home while you still owned your house equaled two years or more (occupancy of home from December 1, 1993, until January 1, 1995, and residence in the nursing home from January 1, 1995, until December 1, 1998).

MULTIPLE SALES WITHIN A TWO-YEAR PERIOD If you sell your principal residence at a gain and you have previously sold another principal residence within the past 24 months and excluded any gain from your income under the current law, you may not claim the full $250,000 exclusion. In effect, the law imposes a two-year waiting period before you may claim the full exclusion, even if you excluded significantly less than $250,000 of gain in the prior sale. However, if your sale is made as a result of certain hardships, you may be entitled to a partial exclusion, described below. Also, if you previously sold another principal residence at a loss within the last 24 months, you may still claim the full exclusion for your current sale. In addition, for purposes of applying the two-year rule, you may disregard any sale of a principal residence before May 7, 1997.

MARRIED TAXPAYERS

Under current law, married taxpayers are treated, in many respects, in the same manner as single taxpayers. Each spouse may exclude from income $250,000 of gain from the sale of his or her interest in a principal residence if he or she: (1) satisfies the ownership and use tests, and (2) has not previously claimed an exclusion for gain realized from a sale occurring after May 6, 1997, and within the two-year period ending on the date of the current sale.

Example: You and your spouse purchased a home for $50,000 in 1975 and took title to the residence as tenants by the entirety. (Tenancy by the entirety is a form of joint ownership. See Chapter 7.) You both have used the home as your principal residence since 1975 but have made no capital improvements to the home since then. Your adjusted basis for the home remains $50,000.

On January 2, 1999, you and your spouse sell the home for $360,000. You pay commissions, legal fees, and other selling expenses of $10,000. For tax purposes, regardless of how you and your spouse divide the sale proceeds, the IRS considers that each of you has sold one half of the home for $175,000. Similarly, you are each entitled to claim one-half the basis in the home, or $25,000. Accordingly, you each realize a gain of $150,000 ($175,000 − $25,000). Whether you and your spouse file joint or separate returns for 1999, you are each entitled to exclude $150,000 of gain from your income.

The current law does provide additional breaks to married taxpayers who file a joint return for the year they sell a principal residence. First, if either spouse meets the ownership test and both spouses meet the use test, they may exclude from their income $500,000 of gain from the sale of a residence *provided that* neither spouse has claimed an exclusion for a prior sale of a residence after May 6, 1997, and within the two-year period ending on the date of the current sale.

Example: Same facts as example above except that title to the residence was always in your name. If you and your spouse file a joint return for 1999, you may exclude from your income the entire $300,000 of gain.

What if only one spouse meets the ownership and use tests or one spouse has excluded gain from another sale within the past 24 months? If the spouses file a joint return for the year of sale, then their exclusion is generally equal to the sum of the exclusions they could have claimed if they had not been married. However, for purposes of applying the ownership test in this case, the IRS treats each spouse as owning the residence for the period he or she actually owned it plus the period his or her spouse owned it. If the spouses file separate returns, each spouse computes the exclusion as a single taxpayer. Of course, if only one spouse actually owns the residence, only that spouse will report any gain from the sale.

Example: You purchased a home in 1980 and have occupied it as your principal residence ever since. On April 1, 1999, you are married, and your spouse moves into the home with you. Your spouse rents out her home. Title to your home remains in your name. On May 1, 1999, you sell your home for $760,000. Your adjusted basis is $260,000. Your gain is $500,000 ($760,000-$260,000).

If you file a joint return for 1999, it appears that you will be allowed to exclude a total of $259,868 of the gain from your income. This amount is equal to the sum of (1) the $250,000 exclusion available to you based upon your ownership and use of the residence for the required two-year periods plus (2) a $9,868 partial exclusion ($250,000 ÷ 24 months), which you may also claim based on your spouse's use of your residence for one month.

In contrast, if you and your spouse file separately for 1999, you will be limited to an exclusion of $250,000. You may not claim any partial exclusion based on your spouse's use of the home.

The tax considerations become more complicated if newlywed taxpayers both wish to sell their separate residences, particularly if either sale is made on or before August 4, 1999. As described in the next section, after that date, the right to claim a partial exclusion is sharply reduced.

Example: Same facts as example above except that on July 1, 1999, your spouse sells her residence for $350,000. Her adjusted basis is $100,000. She satisfies the ownership and use tests for this residence. If she files jointly with you for 1999 and permits you to claim a partial exclusion of $9,868 based on her use of your residence, she will not be entitled to claim a full $250,000 exclusion for her sale of her residence.

She has two choices if she wishes to preserve her $250,000 exclusion. First, she may file separately for 1999. In this case, your exclusion for your sale is reduced to $250,000. Second, while neither the IRS nor the courts have ruled on the matter, it appears that she may file jointly with you for 1999 but request that you not claim the $9,868 partial exclusion based on her use of your residence.

REDUCED EXCLUSION

Even if you fail to satisfy the two-year ownership and use tests or you have excluded from your income gain from another sale after May 6, 1997, and within two years of your current sale, you may still be able to claim a reduced exclusion. A transition rule applies for purposes of determining the amount of your exclusion if on or after August 5, 1997, the date of enactment of the 1997 Act, and before August 5,

1999, you sell a residence that you owned on August 5, 1997. A more restrictive general rule applies to sales after August 4, 1999 (as well as to sales subject to current law made prior to August 5, 1997).

GENERAL RULE Under the general rule, you may claim a reduced exclusion if due to a change in your health or place of employment, you (or your spouse if filing a joint return) do not satisfy the ownership and use tests or are selling your residence within two years after the sale of another residence. The IRS also has authority to issue regulations permitting you (or your spouse) to claim a reduced exclusion if, due to "unforeseen circumstances," you (or your spouse) fail to meet the ownership and use tests or satisfy the two-year waiting period after an earlier sale. However, as of the date this book went to press, the IRS has not issued such regulations or explained the circumstances under which a change in your health or place of employment will permit you to claim the reduced exclusion.

If you do qualify to claim the reduced exclusion and you are single (or married filing separately), you determine the maximum amount of your exclusion by multiplying $250,000 by a fraction. The numerator of the fraction is the lesser of:

- The lesser of (a) the number of days during the five-year period ending on the date of sale of this residence that you used it as your principal residence or (b) the number of days during this period that you owned it; or

- if you have excluded gain from the sale of another residence after May 6, 1997, the number of days between the sale of that residence and the current residence.

The denominator of the fraction is 730 (2 x 365). In effect, you are allowed a pro rata portion of the $250,000 exclusion. Use *Worksheet 10* to calculate the exclusion.

Example: You are single and work in Manhattan. On July 1, 1998, you purchased a home in Yonkers, a suburb of New York City, for $400,000. The home was the first one you ever owned. Shortly thereafter, your employer requests that you transfer to its Philadelphia office. After living in your home for one year, on July 1, 1999, you sell it for $460,000 and move to Philadelphia. You pay no commissions or other selling expenses. Accordingly, you realize a gain of $60,000 ($460,000 - $400,000). You may claim an exclusion for this sale of up to $125,000 ($250,000 ÷ 2). You may therefore exclude your entire $60,000 gain from your income.

If you are married filing jointly, the computation of the reduced exclusion becomes more complicated. You and your spouse may qualify for an exclusion of up to $500,000. Your combined exclusion is generally equal to the sum of the exclusions you could have claimed if you had not been married. However, for purposes of applying the ownership test in this case, you and your spouse are treated as owning a residence for the period either one actually owned it. Refer to *Worksheet 10* to compute your exclusion.

TRANSITION RULE. If you owned a residence on August 5, 1997, and sell it prior to August 5, 1999, even though you do not meet the ownership and use tests, you may claim a reduced exclusion in all events. Your failure to meet these tests need not be due to a change in your health or place of employment or any other unforeseen circumstances. The amount of the reduced exclusion is computed in the same manner as under the general rule. Refer to *Worksheet 10* to compute the amount of your reduced exclusion.

FIGURING YOUR GAIN

In 1997, the Treasury Department estimated that the changes in the law made by the 1997 Act would exempt 99 percent of home sales from capital-gains taxes. But if inflation returns or you do not qualify to claim the full exclusion, calculating your gain will remain important.

To figure the profit or gain on your home, first establish its adjusted *basis,* which in IRS parlance means its total cost. The basis is ordinarily what you paid for your house, including the down payment, the amount of the original mortgage, and closing costs. If you built your house, it includes the cost of land and construction. To this amount, add the value of any additions or permanent improvements— new rooms, new plumbing, wiring, or a finished basement, for example. You can also include the cost of fixtures that can't be removed without damaging the house structure but not the cost of paint jobs and repairs.

Once you've made all the additions to the original cost of your home, subtract certain items if they are applicable. If you have claimed tax deductions for fire, flood, or storm damage, reduce your basis by the amount of those deductions. Moreover, if you deferred gain from the sale of a home under the rollover rules in effect prior to the enactment of the 1997 Act, you must reduce your basis by the amount of gain deferred. Despite the repeal of the rollover rules, you cannot disregard this basis adjustment. You should refer to Form 2119, Sale of Your Home, for the year of the prior sale for the amount of this adjustment. And if you use part of your home for business and have taken deductions for depreciation, subtract the amount of those deductions from your basis. The result is your adjusted basis.

(If you inherited your home, its initial basis is its value in the estate of the person from whom you inherited at the time you inherited it. This is usually the value reported for tax purposes. If there were no estate proceedings, you may need an independent appraisal to assess its value. If you are a U.S. citizen and owned your home jointly with your spouse and your joint ownership was created after 1976, only 50 percent of the home is includible in your spouse's estate. Thus, only this portion receives a new basis on his or her death. But if your joint ownership was created before 1977 or your spouse died before 1982, consult a tax adviser.)

Once you establish your adjusted basis, determine the selling price. You can reduce the gross proceeds from the sale by the amount of any sales expenses, such as real-estate commissions, advertising costs, and legal fees. The gross proceeds minus sales expenses is the amount realized.

Next, subtract the adjusted basis from the amount realized to arrive at the gain. *Example:* If your adjusted basis is $155,000 and the amount realized is $241,000, your gain is $86,000. If you cannot exclude this gain from your income, the gain will be subject to tax at capital-gains rates.

RESIDENCE/BUSINESS TAX RULES

If you have a home office, use part of your home as a professional office, or live in one apartment of the two-family home or apartment house that you are selling, you can claim an exclusion only for the part of your gain that is allocated to your residence. When you sell the property, the IRS may treat the sale as if you had sold two separate properties—your home and your business.

Example: Since 1990, you have owned a building with a retail store on the first floor and an upstairs apartment that you occupy as your principal residence. Your adjusted basis for the residential portion is $60,000 and $40,000 for the business portion (after allowing for depreciation and improvements). You sell the building for $200,000 and allocate $100,000 of the proceeds to each portion. Your realized gain on the business portion is $60,000 ($200,000 divided by 2 equals $100,000, less $40,000 basis). You may not claim the exclusion for this portion of the gain. You may, however, potentially exclude the $40,000 of gain allocated to the sale of the residential portion of the building.

If you have used a portion of your home as a home office, but also used that portion of your home for residential purposes for at least two years out of the five years ending on the date of your sale of your home, you may still be able to exclude substantially all of your gain on the sale of your home from your income. However, under the 1997 Act, you must nevertheless include in your income ("recapture") so much of the gain from sale of your residence as does not exceed depreciation you claimed for periods after May 6, 1997, on the portion of your home attributable to your home office.

Example: You purchased your principal residence for $200,000 on January 1, 1986. From January 1, 1986, until December 31, 1997, you regularly and exclusively used two of the 10 rooms of the house as the principal place of your consulting business. You claimed a deduction for home-office expenses (including depreciation) for each of those years. On June 1, 2000, you sell your residence. You may exclude from your income all your gain in excess of the depreciation claimed on the two rooms for the period May 7, 1997, to December 31, 1997. Because you used the two rooms for residential purposes for at least two years of the five years ending on the date of sale, the gain attributable to this portion of your residence may otherwise be excluded from your income.

HOMESTEAD EXEMPTIONS AND OTHER REDUCTIONS IN STATE TAXES

Many states provide real-estate tax reductions or tax deferrals for homes occupied by senior citizens. These tax breaks are designed to allow older residents living on fixed incomes to remain in their homes, despite the rising burden of local property taxes. These reductions take many forms and often include corresponding state income-tax credits for renters. Most states also provide some kind of arrangement to preserve your benefits while you're in a nursing home.

For example, New York municipalities, at their option, may exempt older, low-income residents from up to 50 percent of their real-estate tax bills. Married couples are eligible for this benefit if either of them is 65 or older; for other joint owners, both must be 65 or older. To qualify, your income must be under $18,500; this figure is periodically adjusted for inflation. The real-estate tax bills you receive from the city or town where you live will tell you how to apply for the exemption.

California residents who are 62 or over and have less than $13,200 of income are entitled to a credit against property tax on the first $34,000 of assessed value. The credit is computed on a sliding scale, from 96 percent for incomes under $3,000 down to 4 percent for higher incomes.

In other states, such as Illinois and Hawaii, the break takes the form of a *homestead exemption,* which eliminates the tax on part of the assessed value of your home. New Jersey gives most homeowners a homestead rebate, with a larger amount going to qualified senior citizens.

One popular retirement destination, Florida, has several layers of homestead exemptions. If you or a dependent are permanent residents of Florida, the first $5,000 of your home's assessed value is exempt from municipal and school taxes. This exemption goes up to $25,000 for all residents. If you occupy the residence yourself, the first $25,000 of assessed value is exempt regardless of your age.

As explained in Chapter 15, states with deferral provisions, such as Georgia and Colorado, let qualified senior citizens postpone paying all or some of their property taxes. The accumulated taxes, plus interest, are a lien against the property that becomes payable when they sell the house or die. The deferral saves cash for those living on fixed incomes, but shifts the tax burden to their children or other heirs.

And some states, such as New Mexico, combine their real-estate and income-tax systems by allowing real-estate-tax rebates (up to $250) as state income-tax deductions. If your rebate is more than your tax, you get a refund.

You can get information on property-tax breaks from your state department of revenue or state agency on aging, listed in Appendix A or Appendix G . If you move to a retirement home in a new area or enter a nursing home or other care facility, be sure to check on your real-estate tax status—the rules may be very different from what you are familiar with.

CONTINUING-CARE
R·E·T·I·R·E·M·E·N·T
COMMUNITIES
AND ASSISTED-LIVING FACILITIES

TODAY, AN INCREASING NUMBER OF OLDER Americans are moving into various types of housing that provide for a continuum of care; that is, apartments that allow you to live independently and then other arrangements that provide for more and more supervision and assistance as you become frailer and unable to care for yourself. About 10 years ago, those arrangements took the form of continuing-care retirement communities (CCRCs). But today, assisted-living facilities make up the fastest-growing segment of the housing market for older adults. In some cases, the distinction between CCRCs and assisted-living facilities is blurring. Nevertheless, you'll need to know about both types as you begin to plan for retirement.

CONTINUING-CARE RETIREMENT COMMUNITIES

These communities come in many shapes and sizes: luxury high rises with balconies, modest mid-rises, one- and two-bedroom cottages with carports and patios, and ranch-like structures with apartment wings radiating from a central common area. Most communities provide transportation, housekeeping services, craft or activity rooms, gardens, libraries, beauty shops, and a steady supply of bridge games, movies, tours, parties, exercise classes, concerts, and religious services. All have communal dining rooms. Increasingly, they are focusing on wellness and disease prevention, and many facilities now have exercise rooms and special exercise programs.

Round-the-clock personnel provide skilled nursing in nursing wings, or on special floors in the main building, or in a separate building that's part of the entire complex.

The communities, built largely with tax-exempt bonds and some conventional mortgage financing, work on the insurance principle of risk pooling. Not all residents will need nursing care, but for those who do, their care is funded with the fees paid by all the residents. In this sense, CCRCs work like any insurance policy premiums paid by all policyholders that are pooled to pay benefits to those who suffer some misfortune. Some CCRCs also work on another insurance principle—the life annuity. When you buy an annuity, you pay an insurance company a sum of money, and the company sends you a monthly check for the rest of your life (see Chapter 4). When you sign a CCRC contract, you receive your payments in the form of services and care. With an annuity, you can't outlive your income; with a CCRC, you can't outlive your lifetime care. What kind of services and how much care you receive depend on the generosity of the sponsor, the facility you select, and the amount of money you pay.

WHAT CONTINUING-CARE RETIREMENT COMMUNITIES COST

There are four basic types of continuing-care retirement contracts:

TYPE A OR 'ALL-INCLUSIVE' These contracts guarantee residents *fully paid* nursing care. If you spend 10 years in the nursing wing, the community is obligated to provide care at no cost other than your monthly fee. You are, in effect, buying a benefit-rich, long-term-care insurance policy.

Some Type A communities provide care for certain acute illnesses and offer other medical services, such as eye and podiatric clinics. Many offer personal care, such as help with bathing, dressing, and taking medications. A Type A CCRC may also provide apartment cleaning, laundering linens, tray service, utilities (though usually not telephones), transportation, private dining rooms, cable television, banks, saunas, and swimming pools. About one-third include three meals a day in the monthly fee; the rest, one or two. Some communities require you to buy a certain number of meals each month, sometimes for an extra charge. Meals not included in the basic fee are also extra.

TYPE B OR 'MODIFIED' These contracts generally do not guarantee unlimited nursing care. Instead, they provide nursing care for only a specified number of days each year or during your lifetime. When the days (usually fewer than 15) are used up, you pay the regular per diem charge for nursing care, although a growing number of communities give discounts from the going daily rate. They may offer CCRC residents a 10-percent discount off the daily nursing-home rate, for example. Many of these communities offer personal care, such as help with bathing and dressing, but fewer than half include those services in the basic fees. Services and amenities offered by Type B communities are similar to those found in Type A facilities, and most include at least one meal a day in the monthly charge.

TYPE C OR 'FEE-FOR-SERVICE' These contracts guarantee access to their nursing wings but usually charge the full per diem rate. Occasionally, you find a Type C community that reduces the daily charge for its residents. These communities typically do not include meals or personal-care services in their basic monthly fees. They do offer some of the same amenities as Type A and B facilities, although they are less likely to provide private dining rooms for parties, swimming pools, and woodworking shops.

TYPE D OR 'RENTAL' With this type of contract, you rent the living unit. There's no "up-front" fee. As you move from one level of care to a higher one, the monthly rent increases.

The major difference among CCRC contracts is the amount of prepaid nursing care the entrance fee buys. Type B and C facilities shift the cost of future care to you. And you may still be at the mercy of Medicaid and face the prospect of spending down your assets so Medicaid will pay your nursing bills (see Chapter 13).

COST OF CCRCS

Entrance fees may be substantial and vary depending on the size of the unit and geographic location of the facility. Expect to see fees in the neighborhood of $50,000 to more than $150,000. Monthly fees vary, too, by size of the living unit. For independent-living units, monthly fees average around $1,170 for a studio apartment; $1,443 for a one-bedroom; and $1,768 for a two-bedroom apartment. Nursing-facility rates average $4,530 a month for a private room; $3,540 for a semiprivate room; and $2,482 for a room shared by three or more people.

Couples almost always pay more than single people, on average $600 more. Older residents usually pay the same entrance and monthly fees as younger ones, even though they have shorter life expectancies and will have less time to use the facilities. On the other hand, older people are more likely to need the expensive nursing care, which communities say justifies charging the same price. Nevertheless, older residents who enter a CCRC and then leave or die before needing nursing care get less for their money. In that sense, going into a CCRC is a financial gamble. A few communities do recognize that younger residents will need services longer and so charge them more. It is rare, however, that people in their late 50s and 60s move into a CCRC. The median age of someone moving in is 78; the average age of all residents is 82.

Once you're in a CCRC, the facility can't retroactively raise the entrance fee, although it may charge a higher entrance fee to newcomers. But monthly fees can and do increase as the cost of providing services increases. Fee increases of between 4 and 6 percent per year have been typical. Sometimes, the frequency and the basis for the increases are spelled out in the contracts. Often, they are not. In terms of equity, your entrance fee buys security rather than real estate, and in most facilities, you don't have an equity interest in your living unit. When you die or leave, the community reclaims the apartment. Whether you or your estate get back any portion of the entrance fee depends on whether your contract specifies the fees are refundable.

REFUNDABLE FEES Historically, CCRC entrance fees were not refundable. If you paid a substantial sum to enter one and died two days after moving in, your heirs would be out of luck. But to gain a marketing edge, many communities now make their fees refundable or at least offer a choice between an entrance fee that is refundable and one that is not.

Refundable fees appeal mainly to those who want to leave an estate. Nonrefundable plans appeal to those who have no heirs and prefer to pay a fee that may be as much as 40 to 50 percent lower. To refund fees and still cover the cost of promised services, communities necessarily must make refundable fees higher. Sometimes, the fees are as much as 65 percent higher. (Thus, facilities with refundable fees may attract wealthier residents.) In some localities, communities refund 100 percent of the fee. You might receive 100 percent if you leave in the first year but only

90 percent or even 80 percent if you leave after that. Or it could be the other way around. You get 80 percent back the first year, 90 percent the next year, and 100 percent the third year. Typically, though, the amount of the refund will decline by 1 or 2 percent a month, so that after a number of years, you are entitled to no refund at all.

Some communities refund entrance fees only if you die; others only if you leave. Still others return your money in either case. Most communities attach an additional string. They refund your money only after your unit is reoccupied, using the entrance fee paid by the new resident to reimburse you.

CONTINUING CARE LOOK-ALIKES

The definition of a CCRC is blurring as more and more retirement communities offer a "continuum of care" but *not* continuing care. This subtle distinction has enormous financial consequences.

CCRC look-alikes outnumber CCRCs. They offer the same services and amenities. Indeed, there may even be a nursing wing or an assisted-living unit down the hall from the residents' apartments. But the financial arrangements are very different from the traditional continuing-care community.

Look-alikes rent their apartments on a monthly basis, but unlike Type D CCRCs, your contract may not offer the assurance of nursing-facility care. You often have neither the burden of an entrance fee nor the protection of a contract or lease. If you need nursing care, you pay the going daily rate—that is, if you can get into the nursing wing. Many communities rent their nursing beds to people who live outside the CCRC. Residents are not assured of a bed in the nursing center, only a priority spot on the waiting list. If the beds are full when you need care, you have to go somewhere else. Other services, including meals, also cost extra.

The number of look-alikes is growing rapidly. Even some traditional communities that have gotten into financial trouble have converted to simpler continuum-of-care arrangements without entrance fees.

Without the protection of a lease, skyrocketing fees could force you to leave if you can't afford the increases. At one facility, monthly fees rose from $950 to $1,500 in four years. In the long run, you may pay more at a CCRC look-alike than at a community charging an entrance fee, especially if you need extended nursing care.

PROFIT OR NONPROFIT?

The continuing-care industry has traditionally been nonprofit, since most communities sprouted from religious and fraternal organizations. The industry is still overwhelmingly not-for-profit, but in recent years, for-profit corporations, notably hotel chains, have begun to supply housing for the elderly. You can find both profit and nonprofit arrangements among all types of CCRCs, including the look-alikes.

Nonprofit sponsors of CCRCs, who believe they have a mission to care for the elderly, don't like for-profit businesses invading their territory and question whether for-profit organizations always have the residents' best interests at heart. However, there's no evidence that for-profit companies have deceived or harmed residents of continuing-care communities, and the nonprofits have had their share of problems. Nevertheless, many residents feel more comfortable with the nonprofit label, which many CCRCs exploit. Some communities, however, are not as nonprofit as they first appear. They may have a nonprofit board of directors, but the community is managed by a for-profit management company hired by the board. It's not always clear whether the board and the management firm are at arm's length. If they aren't, it's possible you will face increased costs or reduced services that wouldn't otherwise occur.

COMMUNITIES IN TROUBLE

Nobody knows how many CCRCs are in financial trouble. If they are having financial difficulties, low occupancy rate is usually the reason. Low occupancy means fewer fees and less money for services. It's a problem that plagues both old and new communities.

If an old community doesn't have adequate reserves to spruce up its aging facilities, it can quickly find itself at a disadvantage when it tries to attract new residents to replace those who leave or die. As with any real-estate development, if the location of a new community is wrong or if the buildings are unattractive, it can fail to attract interested prospective residents. If a community is undercapitalized, too small, fails to project future costs accurately, or fails to project correctly the sources of future dollars to pay those costs, its residents may find that the security they were buying has suddenly evaporated.

How do you know whether a CCRC you're considering is in

financial difficulty? It's not easy to find out. You may have to dig deeply to get the necessary information.

The industry's trade association, the American Association of Homes and Services for the Aging, says that buyers are entitled to specific information about each community. Thirty-seven states regulate CCRCs, and many require a community to give such information to prospective buyers as well as to current residents. Before investing your money, find out what your state requires a CCRC to give you.

Partly in response to prospective state regulations and partly to elevate the quality of the communities, the industry has formed a commission to accredit CCRCs that meet certain minimum standards in the areas of finance, governance, resident life and services, and resident health and wellness. Communities applying for accreditation conduct a self-examination of their operations and open their books and facilities to a two-and-a-half-day inspection by an industry team. So far, some 230 communities have won the stamp of approval.

Between 5 and 10 percent of those applying for accreditation are found unfit, mostly because of too many liabilities and too few reserves to cover their health-care commitments. Accreditation may be a helpful guide to a community's financial picture. Be sure to ask for some official document to prove that the CCRC you're considering is indeed accredited by the Continuing Care Accreditation Commission. (Don't confuse this kind of accreditation with approvals given to a community by a state health department.)

To obtain a list of accredited communities, send a self-addressed, stamped envelope to the Continuing Care Accreditation Commission, 901 E St., N.W., Suite 500, Washington, DC 20004.

Is a Continuing care for you?

A CCRC may be your last residence, and moving into one requires careful planning and shopping to protect the security you're buying. If you wait until the need for continuing care suddenly appears, you may hastily choose the wrong community or may not even be able to get into your first choice. The better CCRCs have long waiting lists, and the larger the unit, the longer the wait. For example, at many CCRCs, there is often a one- to five-year wait for a two-bedroom apartment. All communities have entrance requirements relating to your health and ability to pay. Communities require physical examinations, performed either by your own doctor or by one selected by the community. Some require a psychiatric exam as well. CCRCs also scrutinize your finances. As a general rule, you must have a monthly income that's one- and-a-half to two times the monthly fee. This requirement is intended to assure the CCRC that you can afford the inevitable fee increases.

If you wait until you need long-term care, your health has probably deteriorated to the point where a community will not accept you. Though nearly all CCRCs offer some assistance with activities of daily living and some even offer specialized units for Alzheimer's patients, few communities accept people who are already debilitated by a stroke or Alzheimer's disease and who are almost certain candidates for nursing care. That doesn't mean if you need a wheelchair or a walker to get around, you shouldn't apply. So long as you can care for yourself, many communities will consider you. The community may, however, make you pay extra for nursing care arising from certain health conditions you have when you enter.

If you do qualify for a CCRC, then ask yourself the following basic questions:

• Will you be happy living in a community? Administrators say that people who have worked in large, institutional settings adjust to communal living better than those who have worked and lived alone. Make sure the community has the amenities and services you're looking for. You may want to spend a few nights as a guest to see how residents interact and if the daily routines appeal to you.

• How much prepaid health care do you want to buy? If you like the security of knowing that any long-term care is paid for and you can afford it, go first-class with a Type A contract, bearing in mind that you pay much larger entrance and monthly fees. If you are a risk taker and think you'll need little, if any, nursing care, a contract that does not prefund care through an entrance fee may be a good choice. A facility without an entrance fee may be attractive initially but could cost you dearly later. If you do need care, you may end up paying more than you would have at a community with an entrance fee.

• If you choose a CCRC with an entrance fee, do you want it to be refundable or nonrefundable? If your assets are limited or you don't care about leaving an estate, consider communities with nonrefundable fees, since they are likely to be much lower. If money is no object or you want to leave money to your children, explore communities with refundable fees. (This decision is similar to one you might have to make about an annuity payment.) Both refundable and nonrefundable fees have income-tax implications. Some fees, usually those at Type A facilities, are considered below-market loans to the CCRC and are subject to a tax on the imputed interest. (The IRS assumes that a resident receives something of value instead of interest on the "loan," and therefore "imputes" interest income to the lender.) CCRCs should warn you of this and advise you to consult a tax adviser. On the other hand, a substantial portion of nonrefundable entrance fees is tax-deductible as a prepayment for future health care. A portion of the monthly fee is similarly deductible. Consider this in determining your tax bill in retirement (see Chapter 6).

• Once you make the basic decision, look carefully at the finances of each community you're considering, then evaluate whether each is a good financial investment.

LOOKING AT THE FINANCIALS

It's important that you or your accountant or financial adviser determine how well a facility is doing financially. A poorly run facility could spell trouble later.

Obtain complete audited financial statements and give them to your accountant to examine. These may be in the community's disclosure statement, a thick document available for inspection at the facility. If a community does not have audited statements or if it refuses to give you financial information, look for another community. It's important to obtain financial information, even from communities that don't charge entrance fees. A shaky community may have to raise its monthly fees to the point where you can't afford them, and if the community offers no lease, you might have to find another place to live at a time when you are least able to do so.

Once you get the statements, have your accountant look at the auditor's notes. They often reveal important information about a community's financial health. For example, the notes may disclose how the community treats entrance fees on its income statement. Fees should be amortized over the resident's lifetime, and only a portion recognized as income in any year. If the entire fee is counted as income the year it's received, the community may project an overly rosy financial picture.

Look at the community's debt. A CCRC with heavy debt, few assets, and little income to cover it may be headed for trouble.

Compare the facility's current liabilities with the liquidity it has available to meet those liabilities. A CCRC with plenty of assets in the form of buildings and equipment might not have enough cash on hand to pay everyday expenses.

For nonprofit CCRCs, your accountant should also look at the fund balance. Most nonprofit facilities try to achieve a fund balance close to zero. A negative balance is not necessarily bad, but if the community is running substantially negative balances year after year, ask why.

Ask for a history of fee increases. Most communities raise fees yearly, in line with the cost of living. A community that has not raised its fees in several years could have an inadequate cash flow rather than a benevolent management. It may have inadequate cash to pay its bills.

Find out the occupancy rate. For most facilities, the break-even rate is around 90 percent. If a community's rate is lower than that after several years of operation, the community may be in trouble.

Ask whether the community has conducted actuarial studies and knows whether it has adequate reserves for paying future health-care costs and refurbishing the facility. A community that has conducted such a study has at least thought about how it will fund future costs. You might have trouble getting this information. Persevere or look elsewhere.

Learn who the sponsors and managers are and their experience with CCRCs. Understand the financial structure of the community and know something about the financial entity whose name appears on your contract.

CONTRACT CHECKLIST

When shopping for a continuing-care community, it's critical to review the contract. If you don't have a contract in hand you may be misled by the claims of the facility's sales personnel. Once you obtain a contract, have a lawyer look it over, paying attention to the following provisions:

REFUNDS Are entrance fees refundable? If so, under what conditions? The contract should be clear on the issue.

TRANSFER DECISIONS Contracts should spell out what triggers the transfer of a resident from his or her apartment to the nursing center or assisted-living unit. Many contracts say the community alone makes the decision to transfer. Others require consultation with the resident, his or her physician, and the resident's family. What right of appeal do you have if you don't agree with the community's decision?

AVAILABILITY OF NURSING BEDS What responsibility does the community have to provide nursing care? Contracts should state what your rights are if no beds are available in the nursing center when you need one. Does it guarantee that any off-site care will be comparable in quality?

FEES IF YOU ARE TRANSFERRED TO A NURSING CENTER Residents with Type A contracts who transfer permanently to the nursing center usually pay a monthly fee equal to that for the smallest one-bedroom apartment. In Type B and C communities, residents who go to the nursing center typically pay the normal daily rate for nursing care after any days of prepaid care are used up. (These rates generally range from $50 to $100 a day, depending on the locality.)

FEES IF SPOUSE IS TRANSFERRED TO NURSING CENTER In many Type A communities, if one spouse is in the nursing center temporarily (some facilities use 60 days as the cutoff), the spouse remaining in the apartment continues to pay the regular monthly fee. The spouse in the nursing center pays for only two extra meals. If he or she needs permanent nursing care, the monthly charge then becomes the fee for the smallest one-bedroom apartment. The spouse still living independently continues to pay the regular monthly fee for the apartment. With Type B and C contracts, spouses transferred to the nursing center pay the normal daily charges after any days of prepaid care are exhausted.

FEE INCREASES The contract should specify how the community raises or lowers the monthly fee. Many contracts give communities the right to raise (or lower) fees if the cost of operations increases (or decreases). It should also say how much notice will be given to residents and specify the frequency of increases. It should also explain any caps on the amount of those increases.

To maintain their tax-exempt status, nonprofit continuing-care communities can't evict you if you run out of money. In fact, most contracts say that communities won't evict residents so long as the community's finances are not jeopardized. Some CCRCs have special funds to subsidize residents who fall on hard times.

RIGHTS UPON REMARRIAGE What are your rights if you remarry? Can your new spouse live in the community? This is an important issue often overlooked in contracts.

Some communities stipulate that a new spouse who is not a resident must meet the community's entrance requirements and pay an entrance fee equal to the fee for a studio apartment at the time you moved in. The couple must also pay the monthly fees for a couple. (If the new spouse fails to meet the entrance requirements, you are free to move out.) Other communities have a more reasonable approach. If new spouses don't meet the entrance requirements, they can remain in the community as nonresidents and even receive care in the nursing center if they pay for it themselves.

GROUNDS FOR CONTRACT TERMINATION Generally, communities can ask you to leave if you (1) are disruptive, or (2) lied about your health or finances on the application. For your part, you can cancel during a probationary period of residency, usually seven to 90 days, and the community refunds almost all the entrance fee even if the entrance fee is normally not refundable. If, however, you die during the probationary period, some communities refund nothing.

REQUIREMENTS FOR HEALTH INSURANCE Many communities require you to carry a Medicare-supplement policy in addition to Parts A and B of Medicare. Some even specify the amount of coverage. That requirement, often written into the contract, ensures that the CCRC doesn't have to pay for your acute illnesses.

Some communities, mostly those offering Type B and C contracts, also require you to carry long-term-care insurance. Since these facilities don't fund in advance much, if any, nursing care, the policies help pay for residents' care. Be wary of Type A contracts that make you buy a long-term-care policy. Since you are already prefunding nursing care through the entrance fees, it makes no sense to pay for it twice.

Some facilities that require long-term-care policies want you to buy the one they have preselected. Others may require you to buy a policy, but don't specify which one. In cases where you have a choice, shop carefully, just as you would if you were not going to live in a CCRC (see Chapter 12).

CONTINUING CARE AND MANAGED CARE

If you choose to live in a CCRC and also receive your health care from an HMO, it's vital to know whether your state allows you to return to your home in the CCRC after you've been hospitalized and need skilled-nursing care, a benefit your HMO must provide as part of the Medicare coverage it offers. Six states (Florida, Illinois, Maryland,

North Carolina, Ohio, and Virginia) have passed what is called "return-to-home" legislation, which permits residents of retirement communities to return to their CCRC and receive their skilled care at that facility. If your state has no such law, you may be required to move to a different facility that's part of the HMO's managed-care network—an obvious disruption for you and your family. State laws differ, so it's important to know the particulars that could apply to you. Ask the CCRC for details, and make sure you understand them.

ASSISTED-LIVING FACILITIES

Sometimes consumers confuse assisted-living facilities with CCRCs. It's true that some retirement communities also have assisted-living wings, where residents move when they become more disabled and can no longer live independently. But some assisted-living facilities are not part of any CCRC and operate entirely on their own. These may go by a variety of names—adult congregate living facilities, residential-care facilities, personal-care homes, or board-and-care homes.

Some assisted-living facilities operate without any scrutiny from public agencies. They may not need a license if they serve only a few residents, or they may fall outside of regulation if they do not offer particular services spelled out in a state's law. If you or a family member is considering an assisted-living facility, it's important to know what state regulations apply.

Monthly fees of $3,000 or more are not uncommon. You can't count on Medicare or Medicaid to help pay the bills, as you can for nursing homes. Medicare usually won't pay unless skilled care is delivered in a certified facility, and many aren't certified. Medicaid will pay in some states for certain services provided in these facilities if a resident is poor enough. Like with CCRCs, many people sell their homes and liquidate assets to have enough money to pay for care in an assisted-living facility. If you stay too long and your money runs out, the facility may ask you to move, creating a major dilemma for you and your family.

Choosing a facility can be tricky. There are no objective quality measures and no uniform inspection reports, as there are for nursing homes. (If your state requires inspections and makes the reports public, it's worth your time to look at them.) Most consumers are lured to assisted living by the physical appearance of the facility. While that may be important, it says nothing about the quality of care you will receive once you are there. Physical appearance also says little about your legal rights once you enter the facility.

A few years ago, CONSUMER REPORTS asked the American Bar Association's Commission on the Legal Problems of the Elderly to evaluate a number of contracts obtained from assisted-living facilities. Good assisted living is supposed to foster independence, dignity, privacy, a maximum level of functioning, and connections with the community. But most of the contracts were silent on those issues or appeared to promote the opposite by limiting residents' autonomy and fostering dependence.

ASSISTED-LIVING FACILITY CHECKLIST

The following questions—sometimes answered in the contract, sometimes not—are worth careful consideration before signing up for assisted living.

WHERE WILL THE RESIDENT LIVE? In most assisted living arrangements, residents reside in a unit or room; they have no ownership rights. But contracts should provide for flexibility when it comes to bringing in your own furnishings or modifying the unit, who can come to live or visit, and whether the same unit will be available after a temporary hospital stay. Many contracts are silent on those points. They don't specify the particular unit or room, nor do they mention adapting or customizing the unit or even providing for changes in the household composition that can occur if a resident marries or wants to live with someone. Few make it clear residents can return to the same room after returning from the hospital.

ARE MEALS INCLUDED? Most contracts specify what meals would be provided. But some facilities don't offer special diets, something you should find out about if you have special dietary requirements.

HOW DO YOU GET ABOUT? Whether a resident can leave the facility freely to shop, dine out, attend religious services, or visit a doctor is key to quality of life and independence. Contracts should specify who will provide what kinds of transportation and where. Some contracts are silent on the subject or say it's up to residents to arrange their own transportation. When they do touch on transportation, contracts may impose restrictions and conditions. For example, they may say the facility will provide transportation for medical appointments only on certain days of the week at certain times. Or it may limit transportation within a certain radius of the facility. Or it may say you have to give at least a day's notice before going out.

WHAT SERVICES ARE PROVIDED? Facilities should specify exactly what services—housekeeping, laundry, nursing care, activities, meals—they'll provide, how often, and whether they can stop providing them. Although it's best if a contract specifies when a service can be cut, for example, after a 30-day notice, you are more likely to find them saying services will be provided when the facility deems they are appropriate or are required. The vagueness of those provisions is tailor-made for abuse and neglect, and it's possible for a facility to manipulate the services to meet its financial objectives rather than the needs of its residents.

WILL YOUR PRIVACY BE PROTECTED? Residents need their privacy, but at the same time need some assurance that they're safe. Some facilities do bed checks during the night, a procedure some residents find objectionable. Be sure you understand how the facility you're considering keeps tabs on its residents, day and night. A contract may say little about privacy, but it's important to find out just what you'll be allowed to do or not do.

WHAT'S THE COST? Most contracts spell out the costs of living in the facility, and there are many—entry deposits, cleaning charges, vacating fees, processing fees, and fees that increase as more intensive care is needed. Then there are the optional fees—breakfasts, companion visits, RN/LPN visits, medication administration, help with bathing, dressing, and grooming. Because of the way different facilities bundle services, comparing fees is tricky, perhaps intentionally so. The best way to approach fees is to list all the services and care you or a family member require and then ask the facility how much it will charge to provide what you need. Remember, however, that as you need more care, the price goes up.

CAN YOU SEE YOUR OWN DOCTOR? Most residents prefer to see their own doctor, but in some facilities you may have to use the doctor the facility provides. Contracts may be vague about medical care and fail to explicitly give you the right to choose your own physician. If the contract says you can choose your own, does it then say the doctor must meet standards set by the facility? If a facility requires all residents to use the same doctor, and if you belong to an HMO that requires the use of its own physicians and other providers, you could be caught in the middle, unable to obtain medical care without incurring unnecessary out-of-pocket expenses.

WHO'S IN CHARGE OF MEDICINE? Contracts should say who is responsible for administering, coordinating, and scheduling medications. Is it the facility, the resident or family member, or visiting nurse? In some facilities, you may have to hire a nurse to administer medications, because the facility may only offer assistance in seeing that you actually swallow the medication. If your contract uses the word "supervise," be sure you understand what supervision means.

WHAT IF YOUR HEALTH FAILS? Few contracts specify what happens when a resident's physical or mental status declines. What happens, for example, if a resident's eyesight goes or if he or she can no longer walk to the dining room? Ideally, contracts should specify that an individual program will be devised to accommodate those needs. Instead, the contract might say you can bring in aides and assistants to help with your changing needs. This obviously adds to the cost of care. Many facilities are neither licensed nor equipped to deal with the increasing frailty of their residents. One question to ask when shopping for assisted-living communities: What do you do to accommodate my changing needs? Give some hypotheticals, such as failing eyesight or failing hearing. If the facility doesn't give very good answers or is vague, continue looking for a place that is more attuned to changes in its residents' functionality.

WHO DECIDES ABOUT TRANSFERS? It's not uncommon for residents to live in several units during their stay in assisted living, first in a private unit and then, as their money runs low, in a shared room, perhaps in an undesirable wing or floor. Nor is it uncommon for residents to be shipped off to a nursing home or placed in a higher level of care as their physical or mental capacity declines. Knowing who makes the decisions about transfers, the factors they're based on, and whether a resident has any say in the matter is crucial.

Ideally, the facility should provide for a committee composed of facility staff and the resident or the resident's representative to make the tough choices. Residents should be allowed to have a say when such transfers are recommended in nonemergency situations. Contracts, however, often put the decisions in the hands of the facility and sometimes in the hands of just one person, the facility's physician, without providing for consultation. Beware of contracts that say the decisions are "determined" by the facility.

CAN THEY KICK YOU OUT? Contracts should allow for a minimum of 30 days' notice if the facility wants to end the agreement, something the facility should have the right to do if a resident fails to pay or harms others. They should also provide for a probationary period to see if a resident is suited to assisted living. If not, they should offer a prorated refund of fees. If you find a contract that calls for less than a 30-days' notice, consider whether you can find other living arrangements in the time the contract allows.

If you don't like the contract provisions, see if you can modify or eliminate them. If the facility refuses to change any provisions you can't live with, look for another that offers a more resident-friendly agreement. Don't forget to obtain a copy of the rules and policies that pertain to life in the facility. The contracts often say that the rules are just as binding as the contractual provisions.

PART FOUR

ESTATE PLANNING

18

TRANSFERRING YOUR
E·S·T·A·T·E

ESTATE PLANNING IS AN INTEGRAL PART OF
retirement preparation. It involves gathering information about your
assets, providing for your family's financial needs, making sure the
right people benefit from your estate, and appointing the appropriate
executors, trustees, and guardians to carry out your wishes.

Estate planning can include writing a will, giving away assets
while you're alive, setting up a trust for someone to manage your
money, and minimizing taxes. (Many estates do not have to pay
federal estate taxes, but they may be subject to state death taxes and
both state and federal income taxes. Good planning can minimize
the bite.)

You almost always need the help of a lawyer if your family situation or your financial circumstances are complicated. For example, a lawyer will usually be required if you've been married more
than once, have children from a previous marriage, own an interest
in a closely held corporation or partnership, own investment real
estate, or have significant assets in more than one state. Furthermore, if you have a qualified pension or profit-sharing plan, you
should consult with an accountant or tax adviser before choosing
payout provisions (see Chapter 3). Also, if any of your proposed beneficiaries is disabled or incompetent, you should consult with a
lawyer to address his or her special needs.

SETTING UP AN ESTATE PLAN

Estate planning should focus on the following:

THE RIGHT BENEFICIARIES Provide for the most important beneficiaries first—usually your spouse and children—before leaving any property to others. Then consider the possibility that your spouse or one or more of your children may not survive you. Who should receive your property then?

THE RIGHT PLAN Don't hesitate to use trusts or other tax-saving or property-management arrangements just because they are complex. You may, for example, want to establish a trust for a child you believe will squander the family fortune. At the same time, don't make your affairs unnecessarily complicated. If a trust isn't really necessary, it's foolish to spend money setting one up and paying the annual costs of administration.

COMPETENT MANAGEMENT Pick one or more executors (and trustees, if necessary) who can manage your estate effectively and who are acquainted with your family's needs. Competent trustees are especially important if your heirs include minor children or grandchildren or other beneficiaries who are inexperienced in handling money.

LIQUIDITY After you figure the taxes and administrative expenses that will be charged to your estate, make sure that there are enough liquid assets to pay them. If a large part of your estate consists of a family business or investment real estate, there may be insufficient cash at your death to cover these expenses. Federal estate taxes are ordinarily due nine months after a person's death (though installment payments are permitted in certain cases). Your executor may not be able to sell your business at a fair price within this period.

If you lack sufficient liquid assets, one option is to buy life insurance. With proper planning and sufficient coverage, your heirs may be able to keep the family business. Other ways to find cash include drawing up a shareholders' or partners' agreement during your lifetime or a corporate stock-redemption plan to tap the cash in the business after your death. You will need professional help for both of these options.

WHAT ESTATE PLANNING COSTS

The cost of planning your estate and drawing up a will varies, depending on the complexity of your situation, where you live, and your lawyer's customary fee. Some lawyers regard wills as loss leaders and charge a small fee in the hope of someday handling your estate. If a lawyer insists on being named executor of your estate, a seemingly cheap will could turn out to be very expensive. Furthermore, you may not want your lawyer as the executor of your estate. He or she may have personal interests that conflict with your interests or those of your beneficiaries.

Some lawyers charge a flat fee—for example, $500 for a simple will or $750 for a will with trusts. Others charge an hourly rate. A simple will may cost less than $500 in a small town or significantly more in a large city. If you want to create trusts for your spouse and children or you have a complex estate in need of tax planning, the cost could easily exceed $1,000, and you may also require help from a financial planner or an accountant, which would increase the cost.

If you don't have a lawyer, ask friends for references. If that doesn't work, contact your local bar association; most have referral services. When you find a lawyer, ask what his or her charges will be. If the lawyer can't give a precise figure, find out the basis for the fee and how long it will take to draw up your plan. If you don't get satisfactory answers to your questions about fees, find another lawyer.

MAKING A WILL

Some of your property automatically passes to others whether or not you write a will. For example, joint accounts with right of survivorship pass to the surviving joint owner, and "in trust for" bank accounts go to the named beneficiary (see Chapter 7). The proceeds from life-insurance policies, pension and profit-sharing plans, and IRAs also go to the person you name as beneficiary.

None of these devices alone, however, may be sufficient to dispose of your entire estate. Even if you have put all your investments into joint accounts, you still must decide who gets your furniture and other personal property. If the person who is the joint owner of your accounts (usually your spouse) dies before you do, you definitely need a will to establish who inherits your accounts.

It is important for everyone to legally establish who is to receive his or her property and who will manage that property after your death. Property that does not automatically pass to others can be disposed of in several ways.

One way to establish who will receive your property is to set up a trust during your lifetime—a *living trust*—and transfer your assets into the trust. During your lifetime, you can retain complete control over the assets. Upon your death, the trust property will continue to be managed by someone you designate as the successor trustee and will ultimately pass to those beneficiaries you have designated in the trust instrument, either outright or in further trust. (See Chapter 19 for a more detailed discussion of the use of trusts.)

A more common way to dispose of property at death is through a will. In your will, you designate who will receive your property, how it will be distributed, whether outright or in trust, and you name someone as your executor to manage your estate.

You can also use a combination of a trust and a will to dispose of all your assets. Those assets that you have transferred to a trust during your lifetime will pass according to its terms; any remaining assets will pass according to the provisions of your will.

If you don't have a will when you die, you are said to die *intestate,* and any property in your name passes according to the intestacy laws of your state. These laws are rigid, and you run the risk of having your estate disposed of in a way you do not approve.

If you are survived by both a spouse and children, under most state intestacy laws, all usually share your estate. In some states, the division is equal; in others, children receive larger shares than a surviving spouse. If you have no spouse, your children generally inherit the entire estate. If your children are under 18, the court may appoint a guardian to manage their inheritance until they turn 18. At that time, they have control over the property. The court also appoints a guardian to supervise the daily activities of minor children who have no living parents. (If you had a will, the guardian would be someone selected by you.)

If you have no spouse or children and you die intestate, your estate usually passes to your closest surviving relatives. In some states, however, distant relatives may not receive a thing, and your estate could *escheat* to the state, meaning the state gets whatever property you leave.

Intestacy laws typically grant the right to become administrators or personal representatives to those who inherit. Under certain circumstances, the public administrator or chief financial officer of the county is named as administrator. Administrators control the estate. If your assets pass to a group of heirs, such as your children or your brothers and sisters, they all have the right to administer your estate. Obviously, this can lead to trouble. If the heirs can't agree, or if the estate involves conflicts that can't be resolved amicably, the court could appoint someone else to manage your estate.

There are other reasons not to rely on intestacy laws. These laws create an "average" estate plan that may or may not fit your needs. Even if you are pleased with the state-mandated plan where you live now, after you retire, you might move to a state whose intestacy laws are unsatisfactory.

For example, your assets may pass to some relative who doesn't need the money. Your children may receive more than your spouse, or they may inherit your money outright when they might be better served by a trust. Your parents may inherit your assets, which could be depleted paying for their nursing-home expenses. Or your aged parents could end up as guardians for minor children.

Nor do intestacy laws recognize common-law marriages, nonmarital relationships, or other nontraditional arrangements. Unless each partner in such an arrangement has a will, the survivor usually cannot inherit the estate of the first to die. Finally, you may lose significant tax-planning opportunities if you die without a will.

When you write a will, you decide who gets your assets and who manages them. The first step is to figure out what assets you have and how liquid they are.

Use *Worksheet 8*, "Estate planning: taking stock of your assets and liabilities," in the back of the book, to determine the current value of your assets, project what your assets and liabilities are likely to be when you die, and estimate the remainder after all bills and taxes are paid. You can give this worksheet to your attorney or tax adviser to use as a starting point in devising your estate plan.

Your will should be flexible enough so that it can carry out your wishes whether your death is untimely or far in the future. It should be reviewed periodically as your personal or financial situation changes or if there are new developments in the tax law that affect you.

If the calculation shows that your spouse will need most or all of your assets to live on, then you probably want to leave those assets to him or her, either outright or in trust or in some combination of both. If there's more than enough for your spouse, then consider leaving money to your children, friends, or favorite charities. (You should discuss the estate-tax impact of these alternative dispositions with your lawyer.)

If the worksheet reveals that your assets are substantial and that you can amply provide for your spouse and children, your next step is to consider how your estate can save on taxes.

PROBATE AND NONPROBATE ASSETS

After completing *Worksheet 8*, make a list of your probate and nonprobate assets on *Worksheet 9*, "Probate and Nonprobate Assets," in the back of the book. *Probate* assets are those that pass to your heirs under the terms of your will. (Probate is the process by which a court validates your will and makes sure that your wishes are carried out.) *Nonprobate* assets pass directly to a named beneficiary. For example, if most of your property is in joint accounts and you don't want the joint tenant to retain ownership of the property, change the ownership of those assets. (Even though nonprobate assets don't pass under the terms of your will, they often become part of your estate for purposes of calculating estate taxes.)

Nonprobate assets include:

JOINT ACCOUNTS AND OTHER PROPERTY HELD JOINTLY WITH RIGHT OF SURVIVORSHIP Any residence, bank accounts, stocks, mutual funds, or other assets held jointly with right of survivorship automatically pass to the surviving joint tenant. They are not controlled by your will, although when the survivor dies, the disposition of the asset may be covered by his or her will.

Under current law, half the value of assets owned jointly with your spouse is included in your gross estate for calculating federal estate taxes. (Special rules will apply in the case of a spouse who is not a U.S. citizen.) Whether these assets are counted in figuring state death taxes depends on your state's law. If you own property with someone other than your spouse—for example, your child—the entire value is taxable in your estate, unless your child can prove how much he or she contributed toward the purchase of the asset.

LIFE INSURANCE Life insurance proceeds can be nonprobate property, or they can pass under your will. As explained in Chapter 19, they can also be payable to a trust. If you name a beneficiary when you take out the policy, the proceeds go to that person when you die. For life insurance to pass under your will, you must designate your estate as the beneficiary.

In computing federal estate taxes, life insurance is considered part of your estate if you retain an "incident of ownership" over the policy, whether that be actual ownership or some lesser measure of control, such as the right to change beneficiaries or borrow against the cash value. To keep life insurance out of your estate, you must make an irrevocable transfer of ownership and control of the policy more than three years before you die. (The owner has the right to decide who gets the benefits. The owner and the insured—the person on whose life the policy is written—need not be the same.) Making gifts of life insurance to children is one way to minimize estate taxes. Another is to create an irrevocable life insurance trust as described in Chapter 19.

QUALIFIED PLANS The proceeds from pension and profit-sharing plans, IRAs, 401(k) plans, and SEP arrangements are nonprobate assets that pass to the named beneficiary in each instance. You can, however, leave these assets to a trust created during your lifetime or by your will, or you can name your estate as the beneficiary. Your choice of beneficiary will often have significant income as well as estate-tax consequences, so you may want to consult with a specialist in this area before making a final decision.

The assets from your qualified plan are subject to estate as well as federal income taxes (with an offset for any estate taxes paid). No estate taxes are due, however, if the payout qualifies for the "marital deduction" (see page 276). If, on the other hand, you designate someone other than your spouse as the beneficiary, both estate and federal income taxes may be due.

IN TRUST FOR ACCOUNTS These accounts, also called Totten Trusts, are not true trusts. During your lifetime, you have complete control over the account, and the income from the account or "trust" is taxable to you. When you die, the account becomes part of your taxable estate, and the beneficiary designated on the account becomes the new owner of the account. The beneficiary has no tax liability or ownership rights during your lifetime, since you have the power to take back the account at any time.

SELECTING A TRUSTEE OR EXECUTOR

Every estate has an executor or personal representative who is responsible for managing the assets, paying the estate's bills, including taxes, and making distributions. Usually, the executor hires a lawyer or accountant to help with these tasks. The estate pays the fees of these professionals.

When you establish a trust, you name a trustee to manage the trust's assets. The trustee invests the trust's assets and pays out income and principal as spelled out by the terms of the trust.

If you have minor children, you also need to name a guardian for them. You can select one person to care for the child and another to manage the child's money; one person may not be suitable for both tasks. It is permissible, however, for the same person to act in both capacities.

In naming an executor or a trustee, you should select someone who is responsible and financially sophisticated. Many banks and investment firms may also serve as executors and trustees. Most state laws contain a schedule for the compensation of executors and trustees, and you should ask your lawyer about these fees. Selecting a close relative who does not intend to charge a fee may be the least expensive route to go but may not be your best choice if he or she is not well-suited for the job.

ESTATE TAXES

Under current law, your estate may be subject to five different taxes:

FEDERAL ESTATE TAXES The federal estate tax is a progressive tax based on the value of your taxable estate. The maximum stated rate is 55 percent, which is imposed on the portion of your taxable estate in excess of $3 million. In 1998, estates under $625,000 are not required to file a federal estate-tax return and are exempt from federal estate taxes. (This exemption will increase, in stages, to $1 million in 2006. See page 276.)

STATE DEATH TAXES Every state imposes one of three kinds of death taxes: estate taxes that equal the "state death-tax credit" allowed by the federal government, estate taxes calculated without reference to the federal credit, or inheritance taxes that are levied against what each heir receives.

In states with inheritance taxes, the tax on a spouse's share of an estate is likely to be lower than the tax on the portions inherited by other heirs, or it may not be taxed at all. Many states tax the shares received by relatives at lower rates than shares received by unrelated beneficiaries.

A majority of states, however, impose a tax equal to the state death-tax credit allowed for federal estate-tax purposes. *Example:* Suppose your estate owes federal estate taxes of approximately $362,000 before allowance of any credit (including any credit for state death taxes). According to IRS tables, the maximum credit for state death taxes in this case is $35,143. The amount of federal tax due is reduced by the state credit, and the state then imposes a tax equal to the amount of the credit, or $35,413. Under this system, if it turns out your estate owes no federal estate taxes, no state estate tax will be due.

GIFT TAXES The federal government and seven states (Connecticut, Delaware, Louisiana, New York, North Carolina, South Carolina, and Tennessee) currently tax certain substantial gifts you make during your lifetime. (The New York gift tax will be eliminated effective for gifts made on or after January 1, 2000.)

GENERATION-SKIPPING TAXES The federal government and one-half of the states impose a generation-skipping transfer tax on transfers of assets that manage to escape estate taxes for at least one generation. A typical example of such a transfer is a trust in which the income is payable to your child for his or her life. When the child dies, the trust is then payable to his or her children.

Direct transfers of assets made to a grandchild or descendant two or more generations younger than you may also be subject to this tax. The federal government allows certain exemptions from the tax, the most important being a $1 million exemption for all generation-skipping transfers made during your life or upon your death. (Beginning in 1999, the amount of this exemption will be indexed for inflation.) Unlike the federal estate tax that is a progressive tax, the generation-skipping tax is imposed at a flat 55-percent rate on all transfers that are subject to the tax.

INCOME TAXES The federal government and the states treat estates and trusts as separate taxpayers. After you die, your estate may well be subject to both federal and state taxes on its income.

PENSION-PLAN EXCISE TAXES The Taxpayer Relief Act of 1997 (the "1997 Act") repealed the 15-percent excise tax on distributions from retirement plans. Similarly, the 1997 Act repealed an additional 15-percent estate tax calculated on the balance of your interests in qualified plans and IRAs at your death.

CREDITS AND DEDUCTIONS

One or more of these taxes bite into many estates. But the government has provided credits and deductions that minimize the pain.

UNIFIED CREDIT The 1997 Act made significant changes in the unified credit. In 1998, this credit exempts the first $625,000 of any estate from federal estate taxes.

This credit will increase in stages, so that for a person dying in 2006 or thereafter, the first $1 million of his or her estate will be exempt from estate tax. For someone dying before 2006, the exemption amounts are as follows:

Year of Death	Exemption Amount
1998	$ 625,000
1999	$ 650,000
2000	$ 675,000
2001	$ 675,000
2002	$ 700,000
2003	$ 700,000
2004	$ 850,000
2005	$ 950,000
2006	$1,000,000

Most individuals don't have estates this large. But if you own a house and receive a generous lump-sum pension payment or own a large life-insurance policy, an estate of these amounts is quite possible. (Note that as of September 1998, federal legislation was being considered that would affect the amount in 2006; consult your tax adviser for further information.)

The same credit applies to gift taxes. During your lifetime, you can make gifts beyond the $10,000 annual exclusion (described below) up to the exemption amount and escape federal gift taxes on the money (or property) you give away. However, any amount of the unified credit that you use for lifetime gifts will be subtracted from the total available to your estate at death.

THE UNLIMITED MARITAL DEDUCTION This deduction allows you to give any amount to a spouse when you are alive or when you die and pay no taxes on the amount given. You can give your spouse $100 or $1 million, either outright or as part of a qualified trust, and the gift is exempt from federal gift or estate taxes. (Most states also allow a similar exemption.) If you leave all your property to your spouse, the deduction results in no estate taxes being due.

If your spouse is not a U.S. citizen, you are eligible for the unified credit, but usually you cannot exempt further assets from taxation (unless you use a Q-DOT—see Chapter 19). Lifetime gifts to a noncitizen spouse are limited to $100,000 per year. In other words, the unlimited marital deduction generally doesn't apply to transfers to your spouse if he or she is not a U.S. citizen.

ANNUAL GIFT-TAX EXCLUSION This provision lets you give up to $10,000 a year to children, other relatives, or anyone else. Married couples can give an individual up to $20,000 annually by splitting their gifts. (The gift-tax annual exclusion will be indexed for inflation for years beginning in 1999.) If your gift exceeds the amount of the exclusion, the unified credit comes into play—the value of your gift in excess of the exclusion is charged against the credit. Of course, that reduces the credit available to offset estate taxes, as we have noted.

In states that impose gift taxes, taxpayers can also make use of a state gift-tax exclusion.

DEDUCTION FOR QUALIFIED FAMILY-OWNED BUSINESS INTERESTS The 1997 Act, as amended, permits an estate to claim a deduction for the value of "qualified family-owned business interests." In order to be eligible for this deduction, the value of these interests (those in the estate as well as those that the decendent gave to his or her family during his or her lifetime) must comprise more than 50 percent of the decendent's adjusted gross estate and meet certain other requirements. The maximum available deduction for family-owned business interests is $675,000. The amount of this deduction will reduce the available unified credit (see page 276). For example, if an estate is allowed a maximum qualified family-owned business deduction of $675,000, then the applicable unified credit for that estate is $625,000 (regardless of when the decendent dies). If an estate included less that $675,000 of qualified family-owned business interests, the applicable unified credit is increased, on a dollar-for-dollar basis, from $625,000 up to the maximum amount generally available for that year, but the total of the deduction and the credit cannot exceed $1.3 million.

There are complicated requirements and many special rules that apply to the use of this exclusion, and you should consult with your attorney to determine if your estate qualifies.

PLANNING FOR TAX SAVINGS

The marital deduction lets you defer estate taxes if you leave everything to your spouse. When the spouse dies, his or her estate is taxed on the value of the property he or she held at his or her death. There are ways, however, to minimize those estate taxes.

BEGIN USING THE UNIFIED CREDIT DURING YOUR

LIFETIME The federal government doesn't care whether you use the unified credit during your lifetime or at death. Removing assets from your estate while you are alive and allowing them to escape estate taxes makes sense for many people. Any appreciation and income aren't subject to taxes. If both the appreciation and income are considerable, the tax savings can be great, as well. Life insurance and interests in a family business are examples of assets that can be disposed of during your lifetime at a significant tax savings. Depending on the type of asset given and the form of ownership following the gift, substantial discounts may be available in valuing the gift to reduce the amount of the credit that you use.

CREATE A BYPASS TRUST TO MAXIMIZE THE UNIFIED CREDIT Consider a bypass trust to avoid having money left to a spouse being taxed as part of his or her estate. A bypass trust is a trust that consists of property equal in value to the exemption amount available. Such property will not be taxed in your estate or in your spouse's estate, even if your spouse is the beneficiary of this trust during his or her lifetime. Couples with large estates, generally $1 million or more, find this device useful. *Example:* When you die in 1998, your estate is valued at $1.25 million, and your spouse has no other assets. Your will provides that $625,000 of your estate will be transferred to a bypass trust. You leave the balance of the money to your spouse. You can leave the money to your spouse outright or create a Q-TIP trust (see Chapter 19). The money left to your spouse will qualify for the marital deduction. The use of the bypass trust and the marital deduction allow your estate to escape all estate taxes. When your spouse dies, his or her estate contains only the $625,000 that was not part of the bypass trust (assuming no appreciation in value). Since the spouse's estate is eligible for its own exemption amount of at least $625,000, no estate taxes will be due from either estate.

Without a bypass trust, if you leave your estate to your spouse, it is still not subject to taxes, but your spouse's estate will be. Assuming no change in the estate's value, the entire $1.25 million will pass to your spouse and be taxable when your spouse dies. For example, if your spouse dies in 2001, then after deducting the $675,000 exemption amount available in that year, your spouse's taxable estate will total approximately $575,000. Approximately $198,000 in federal estate taxes will be due, and less will be available for your children or other beneficiaries.

To make a bypass trust work, you must have enough assets in your own name to fund the trust. To do that, you may have to split joint accounts or name your trust as the beneficiary of some of your life insurance. You may also have to rearrange your assets if you want the bypass trust to come into play no matter whether you or your spouse die, first. The spouse with the larger estate can take advantage of the unlimited lifetime marital deduction to shift assets to the other spouse so he or she has at least an amount equal to the exemption amount ($625,000 in 1998) in his or her own name.

MAKE THE MOST OF THE GIFT-TAX ANNUAL EXCLU- SION As mentioned, you can give away $10,000 each year. (Married couples can give away $20,000.) A couple with two married children who each have two children of their own can make eight potential gifts each year (if the spouse of each child is included), amounting to a total of $160,000. Obviously, not everyone is in a position to give away $160,000 annually, but if you can afford to give away some of your money and won't need it for living expenses, gifts to family are one way to keep your money from the IRS.

But don't be pressured into giving away so much that you are left to depend on others. Many overly generous parents have given most of their assets to their children only to find they later need that money.

SPECIAL GIFTS

LIFE INSURANCE You can give away life insurance, keep it out of your estate, and incur no estate tax and little or no gift tax. The primary value of life insurance isn't realized until after your death. Before Congress allowed the unlimited marital deduction, one spouse often transferred ownership of a policy to the other to cut estate taxes. Since the marital deduction makes that unnecessary (if you own the policy and your spouse is the designated beneficiary, the payment of the proceeds will qualify for the marital deduction), the usual recipients of life-insurance gifts are now children or irrevocable insurance trusts.

Think long and hard, however, before relinquishing the ownership of a policy. If you retain ownership, you can borrow against the policy and change the beneficiary. You lose these rights when you transfer ownership. If you transfer and later change your mind, you might be able to persuade a family member to return the policy. But if you give the policy to an insurance trust, the trustee may not have the power to return it or to change the terms of the trust. (As we note in Chapter 19, any trust you have the power to change or revoke is subject to estate taxes.)

Example: You have total assets in your name of $1.5 million, including $300,000 of whole-life insurance and joint property with your spouse totaling $250,000. Your spouse has no other assets. When you die, you leave the entire estate to your spouse, outright, except for the exemption amount that is placed in a bypass trust. If you were to die in 1998, there would be no estate taxes at your death, since the unlimited marital deduction applies to the amounts left to your spouse.

If your spouse's estate does not fluctuate in value, then when your spouse dies, his or her estate will be valued at $875,000 ($1.5 million minus the $625,000 exemption amount in the nontaxable bypass trust). If your spouse also dies in 1998, his or her estate would be subject to estate taxes of about $68,600.

If your spouse won't need the income from the life-insurance policy, you could transfer ownership of the insurance to your children, thus removing $300,000 from both your estate and your spouse's estate. Depending on the current cash value of the insurance, you may use some of your unified credit in making the gift, but probably not much. Of your $1.2 million estate, $625,000 is placed in the bypass trust and the remainder passes to your spouse outright. The balance of the unified credit and the marital deduction protect the money from estate taxes when you die, and there may be no estate tax due when your spouse dies.

However, if your spouse needs the income from the insurance to live on, you might be better off creating an irrevocable insurance trust, which provides your spouse with necessary income. The trustee can also have the power to invade the principal in the trust for your spouse's benefit, but the trust is not subject to estate taxes on your death. When your spouse dies, the trust passes to your children.

INTEREST IN A FAMILY BUSINESS Interests in a family business are well-suited for gifts. By making small gifts of stock to your children, for example, you can eliminate future appreciation in stock values from your estate. The same applies to interests in real estate.

The complicated part of making such gifts is valuing the assets. The IRS requires that all assets be valued at *fair market value,* that is, the price a willing buyer would pay a willing seller. When estimating the value of your home or other real estate, use the price you would receive if you sold it minus the mortgage amount. (You cannot use the original cost.) Special rules govern certain qualified real property (that is used in a trade or business) and farms, which may be taxed (for estate-tax purposes) based on their business or agricultural value rather than their full market value. In valuing a business, the IRS usually looks not only at the book value but also at earnings and comparable businesses to determine what gift or estate taxes are due.

A few strategies can help reduce taxes. Discounts are generally available because of the lack of marketability of most family business interests, and minority discounts may also apply. A binding buy-sell agreement can effectively fix the value of your interest for estate-tax purposes as long as you follow certain statutory requirements. It can also protect your family by assuring that they won't be locked into the business as absentee owners and that they will receive the current value of the stock when it's sold. You should consult with your tax adviser before proceeding in this area.

GIFTS TO CHILDREN OR GRANDCHILDREN These gifts reduce your taxable estate and may also save some income taxes. However, changes in the tax laws made in 1986 have made any income-tax savings harder to come by. Children and parents are very often in the same tax bracket now, and the so-called kiddie tax causes most investment income earned by children under 14 to be taxed at their parents' rates. However, it may still be possible to lower your tax bill by transferring assets to children or grandchildren. (Gifts to grandchildren or younger descendants may also be subject to the generation-skipping transfer tax. See page 275.)

If you pay someone's school tuition or medical expenses, those payments don't count against the $10,000 annual gift tax exclusion or the unified credit. You must, however, pay the school or medical provider directly. This can be a valuable provision as you move into retirement. You may, for example, continue paying for a child or grandchild's education or a relative's medical expenses, in effect giving away more than $10,000 a year.

OTHER PLANNING CONSIDERATIONS

There are many other facets of estate planning to consider as you near retirement. Your lawyer or tax adviser can explain them in detail. Here are a few of these considerations:

SECOND FAMILIES If you or your spouse have children from previous marriages, you may want to leave part of your estate to them. You can make these provisions in a prenuptial agreement or through your will. You can, for example, earmark a life-insurance policy or other assets for one set of children and leave the balance of your estate to the other.

RIGHTS OF A SPOUSE In almost every state, a surviving spouse who does not receive at least some benefits from a deceased spouse's estate has the right to elect against the spouse's will to claim a share of the estate. Most states allow people in this predicament to claim up to one-third of the estate. If you are planning to remarry, you might ask your prospective spouse to waive any elective rights through a prenuptial agreement. That way, you can preserve your assets for your children from a prior marriage. In some states, a spouse's elective share can be left in a trust; in others, it must be given to the spouse outright.

Children and other relatives usually have no elective rights. If you cut children out of your will, they can try to prove your will was invalid, alleging that you were mentally incompetent when you signed it or were pressured by those who do stand to inherit. If children succeed in the legal battle, a court can set aside your will, causing your estate to pass according to the intestacy laws.

COMMUNITY PROPERTY Arizona, California, Idaho, Louisiana, Nevada, New Mexico, Texas, Washington, and Wisconsin are community-property states. That means husbands and wives each own half of their community property, or property that was acquired during marriage. A spouse can own separate property if it was acquired before marriage or by a special agreement. If a spouse in a community-property state dies, only half of the community property is included in his or her estate for tax purposes.

MOVING TO ANOTHER STATE Moving to another state can complicate estate planning. You may have to comply with your new state's requirements. A spouse's elective rights may be different, and if you move to a community-property state, you may have to rearrange your estate plan to suit the different laws. It may also be easier to file a will for probate if it is prepared and signed in the new state.

PROVISIONS FOR CHARITY Any assets you give or leave to a qualified charity will not be subject to gift or estate taxes. Significant income-tax benefits are also available for lifetime gifts, although limitations apply. Before leaving significant gifts (such as paintings and other art) in your will, however, be sure the charity is willing to accept them. Many museums and charities are very selective about their acquisitions and sometimes refuse a bequest unless it is accompanied by a cash gift for maintenance. If the charity you pick refuses your gift, the court may have the power to choose another charity—perhaps one you might not have approved of.

You can also leave a gift to charity through a trust. Here, the tax rules are very complex, so consult a lawyer first. Some charities have special arrangements for these types of gifts. These include annuity programs and pooled-income funds. The charity may also be able to give you guidance.

FEDERAL ESTATE-TAX AUDITS The odds of an estate-tax audit aren't great for most estates. The IRS usually examines only those returns that report large taxable estates or raise significant issues of law or fact, such as the valuation of a family business or real estate, deductions for loans to family members, and the taxability of trusts in which the decedent retained an interest or power.

During an audit, an examiner meets with the estate's lawyer or accountant. When valuation is an issue, the IRS calls on appraisers to prepare a report. The estate hires an appraiser, too. The tax examiner then evaluates both reports and makes a decision. If the estate and examiner still disagree, the decision can be appealed.

KEEPING YOUR ESTATE PLAN UP TO DATE It is important to keep your will current. Given the many changes made by the 1997 Act, it is advisable to have your will reviewed at this time. Normally, reviewing your will every three to five years is sufficient for most people. But if your financial or family situation is complicated or changes, more frequent review is probably necessary. Certain events should automatically trigger a new look at your will. These include: divorce or remarriage; new children or grandchildren you haven't provided for; a significant increase or decrease in assets; changes in estate-tax and pension laws; a move to another state; and the death of a designated trustee or executor.

SETTING UP A
T·R·U·S·T

SOONER OR LATER, WE ALL MUST CONSIDER where we ultimately want our money to go. For many people, a simple will is the easiest and most suitable way to dispose of assets. For others, a will is not enough. In certain situations, the creation of a trust can offer more protection to both heirs and assets.

There are two major reasons for setting up a trust: managing assets and saving taxes. Although trusts come in many forms, almost all are designed to accomplish either or both purposes.

Long before there were income and estate taxes, trusts were used to preserve family lands for future generations. They are still used to control family fortunes. But you don't need millions to use some kinds of trusts. Trusts can help you provide for children, grandchildren, other relatives, friends, or charities. They can be a central feature of your estate plan. For example, if your spouse is elderly or infirm and is unable to manage his or her assets, you might want to create a trust for your spouse's benefit rather than leaving property outright to him or her. Also, a trust would be appropriate to provide for the needs of a disabled child. You should recognize, how-ever, that for all their good points, trusts usually involve some expense and inconvenience. Sometimes you may prefer a less-expensive and easier way to safeguard modest amounts of money.

TRUST BASICS

A trust is a legal arrangement under which one person transfers ownership of assets to a trustee, who can be an individual or a corporation (generally a bank or trust company). The trustee then manages the assets for the benefit of yet another individual, who is known as the beneficiary. (As will be discussed later, in certain cases, the person who establishes the trust is also the beneficiary.) A trust created during your lifetime is called an *inter vivos* or *living* trust. A trust that is created under your will is called a *testamentary* trust. A few trusts have characteristics of both living and testamentary trusts. You set them up while you are alive, but they don't become effective until after your death. (Some types of insurance trusts are examples of these.)

Trusts can be *revocable,* which means you can change or terminate them, or they can be *irrevocable,* which means you can't.

REVOCABLE TRUSTS

These trusts are used primarily to manage assets. For instance, if you are concerned that someday you may be unable to manage your money, you can set up a revocable trust. With this arrangement, you can name yourself as one of the trustees (many states require that there be another trustee acting with the person who creates the trust) and take an active role in managing the trust's assets. If health problems eventually force you to give up your role as trustee, the successor or co-trustee takes over. Sometimes you can write a revocable trust so that you can continue as a trustee, but the power to handle the trust's investments goes to a bank or to another person.

Revocable trusts can be useful if you own assets such as residences or a business located in several states. If you travel extensively or find it inconvenient to look after property located where you no longer live, a family member or an independent trustee in the area can help manage it for you. Also, as discussed below, having this property in a revocable trust could avoid the need for additional probate proceedings following your death.

Revocable trusts don't save income taxes during your lifetime. If you retain the right to receive income or decide how income or principal should be used, or even retain the right to vote stock in a family business, you have to pay taxes on the income generated by the trust's investments. The IRS still considers you the owner of the assets in the trust. That's the case even if someone else actually receives the income.

A TRUST TO AVOID PROBATE Revocable trusts are a kind of living trust, and living trusts can be distributed after your death without any court proceedings. In other words, they can avoid probate, which can be a major advantage in certain instances. If the trust is to continue for the benefit of others after your death, the trustee simply continues to administer the trust assets for them. If the trust is to end with your death, the trustee follows the instructions in the trust agreement for making a final distribution.

An additional advantage of a revocable trust is privacy. When a will is offered for probate, it generally becomes a matter of public record. Because a revocable-trust agreement ordinarily does not have to be filed with the court, its terms remain private.

Transferring an estate through such a trust may be less expensive and faster than probating an estate even though there may be no tax savings. If, for example, the trust is set up for your spouse and children, the trustee can begin paying them income almost immediately instead of waiting for the settlement of your estate. (You should, however, compare the costs of probate with the expenses of setting up and administering the trust.)

If you own property in another state, putting it into a revocable trust may avoid probate proceedings in both states. *Example:* You own a condominium in Florida and a single-family house in Michigan. Even though you are a legal resident of Florida, proceedings will be required in both Florida and Michigan to transfer ownership of your homes. But if you transfer your homes to a revocable trust, the homes will pass without the requirements of probate proceedings in both states. Furthermore, use of a revocable trust will save the commissions to be paid to an executor under your will. However, the trustee of your revocable trust may be entitled to these commissions (see page 288, for a discussion of trustees' commissions), and your estate could still face substantial bills for legal and accounting fees.

Moreover, while transferring property to a revocable trust will avoid probate, the transfer will not reduce your federal estate and state death tax bill. (Assets transferred to a revocable trust are not considered completed gifts at the time of the transfer for federal gift-tax purposes. No gift tax will be due when you create the trust, but all of the trust's assets will be included in your estate for federal estate-tax purposes.)

DRAWBACKS OF REVOCABLE TRUSTS Not all assets are suitable for transfer into a trust. For example, if you and your spouse own all of your property jointly or if your main source of retirement income is pension payments that can't be transferred to a trust, a revocable trust may be unnecessary or inappropriate.

If you decide to establish a revocable trust, you may have to transfer a number of bank accounts or securities and set up a system for record keeping. Whenever you purchase a new investment that goes into the trust, you have to register it in the name of the trust. If you have a mortgage on a home that you want to transfer to the trust, you should check to make sure that the bank won't call in your loan or require you to refinance as a result of the transfer.

As we have pointed out, in certain states, you cannot be the sole trustee. But you may not want a co-trustee interfering in your financial affairs while you are alive. Before you decide to set up a trust, you should check with your lawyer to determine if you live in a state requiring a co-trustee.

Creating a revocable trust also can be expensive. You will have to pay a lawyer to draft the trust and a backup will to cover any assets not placed in trust. That can cost from a few hundred dollars to several thousand. You may incur costs transferring assets to the trust (legal and real-estate recording fees, for example), and you may have to pay the trustee for his or her services. In many states, trustees' commissions are governed by statute. Trustees are often entitled to annual commissions (based on the value of the trust assets each year), and in some states they are entitled to an additional commission on the termination of the trust that is based on the value of the assets distributed. A family member may not charge you for serving as a trustee, but a lawyer or a bank usually will. Bear in mind that although trustee commissions may appear to be lower than commissions paid to an executor who administers your estate, trustee commissions are often paid annually, and over the term of the trust, they can add up to much more than a one-time executor's commission.

If the trust must file income taxes, consider the extra cost of having someone prepare the returns each year. Finally, it is important that you coordinate your will with any trust you set up in order to avoid potential tax and other problems.

ALTERNATIVES TO REVOCABLE TRUSTS A revocable trust is not the only way to provide for someone to manage your financial affairs. As noted in Chapter 7, you can give someone a durable power of attorney. However, if you have many types of investments or business and real-estate interests that require active management, a revocable trust may be more suitable.

You may also allow the court to appoint a guardian, conservator, or committee to manage your affairs (see Chapter 7). But since court proceedings are necessary to appoint a guardian, conservator, or committee, there can be a long delay before any bills are paid, causing a potential hardship for family members. Court proceedings are also costly. The bill, which can include fees for lawyers and medical witnesses, usually far exceeds the cost of drafting a trust. If relatives fight to control your financial destiny, costs can mount. So can the delay.

A trust is a much more efficient way to deal with the problem of incapacity. When you are no longer able to handle your affairs, your co-trustee can begin immediately to act on your behalf. For example, you could set up the trust in such a way that the co-trustee assumes full control if two doctors certify you no longer have the mental capacity to manage the trust. Your co-trustee can then begin to collect your income and pay bills, including those from hospitals and nursing homes.

Setting up a trust before problems arise can also protect you and your family from an unpleasant and expensive battle, which may also draw unwanted publicity about your physical and mental abilities as well as your financial affairs. A trust also allows you to choose the person you want to handle your financial matters. If you appoint a co-trustee to act with you while you are competent, you can see how he or she handles the duties assigned by the trust. If you are not satisfied with the trustee, you can appoint another or revoke the entire trust.

IRREVOCABLE LIVING TRUSTS

During your lifetime, you can create another kind of trust, an irrevocable living trust. If you cannot change the terms of the trust or terminate it, the trust is *irrevocable.*

Unlike revocable trusts, which are used primarily for management purposes, irrevocable trusts have several other uses. You can use them to manage assets and provide income for a beneficiary—usually someone other than yourself. In addition, you can use them to remove property from your estate and reduce your estate-tax bill.

Irrevocable trusts are rarely used just to save on income taxes, since you would have to relinquish all of your control over the assets and all of your rights to the income. In addition, under current law, trust income not distributed to a beneficiary is taxed to the trust at higher rates than the rates applicable to individuals with equivalent amounts of income. For example, for 1998, taxable income of a trust in excess of $8,350 was subject to tax at a rate of 39.6 percent. In contrast, a single individual paid tax on any income at that stated rate only if his or her taxable income exceeded $278,450.

You can set up an irrevocable trust to benefit specific people. For example, you may want to provide for a grandchild's education or a relative's medical needs. A trust allows you to make gifts to beneficiaries, during your lifetime, in a way that allows you to limit their use of the funds. Using a trust, you can control how the funds should be administered and distributed. If you make outright gifts, you lose this power. Suppose you have a child who can't manage money. Creating an irrevocable trust lets you set aside a fund that no one, including the beneficiary or his or her creditors, can touch. In each case, you will need the advice of a lawyer experienced in this area to make certain that the trust will accomplish your goals.

WEIGHING THE PROS AND CONS Creating an irrevocable trust is a serious step. Once you set one up, it's hard to undo it. Sometimes the only way to reverse a trust is through a court proceeding, which can be costly and time-consuming. Although you sometimes can break a trust by obtaining the consent of all of the beneficiaries, this escape hatch won't do much good if you've named minor children, grandchildren born and unborn, or remote descendants as beneficiaries.

Even if the trustee has discretion to distribute all of the trust property to the beneficiary, thereby terminating the trust, this may not be in the beneficiary's best interests or may be impractical, if, for example, the beneficiary is a minor. It may also be contrary to your original intent in establishing the trust.

Before deciding to set up such a trust, think through your objectives carefully. If you want to save income taxes, are you sure you can live with the loss of control over your assets? Can you do without the income they would generate? If the answers are no, then be sure you have other good reasons for establishing an irrevocable trust. If you create a trust intending primarily to benefit your children but you still control the income or disposition of principal, you may find yourself facing a cash drain: because you have relinquished the rights to receive the income but are required to pay the income tax on it.

Be sure you understand which powers you can retain and which you can't. For example, if you are a trustee of a trust you've created, you may still have to pay taxes on the trust's income even if the income is not payable to you. Holding the purse strings on the assets in the trust may subject them to estate taxes in your estate as well. If you give away your assets to an irrevocable trust, the tax law may require you to file a gift-tax return and use some of your available unified credit. Federal and state gift taxes may even be due. A lawyer who specializes in trusts can help you weigh all of the consequences of creating the trust.

Also consider whether you can continue to pay the ongoing expenses of the trust. You not only have to pay a lawyer to draft the trust agreement, but you also need someone to prepare the trust's annual tax returns. The trust may have other record-keeping expenses, as well. Don't forget trustees are also entitled to commissions for their services. State law usually determines the amount. In some states, however, a court that supervises the trust's administration sets the fee. A few states, such as New York, let banks that act as trustees charge more for their services than individuals who perform the same services. Sometimes family members or friends are willing to act as trustees. But remember, you may be giving up competent and expert management to save a few dollars on fees, and individual trustees often use trust funds to hire investment advisers and accountants to do the work. An inexperienced trustee could easily be more costly in the long run.

TYPES OF IRREVOCABLE TRUSTS You can set up a trust for a child or grandchild that could help pay for college or other benefits for him or her. The gift-tax exclusion allows you and your spouse to give up to $20,000 each year to certain types of trusts and escape gift taxes. Furthermore, the assets in such a trust will not be includable in your estate for tax purposes and will thus escape estate taxes on your death.

By shifting assets to the trust, you may also avoid taxes on the income they generate. If you give up control over both the income and assets of the trust, your children or grandchildren, or the trust itself, will be responsible for these taxes. If they are in a lower tax bracket, your family will save taxes. (Keep in mind, however, that under current law, trust income that is not distributed to a beneficiary is taxed to the trust at higher rates than the rates applicable to individuals with the same amount of income.) You should also be aware that if you set up a trust for children or grandchildren who are under 14, any income they receive is taxed at their parents' rates. If the child or grandchild is 14 or over, the income from the trust will be taxed at his or her own rate.

However, if trust income is used to discharge a legal obligation of the beneficiary's parent, such as for necessities like food and clothing, the IRS takes the position that the income should be taxed to the parent. Whether college is a legal obligation of support is a matter of state law. For example, in deciding this issue, the New York courts have looked at factors such as the parents' economic status, their educational background, the rate of college attendance in their community, and their child's academic abilities. You should consult with your lawyer to find out what your state's law provides.

If you want to place more than $20,000 per year in trust for the benefit of a child or grandchild, you may do so. However, you will use up a portion of your gift-and-estate tax unified credit. If the gift exceeds your available exemption amount, gift tax will be due. A separate generation-skipping tax may also apply to a very large gift to a trust for the benefit of a grandchild, although everyone has a $1 million exemption from this tax (see Chapter 18).

GRATS, GRUTS, QPRTS

These trusts are sophisticated irrevocable arrangements created primarily to save gift and estate taxes. Each of these names is an acronym: GRAT for grantor-retained annuity trust, GRUT for grantor-retained unitrust, and QPRT for qualified personal-residence trust. In setting up the GRAT or GRUT, you retain the right to receive an annuity or percentage payment from the trust for a specific period of years that you select. With a QPRT, you simply retain the right to use your home for a specific period of years.

Under the terms of each of the these trusts, if you live for the specified time period, your interest in the trust's assets ends, and the assets pass to the named beneficiaries. If you die before the trust term ends, the assets revert to your estate. But in determining its estate tax, your estate will be no worse off than if you had not created the trust.

When you establish the trust, the tax law considers that you have made a gift of the property you place in the trust. Provided that the trust satisfies the requirements of the tax code for a GRAT, GRUT, or QPRT, you are allowed to discount the value of the gift made to your beneficiaries. The valuation tables published by the IRS assume that until the trust terminates, it will produce a constant rate of return based on the interest rate in effect when it is created. The gift-tax value of the assets ultimately passed along to the beneficiaries is equal to the total value of the assets transferred to the trust less the value of the interest you retain as determined under the IRS valuation tables. The greater the income interest you retain, the lower the value of the gift of the remainder. Moreover, you may claim a further discount to account for the possibility that the assets will return to your estate if you do not survive until the trust terminates. If you are still living when the trust ends, you have removed from your estate an amount equal to (1) the entire value of the property you put into the trust and (2) the increase, if any, in its value during the term of the trust reduced by (3) the amounts you received from the trust during its term.

The potential gift- and estate-tax savings are substantial. But get competent legal advice. This is a tricky subject, and many technical rules apply. Generally, these trusts are more appropriate for people with estates in excess of the exemption amount.

CHARITABLE TRUSTS Significant tax savings may also be available if you create a trust that includes a charity as a beneficiary. If the charity receives its income interest first, the trust is known as a charitable lead trust. If you or someone else receives the income before the assets are eventually paid over to the charity, the trust is a charitable remainder trust. In either case, the amount payable to the income beneficiary may be a fixed percentage of the net fair market value of the assets, recalculated each year based on (1) the value of the trust on any one date during the taxable year of the trust or (2) the average values of the trust on more than one date during the taxable year of the trust (so long as the same valuation date or dates and valuation methods are used each year) (a "unitrust" amount) or fixed as a dollar amount or as a percentage of the initial value of the assets (an "annuity" amount).

Properly planned and drafted, charitable lead and remainder trusts may result in very favorable income-, gift-, and estate-tax consequences. For example, some people transfer highly appreciated assets to charitable remainder trusts. These assets may then be sold by the trustee and reinvested without the payment of capital-gains taxes by the donor or the trustee. But these trusts are not for everyone, and you may want your heirs to receive as much of your property as possible even if additional taxes are due. The rules governing these trusts are complex, and you will need expert advice before setting one up.

TRANSFERS TO TRUSTS AND MEDICAID ELIGIBILITY

As discussed in Chapter 13, Medicaid may eventually step in to pay for most long-term nursing care after all your assets are depleted. Some people try to avoid a Medicaid spend-down by putting their assets in a trust. Doing so is tricky, and you must conform to the rules set by federal and state law or else you may find yourself ineligible for Medicaid during the penalty period described below.

If you retain any interest in or control over the assets that make up the principal of the trust or if the trustee has the authority to make any distributions of principal to you from the trust, Medicaid will consider the trust principal to be an asset of yours in determining your eligibility for benefits. If you retain no interest or control in the principal or income of the trust, then you may be able to preserve the trust's assets for your heirs. However, setting up a trust from which you cannot use any of the income or principal may mean a lower standard of living in retirement, especially if you never need long-term care.

What if you retain an interest only in the income of a trust which you have established? While the Medicaid statute is not entirely clear on this point, it appears that, after the penalty period described below, the principal of the trust will no longer be considered an asset of yours in determining your eligibility for benefits. You should, however, consult with a local attorney regarding this matter.

If you decide to transfer your assets to a trust in which you relinquish an interest in principal (or principal and income), and the transfer occurs fewer than 60 months before you apply for Medicaid, you may be temporarily ineligible for Medicaid. Your period of ineligibility (measured in months) begins on the first day of the month after you transfer the assets and is ordinarily determined by dividing the value of the assets you transfer by the average monthly cost of nursing home care in your area. Depending on the laws of your state, the time limit may not apply if you receive care in your home or in a Medicaid-approved program such as an adult day-care or respite care center.

Obviously, it's difficult, if not impossible, to predict when you might need nursing home care. Transferring assets to a trust years before you're confined to a nursing home can deprive you of money you will need to maintain a comfortable standard of living before and during retirement.

As you can see, setting up a so-called Medicaid trust is compli-

cated and has several disadvantages. Use of these trusts and other planning techniques has also been highly controversial. In 1997, Congress
passed legislation making it a crime for anyone (including an attorney)
to charge a fee and knowingly and willfully counsel or assist an individual to dispose of assets so that he or she might become eligible for
Medicaid, if the disposition of assets actually resulted in a period of
Medicaid ineligibility for that individual. The New York State Bar
Association and another plaintiff brought suits challenging this law as
unconstitutional. In response, Attorney General Janet Reno announced
that the Justice Department would not enforce it. Therefore, the new
law will most likely not eliminate the use of Medicaid planning techniques. However, as we went to press with this edition, the law has not
been repealed or the suits formally resolved. You should consult your
adviser for further information.

An alternative to transferring your assets is a long-term-care insurance policy that helps defray nursing-home expenses. But as we note in
Chapter 12, these policies, too, have their drawbacks. In short, there is no
perfect way to protect your assets from a Medicaid spenddown.

GIFTS TO MINORS

Instead of setting up a trust for the benefit of a minor, consider making
a gift under the Uniform Transfers to Minors Act, known in some
states as the Uniform Gifts to Minors Act. This may be a good choice
if you have little money to spare and still want to do something for a
minor child or grandchild. If you have less than $20,000 to give away,
a gift made under the act may be the best route to go.

You can set up a Uniform Transfers (Gifts) to Minors account at a
bank or a brokerage firm with any amount of money or securities.
Many states allow residents to transfer insurance policies, real estate, or
even limited-partnership interests to these accounts.

Under the Uniform Transfers or Uniform Gifts rules, you can
give money to a "custodian," who must use it for the child's health,
welfare, and education. You can be the custodian yourself. However, if
you are and you die before the child reaches the age of majority, any
money or property in the account at your death would be included in
your estate and might then be subject to estate taxes.

When the child turns 21 (or 18, depending on the law in your
state), the money remaining in the account automatically belongs to

the child. Therein lies the major disadvantage of these accounts. A child turns 21 (or 18) and comes into a large sum of money that he or she may not be ready to handle. If you're worried about this possibility, it's better to put money into a trust where the child has far less control over the assets. If you establish a trust, you may defer the distribution of the trust property until the child reaches a more suitable age.

A child has to pay taxes on the income from the assets in a Uniform Transfers or Uniform Gifts account. Until the child reaches 14, the child's tax rate on income above a minimum threshold is the same as that of the child's parents.

TESTAMENTARY TRUSTS

A testamentary trust is created under your will and becomes irrevocable upon your death. But while you are alive, you can change the terms of your will whenever you like. Testamentary trusts can save both income and estate taxes and preserve assets for your family. The following testamentary trusts are sometimes used for saving taxes:

CREDIT SHELTER OR BYPASS TRUSTS As explained in Chapter 18, you may establish a credit-shelter or by-pass trust under your will for the benefit of your spouse, if he or she survives you. The amount of property transferred to such a trust ordinarily will not exceed the exemption amount ($625,000 in 1998). Such a trust takes advantage of the federal unified credit by allowing assets to escape estate taxes in your surviving spouse's estate. In contrast, if you simply leave all of your property outright to your spouse, you will have wasted your unified credit. In 1998, proper use of this trust permits up to $1.25 million of a couple's assets to pass free of federal estate tax to their children, instead of only $625,000. (See Chapter 18 for the schedule of increases in the unified credit.)

QUALIFIED TERMINABLE INTEREST PROPERTY (Q-TIP) TRUST Leaving your property to a Q-TIP trust is an alternative to leaving it outright to your surviving spouse. If you leave property in a Q-TIP trust, your estate may still claim the marital deduction and you may control the management of the property following your death and its disposition following the death of your spouse. After the death of your spouse, the trust property may be distributed outright or continue in further trust for your family, other beneficiaries, or charity. You may wish to create continuing trusts under your will for purposes of managing your assets or to save taxes.

For a trust to qualify as a Q-TIP, all the income from the trust must be paid to your surviving spouse, at least annually. In addition, the trustee may have discretion to use principal as needed for your spouse's benefit. The executor of your estate must elect to qualify the trust for the marital deduction. Any assets remaining in the Q-TIP trust when your spouse dies are taxed in his or her estate.

Example: Suppose your spouse does not have the experience to manage assets or finances. So you decide to leave your entire estate to him or her by creating two trusts under your will—a Q-TIP and a bypass trust. You name your spouse and your bank as co-trustees. Your spouse receives all the income from both trusts. You may also give the bank discretion to distribute the principal from either trust to your spouse. The assets in both trusts escape federal estate taxes following your death. When your spouse dies, the assets in the bypass trust also escape taxation, but the assets in the Q-TIP trust do not. The remaining assets in both trusts then pass to your children.

You might want to give your spouse the power to dispose of part or all of the assets in the trusts under the terms of his or her will. But this power, technically known as a *power of appointment,* can result in significant estate and income taxes if you're not careful. Discuss this with an attorney before granting such powers.

CHARITABLE TRUSTS You have the same opportunity to create charitable lead or remainder trusts in your will as when you are living. For a discussion of such trusts, see page 293.

QUALIFYING DOMESTIC TRUSTS (Q-DOT) If your spouse is not a U.S. citizen, this kind of trust preserves the marital deduction. (The unlimited marital deduction isn't otherwise available to spouses who are not U.S. citizens.) Without a Q-DOT, the portion of your estate passing to your spouse that exceeds the exemption amount is subject to federal estate taxes.

A Q-DOT is similar to a Q-TIP. The surviving spouse must receive all the income during his or her lifetime, and the executor of your estate must choose to qualify the trust for the marital deduction. Using the Q-DOT results in a tax deferral until the surviving spouse receives certain principal payments or dies. There are many technical requirements that must be met to establish a valid Q-DOT, so you should seek legal advice before setting up a Q-DOT.

INSURANCE TRUSTS

You can set up an irrevocable insurance trust to own and be the beneficiary of a policy of insurance on your life. You can design this trust so that the policy is removed from your own taxable estate and also from the estate of your spouse or other beneficiaries, thereby saving estate taxes. (But again, to achieve any tax savings, you must give up ownership of the policy and control over the trust. You should not serve as the trustee, for example.)

Transferring a policy to the trust has estate- and gift-tax implications. Your taxable estate will include any existing policy you place in a trust within three years of your death. It's usually safest to have the trust buy a new insurance policy rather than transfer an existing policy into the trust.

If you use an existing whole-life policy with a high cash value, there may be gift-tax consequences. If you have an old policy that you want to put into the trust, you may want to borrow the cash value before putting the policy in the trust, thus eliminating the potential for gift taxes. Remember, however, that any outstanding policy loans reduce the amount of the death benefit available to your heirs. Also, if you retain the money that you borrow out of the policy, it will be included in your estate.

You may also want to pay the insurance premiums out of income from other assets you put into the trust. If you pay the premiums with your own money, the payments may be considered gifts to the trust and subject to gift taxes unless the trust permits the beneficiaries to withdraw funds as they are added each year. As you can see, a trust must be properly drawn to avoid these problems. If the trust agreement is properly drafted (and you survive for three years after the transfer of the policy to the trust, in the event that the trust does not buy the policy), the value of the policy and other assets put in the trust should not be included in your estate and should pass to the designated beneficiaries free of estate and inheritance taxes.

As an alternative to an irrevocable insurance trust, you can establish a revocable trust that does not actually own the insurance policy, or you can create a trust under your will to take effect following your death. You name the trust the beneficiary of the policy, and when you die, the trust collects the proceeds. Essentially, the trust is inactive during your lifetime, but acts as a receptacle to consolidate your assets after your death. Although there are no estate-tax benefits for such trusts, they can be useful when no estate taxes will be due and you want a trustee to manage the proceeds from the policy for the benefit of your beneficiaries.

USES OF INSURANCE TRUSTS Establishing an insurance trust can serve many purposes. Suppose you are married to your second wife and have two teenage children from your first marriage. Your wife will need the income from most of your estate to live on. You can create an irrevocable insurance trust that owns a policy on your life. When you die, the proceeds from the policy will be held in the trust, with the income paid to your wife for her lifetime. At her death, the assets pass on to your children free of estate taxes.

Suppose you want to consolidate assets to simplify probate proceedings. You create a revocable living trust and fund it with cash and securities. You retain ownership of the policy, but name the trust as the beneficiary of the policy. The person you name as trustee can now manage all your assets and avoid delay at probate. But keep in mind that a revocable trust won't save any taxes.

Another useful form of insurance trust is a second-to-die policy, insuring the lives of both you and your spouse. On the death of the surviving spouse, the proceeds would be payable to the trust and would ultimately pass to your children. The proceeds could be kept out of both spouses' estates and could serve to "reimburse" your children for the estate taxes that will be payable at the death of the surviving spouse.

ADMINISTRATION AND RECORD KEEPING

If you set up a trust, revocable or irrevocable, good record keeping is essential. To achieve savings on taxes and probate costs, the trust must have a separate identity and will generally be required to file its own tax returns. Comingling trust assets with nontrust property could render the trust ineffective for accomplishing your goals.

WHO SHOULD BE THE TRUSTEE?

You may act as a trustee of a revocable trust. Depending on your state law, you may or may not be able to act as the sole trustee of your trust. If you cannot be the only trustee, you usually can share the trustee's duties with someone else. If you establish an irrevocable trust, you ordinarily should not serve as a trustee if you wish to keep the trust property out of your taxable estate. If you cannot or do not want to be a trustee, here are some possible choices:

A SPOUSE, ADULT CHILD, OR OTHER RELATIVE The cost may be right, but guard against potential conflicts of interest, and consider the qualifications of the trustee. You may not save any money in the end if your trustee exercises poor judgment or must pay high fees for investment, accounting, and legal advice.

A LAWYER, ACCOUNTANT, OR OTHER PROFESSIONAL If you decide to go this route, ask the professional in advance how the trust will be billed for various services. Will the trust pay both a trustee's commission and legal or accounting fees? If so, the total costs may be too high.

A BANK OR TRUST COMPANY If you plan to transfer a substantial amount of money to a trust, choosing a bank often makes a lot of sense. A bank usually takes care of all investments, accounting, and tax-filing requirements as part of its fee. However, most banks charge a minimum fee, so it's usually not economical to appoint a bank as trustee of a modest trust. Nor may a bank be the best choice if you anticipate complications in administering the assets held in trust or if the beneficiaries have very specific needs or issues that could require significant personal attention. Closely held business or real-estate interests can complicate a trust. If you decide on a bank, check its investment track record to determine if you are satisfied with its performance prior to naming it in the trust instrument. If the investments it has managed have performed poorly, you may want a different bank or someone else to act as trustee. It is also useful to meet with members of the appropriate department at the bank to acquaint yourself with their procedures for administering a trust.

WORKSHEETS

These worksheets can help you plan retirement finances. Make extra copies of blank worksheets so you can try scenarios and update scenarios as circumstances change.

WORKSHEET 1 •	ASSESS INCOME AND EXPENSES BEFORE RETIREMENT

Date _____

MONTHLY INCOME

Wages or self-
  employment
  income $ _____
Interest   _____
Dividends   _____
Rental income   _____
Annuity income   _____
Trust income   _____
Other income   _____

MONTHLY EXPENSES

Housing $ _____
Utilities   _____
Real-estate taxes   _____
Repairs, upkeep   _____
Food   _____
Clothing   _____
Laundry, cleaning   _____
Personal care   _____
Commuting   _____
Entertainment   _____
Vacation, travel   _____
Hobbies, sports   _____
Other travel   _____
Health insurance   _____
Auto insurance   _____
Life insurance   _____
Homeowner's
  insurance   _____
Newspapers,
  magazines, books   _____
Education expenses   _____
Contributions   _____
Credit cards,
  other debts   _____
Income taxes   _____
Savings,
  investments   _____
Miscellaneous   _____

TOTAL MONTHLY
  INCOME $ _____
                        x 12

TOTAL ANNUAL
  INCOME $ _____

TOTAL MONTHLY
  EXPENSES $ _____
                        x 12

TOTAL ANNUAL   EXPENSES
                  $ _____

WORKSHEET 2 · SAVINGS, INVESTMENTS, AND PENSIONS

TYPE OF ACCOUNT	WHERE HELD	ACCOUNT NUMBER	AMOUNT
Regular checking			
NOW account checking			
Bank money-market deposit account			
Bank savings account			
Certificates of deposit			
6-month			
1-year			
1½-year			
3-year			
5-year			
Other			
Credit-union savings account			
U.S. Treasury bills			
U.S. savings bonds			
Money-market mutual fund			
Tax-exempt money-market fund			
Bond mutual funds			
Stock mutual funds			
Other mutual funds			
Cash-value life insurance			
Deferred annuities			
401(k) plan			
Defined-contribution plan other than 401(k)			
Stocks (list separately)			
Bonds (list separately)			
Expected monthly benefit from pension plan			

Date _____

INTEREST RATE/ RATE OF RETURN	DATE MATURES (IF APPLICABLE)	TAX- EXEMPT?	TAX- DEFERRED?
_____	_____	_____	_____
_____	_____	_____	_____
_____	_____	_____	_____
_____	_____	_____	_____
_____	_____	_____	_____
_____	_____	_____	_____
_____	_____	_____	_____
_____	_____	_____	_____
_____	_____	_____	_____
_____	_____	_____	_____
_____	_____	_____	_____
_____	_____	_____	_____
_____	_____	_____	_____
_____	_____	_____	_____
_____	_____	_____	_____
_____	_____	_____	_____
_____	_____	_____	_____
_____	_____	_____	_____
_____	_____	_____	_____
_____	_____	_____	_____
_____	_____	_____	_____

WORKSHEET 3 · ESTIMATE EXPENSES AFTER RETIREMENT

Date _____

MONTHLY EXPENSES

Housing _____
Utilities _____
Real-estate taxes _____
Repairs, upkeep _____
Food _____
Clothing _____
Laundry, cleaning _____
Personal care _____
Commuting _____
Entertainment _____
Vacation, travel _____
Hobbies, sports _____
Other travel _____
Health insurance _____
Auto insurance _____
Life insurance _____
Homeowner's insurance _____
Newspapers, magazines, books _____
Education expenses _____
Contributions _____
Credit cards, other debts _____
Income taxes (federal and state) _____
Savings, investments _____
Miscellaneous _____

Total monthly expenses _____

x 12

Total annual expenses _____

WORKSHEET 4 · SCENARIOS FOR RETIREMENT

Your needs and resources may change during retirement. Your health-insurance costs will certainly change. Complete a column of the worksheet for each period after retirement when you expect a significant shift. If you need more columns, make extra copies of the worksheet.

TIME FRAME

Retirement date: _____
Years from now: _____

NEEDS IN RETIREMENT

This section adds up expenses. Include health-insurance premiums but not income-tax payments—those will be deducted later. Use Worksheets 1 and 3 to help figure expenses. If expenses add up to more than income, go back over your figures and see what you can change.

	RETIREMENT PHASE 1	RETIREMENT PHASE 2
Monthly expenses	_____	_____

RESOURCES IN RETIREMENT

This section adds up income and other resources in the different phases of retirement. Use Worksheet 1 to help estimate income.

	RETIREMENT PHASE 1	RETIREMENT PHASE 2
Monthly Social Security benefit
(Get this from the Social Security Administration (800 772-1213) or use an estimate from Table 1 on page 32.)	_____	_____
Monthly pension
(Ask your personnel department for two kinds of estimate: as a single-life annuity or as a 100 percent joint-and-survivor annuity. See page 89.)	_____	_____

Continued on next page

	RETIREMENT PHASE 1	RETIREMENT PHASE 2
Monthly employment earnings *(If you or your spouse plans to work full-time or part-time after retirement)*	_____	_____
Monthly income from investments *(See below)*	_____	_____
Total monthly income	_____	_____
Estimated income taxes *(Get figure from expert or use rough estimate of 20% of total income)*	_____	_____
Net income	_____	_____

FIGURING INVESTMENT INCOME

YOUR HOUSE

Fill this section out if you plan to sell your house when you retire.

Current market value of house	_____	
Less broker's fees *(estimate 6% of sale price)*	_____	
Less taxes and other fees *(estimate 2% of sale price)*	_____	
Less other closing costs	_____	
TOTAL PROCEEDS FROM HOUSE		_____
Less tax, if any, on any profit	_____	
GROSS PROCEEDS FROM HOUSE		_____
Less mortgage balance at date of sale *(Get from bank or estimate 1)*	_____	
Adjusted for 3% annual inflation *(Multiply mortgage balance by Factor A, page 310, for the number of years to retirement)*	_____	
Net proceeds from house *(in today's dollars)*	_____	

Cost of new house (if any) _____
Plus closing costs _____
(Estimate 4% of price)
Moving expenses _____

TOTAL NEW HOUSE COST _____

PROCEEDS FROM SALE OF HOUSE TO INVEST _____
*(If new house cost is less than
present house value)*

SAVINGS AND INVESTMENTS _____
Use Worksheet 2 to help figure this

Current savings _____
*(Savings, profit-sharing, 401(k), IRAs,
other investments)*
Adjusted for investment growth at 4% _____
more than inflation *(multiply by factor B,
page 310, for the number of
years to retirement)*

Future savings _____
*(Amount you or your employer adds
to savings each year times number of
years to retirement)*
Adjusted for investment growth at 4% _____
more than inflation *(multiply by factor C,
page 310, for the number of
years to retirement)*

Total accumulated savings _____
*(Add amounts from sale of house,
current savings, future savings)*
Less your one-time needs at _____
retirement

Total accumulation _____
Yearly income *(multiply by 4% to provide
a flow of income that will keep up with inflation)*

MONTHLY INCOME _____
(Divide yearly income by 12)

Try out different scenarios. If you have more than enough money for
one phase of retirement but not another, move some money from one
phase to another.

FACTORS FOR WORKSHEET 4

Years to retirement	Factor A[1]	Factor B[2]	Factor C[3]
1	0.971	1.040	1.020
2	0.943	1.082	2.081
3	0.915	1.125	3.184
4	0.888	1.170	4.331
5	0.863	1.217	5.525
6	0.837	1.265	6.766
7	0.813	1.316	8.056
8	0.789	1.369	9.399
9	0.766	1.423	10.794
10	0.744	1.480	12.246
11	0.722	1.539	13.756
12	0.701	1.601	15.326
13	0.681	1.665	16.959
14	0.661	1.732	18.658
15	0.642	1.801	20.424
16	0.623	1.873	22.261
17	0.605	1.948	24.171
18	0.587	2.026	26.158
19	0.570	2.107	28.225
20	0.554	2.191	30.374
21	0.538	2.279	32.609
22	0.522	2.370	34.933
23	0.507	2.465	37.350
24	0.492	2.563	39.864
25	0.478	2.666	42.479
26	0.464	2.772	45.198
27	0.450	2.883	48.026
28	0.437	2.999	50.967
29	0.424	3.119	54.026
30	0.412	3.243	57.207
31	0.400	3.373	60.515
32	0.388	3.508	63.955
33	0.377	3.648	67.534
34	0.366	3.794	71.255
35	0.355	3.946	75.125
36	0.345	4.104	79.150
37	0.335	4.268	83.336
38	0.325	4.439	87.690
39	0.316	4.616	92.217
40	0.307	4.801	96.926

[1] *The present worth of $1 payable at the future retirement date, discounted at 3 percent per year as an estimate of inflation.*

[2] *The amount $1 invested today will grow to at the future retirement date, compounded at 4 percent to reflect the expected investment return in excess of the rate of inflation.*

[3] *The amount to which $1 invested each year until your retirement date will grow, compounded at 4 percent to reflect the expected investment return in excess of the rate of inflation.*

WORKSHEET 5 • LIFE INSURANCE VERSUS ANNUITY

This worksheet helps you determine whether you are better off taking an insurance policy or a joint-and-survivor annuity from your pension. The example provided will guide you through the calculations.

	EXAMPLE		YOUR SITUATION	
	MONTHLY	ANNUAL	MONTHLY	ANNUAL
AMOUNT OF MONTHLY PENSION TO EMPLOYEE (LIFE ANNUITY)	$1,000	$12,000	$_____	$_____
AMOUNT OF MONTHLY PENSION TO EMPLOYEE (50-PERCENT JOINT-AND-SURVIVOR)	$900	$10,800	$_____	$_____
AMOUNT OF MONTHLY PENSION TO SPOUSE (50-PERCENT JOINT-AND-SURVIVOR)	$450	$5,400	$_____	$_____

STEP 1. Find the difference between your annual pension if you take a life annuity or if you take a joint-and-survivor annuity. In our example, the difference is $1,200 ($12,000 - $10,800 = $1,200).

STEP 2. Ask your insurance agent how large a policy you can buy with the difference. You should compare several companies. Enter the amounts below. In our example, we have assumed the $1,200 buys a $20,000 whole life policy.

AMOUNT OF LIFE INSURANCE POLICY	EXAMPLE $20,000	COMPANY A $_____	COMPANY B $_____

STEP 3. How large an annuity guaranteed for your spouse's life does the face amount of the policy buy? Ask the agent. (You are converting the policy into monthly payments for your spouse.)

Use the annuity rates for your spouse's sex and age at retirement, and enter the amounts below. In our example, the $20,000 death benefit could be converted into a life annuity paying $200 a month.

AMOUNT OF LIFE ANNUITY PER MONTH	EXAMPLE $200	COMPANY A $ _____	COMPANY B $ _____

STEP 4. Compare these amounts to the amount of monthly income your spouse receives if you take the joint-and-survivor annuity. In this example, the joint-and-survivor annuity pays $450 a month, making the joint-and-survivor annuity the better buy.

| **WORKSHEET 6** • LONG-TERM-CARE POLICY CHECKLIST |

Use this worksheet to help compare features of a long-term-care policy. The example shows what kinds of information should be included. Annual premium is standard rate for age 65. Subtract 10% for preferred rate, additional 10% for special discount.

	EXAMPLE	POLICY 1	POLICY 2
COMPANY	Equitable Life & Casualty		
POLICY NAME	EquiCare 2002		
DAILY BENEFITS			
Nursing-home care Percentage of eligible charges paid	Actual expenses up to $100 a day 100%		
Home care Percentage of eligible charges paid	Same		
Assisted-living Percentage of eligible charges paid	Same		
MAXIMUM BENEFITS			
Total lifetime benefits	$584,000		
Is this policy a pool-of-money approach?	No		
Number of years for nursing-home benefits	4		
Number of years for home-care benefits	4		
Number of years for assisted-living benefits	4		
ELIMINATION PERIOD	0 days		

Continued on next page

	EXAMPLE	POLICY 1	POLICY 2
GATEKEEPER (BENEFIT TRIGGER)			
Medical necessity	No		
Doctor certification	Yes		
Activities of daily living	Yes		
Number of ADLs needed	2		
Criteria to fail ADLs	Assistance needed in 2 or more		
Are ADLs specifically defined?	Yes		
Is bathing included?	Yes		
RESTRICTIONS ON FACILITIES			
Nursing home	Licensed		
Assisted living	Licensed		
Home-care providers	Licensed		
INFLATION PROTECTION			
Amount of increase	5%		
Compound or simple	Simple		
ANNUAL PREMIUM*			
Without inflation protection	$1,044		
With inflation protection	$1,200		
Tax-qualified	No		
OTHER BENEFITS (list)	1. Optional non-forfeiture benefit		
	2. No pre-existing conditions requirement		
	3. Paid-up survivor benefit		

WORKSHEET 7 • HEALTH INSURANCE ANNUAL FEES

Fill in your annual premiums for a Medicare-supplement policy, an HMO premium, any coverage from your former employer, and coverage for a long-term-care policy. If you take one of the new Medicare+ Choice options, list the premium for that. If you are paying premiums for a spouse, make a copy of the worksheet and fill in the same information for him or her. This assumes you are not required to pay Part A premiums.

	1998	1999	2000	2001	2002	2003
Medicare Part A	0	0	0	0	0	0
Medicare Part B	$526	584	638	707	772	858
Medicare-supplement policy						
Employer-provided coverage						
HMO premium						
Medicare+ Choice option						
Long-term-care policy						
TOTAL						

WORKSHEET 8 • ESTATE PLANNING: TAKING STOCK OF YOUR ASSETS AND LIABILITIES

Use worksheets 2 and 4 to help gather these figures.

Date: _____

	YOURS	YOUR SPOUSE'S	JOINT

REAL ESTATE (TOTAL FOR ALL PROPERTIES)

Market value _____ _____ _____

Less mortgage, including home-equity loans _____ _____ _____

Net equity _____ _____ _____

INVESTMENTS

Stocks and bonds
(total value, from brokerage statement or stock tables) _____ _____ _____

Shares in privately held companies _____ _____ _____

Other business interests and investments *(partnerships, joint ventures, etc.)* _____ _____ _____

CASH *(savings, money-market accounts, checking accounts, etc.)* _____ _____ _____

LIFE INSURANCE *(total face value of policies you own)* _____ _____ _____

	You	Your spouse	Jointly
PERSONAL AND HOUSEHOLD GOODS *(approximate value)*			
Jewelry and furs	_____	_____	_____
Paintings and antiques	_____	_____	_____
Automobiles	_____	_____	_____
Other	_____	_____	_____
AMOUNTS OWED TO YOU	_____	_____	_____
INHERITANCE AND TRUSTS			
Potential inheritance	_____	_____	_____
Interests in trust	_____	_____	_____
RETIREMENT BENEFITS *(those payable upon your death;* *get from the administrator* *where you work)*			
Pension	_____	_____	_____
Profit-sharing	_____	_____	_____
IRA	_____	_____	_____
Keogh	_____	_____	_____
401(k)	_____	_____	_____
Other	_____	_____	_____
MISCELLANEOUS *(any assets not listed above)*	_____	_____	_____
TOTAL ASSETS	_____	_____	_____
LIABILITIES *(substantial amounts* *excluding mortgages)*	_____	_____	_____
VALUE OF YOUR ESTATE *(assets minus liabilities)*	_____	_____	_____

WORKSHEET 9 · PROBATE AND NONPROBATE ASSETS

List assets here to help with your estate planning.

PROBATE ASSETS   **NONPROBATE ASSETS**

WORKSHEET 10 • HOW TO FIGURE THE NEW
REDUCED EXCLUSION

Use the worksheet on this page to figure the amount of your reduced exclusion if **either** 1 or 2 below applies. Enter figures for spouse only if you're filing a joint return.

>   1. You (or your spouse) owned the home on August 5, 1997, sold it before August 5, 1999, and did not meet the ownership and use tests for the maximum exclusion.
>   2. Because of a change in health or place of employment, you (or spouse):

>   a. Did not own or live in the home for a total of at least 2 years within the 5-year period ending on the date of sale, or

>   b. Are excluding gain on the sale of another home after May 6, 1997, and within 2 years of the date of the current sale.

	YOU	YOUR SPOUSE
1. During the 5-year period ending on the date of sale, enter the **smaller** of: • The number of days each person used the property as a main home **OR** • The number of days each person owned the property. If filing jointly and one spouse owned the property longer than the other, both are treated as owning the property for the longer period.	_____	_____
2. Are you (or your spouse) excluding gain from the sale of another home after May 6, 1997, and within 2 years of the date of the current sale? **No**—Skip to item 3. **Yes**—If the other home was sold before this home, enter the number of days between the date of sale of the other home and the date of sale of this home. Otherwise, go to item 3.	_____	_____
3. Enter the smaller number of days from line 1 or line 2	_____	_____
4. Divide by 730 days and enter the results as a decimal	_____	_____
5. Multiply by maximum amount	x $250,000	x $250,000
TOTAL	_____	_____
Add spouses' totals to get **FAMILY TOTAL**	_____	

APPENDIXES

APPENDIX A · STATE AGENCIES ON AGING

ALABAMA
Commission on Aging
770 Washington Avenue,
Suite 470
P.O. Box 301851
Montgomery, AL 36130
(334) 242-5743
(800) 243-5463

ALASKA
Division of Senior Services
3601 "C" St., Suite 310
Anchorage, AK 99503
(907) 269-3680

AMERICAN SAMOA
Territorial Administration
on Aging
Government of American Samoa
Pago Pago, AS 96799
(684) 633-1252

ARIZONA
Aging and Adult Administration
Department of Economic Security
1789 W. Jefferson St., #950A
Phoenix, AZ 85007
(602) 542-4446

ARKANSAS
Division of Aging and Adult
Services
7th and Main Streets
P.O. Box 1437/Slot 1412
Little Rock, AR 72201
(501) 682-2441

CALIFORNIA
Department of Aging
Health Insurance Counseling and
Advocacy Program
1600 K Street
Sacramento, CA 95814
(916) 322-5290

COLORADO
Aging and Adult Services Division
Department of Social Services
110 16th St., Suite 200
Denver, CO 80203-5202
(303) 620-4147

**COMMONWEALTH OF NO.
MARIANA ISLANDS**
Department of Community and
Cultural Affairs
Civic Center
Saipan, CM 96950
(607) 234-6011

CONNECTICUT
Elderly Services Division
Department of Social Services
25 Sigourney Street
Hartford, CT 06106-5033
(860) 424-5274
(800) 443-9946

DELAWARE
Division of Services for Aging and
Adults with Physical
Disabilities
1901 N. DuPont Highway
2nd Fl. Annex Admin. Bldg.

New Castle, DE 19720
(302) 577-4791
(800) 223-9074

DISTRICT OF COLUMBIA
Office on Aging
441 4th St., NW, 9th Floor
Washington, DC 20001
(202) 724-5622

**FEDERATED STATES OF
MICRONESIA**
State Agency on Aging
Office of Health Services
Federated States of Micronesia
Ponape, E.C.I. 96941

FLORIDA
Department of Elder Affairs
4040 Esplanade Way
Building B, Suite 152
Tallahassee, FL 32399
(850) 414-2000

GEORGIA
Division of Aging Services
Department of Human Resources
2 Peachtree St., NE, 36th Floor
Atlanta, GA 30303
(404) 657-5258

GUAM
Division of Senior Citizens
Department of Public Health and
    Social Services
P.O. Box 2816
Agana, Guam 96910
011 (671) 475-0263

HAWAII
Executive Office on Aging
250 South Hotel St., Suite 109
Honolulu, HI 96813-2831
(808) 586-0100

IDAHO
Commission on Aging
700 West Jefferson,
Room 108
P.O. Box 83720
Boise, ID 83720-0007
(208) 334-2423

ILLINOIS
Department on Aging
421 East Capitol Avenue
Springfield, IL 62701
(217) 785-3356

INDIANA
Bureau of Aging and In-Home
    Services
402 W. Washington St., E-431
Indianapolis, IN 46207-7083
(317) 232-7020

IOWA
Department of Elder Affairs
200 10th Street
Clemens Building, 3rd Floor
Des Moines, IA 50309-3609
(515) 281-5187

KANSAS
Department on Aging
New England Building
503 S. Kansas

Topeka, KS 66603-3404
(913) 296-4986

KENTUCKY
Division of Aging Services
Cabinet for Human Resources 275
East Main St., 6 West
Frankfort, KY 40621
(502) 564-6930

LOUISIANA
Governor's Office of Elderly Affairs
P.O. Box 80374
412 North 4th Street
Baton Rouge, LA 70802
(504) 342-7100

MAINE
Bureau of Elder and Adult Services
State House, Station 11
Augusta, ME 04333
(207) 624-5335

MARYLAND
Office on Aging
State Office Building, Room 1007
301 W. Preston Street
Baltimore, MD 21201
(410) 767-1100
(800) 243-3425

MASSACHUSETTS
Executive Office of Elder Affairs
1 Ashburton Place, 5th Floor
Boston, MA 02108
(617) 727-7750

MICHIGAN
Office of Services to the Aging
P.O. Box 30676
Lansing, MI 48909-8176
(517) 373-8230

MINNESOTA
Board on Aging
444 Lafayette Road
St. Paul, MN 55155-3843
(612) 296-2770
(800) 882-6262

MISSISSIPPI
Division of Aging and Adult
   Services
750 N. State Street
Jackson, MS 39202
(601) 359-4929

MISSOURI
Division of Aging
Department of Social Services
P.O. Box 1337
615 Howerton Court
Jefferson City, MO 65102-1337
(573) 751-3082

MONTANA
Division of Senior and LTC/DPHHS
111 No. Sanders Street
P.O. Box 4210
Helena, MT 59604
(406) 444-7781

NEBRASKA
Department on Aging
State Office Building
P.O. Box 95044
301 Centennial Mall South
Lincoln, NE 68509
(402) 471-2306

NEVADA
Division for Aging Services
Department of Human Resources
340 N. 11th St., Suite 203
Las Vegas, NV 89101
(702) 486-3545

NEW HAMPSHIRE
Division of Elderly and
    Adult Services
Department of Health and Human
    Services
115 Pleasant Street
Amex Building No. 1
Concord, NH 03301-3843
(603) 271-4680

NEW JERSEY
Division of Senior Affairs
Dept. of Health and Senior Services
P.O. Box 807
Trenton, NJ 08625-0807
(609) 588-3139

NEW MEXICO
State Agency on Aging
La Villa Rivera Building
228 E. Palace Avenue
Ground Floor

Santa Fe, NM 87501
(505) 827-7640

NEW YORK
State Agency for the Aging
Empire State Plaza, Building 2
Albany, NY 12223-1251
(518) 474-4425
(800) 342-9871

NORTH CAROLINA
Division of Aging
693 Palmer Drive
Caller Box 29531
Raleigh, NC 27626-0531
(919) 733-3983

NORTH DAKOTA
Aging Services Division
Department of Human Services
600 S., 2nd Street, #1C
Bismarck, ND 58504
(701) 328-8989
(800) 755-8521

OHIO
Department of Aging
50 W. Broad Street, 9th Floor
Columbus, OH 43215-5928
(614) 466-5500

OKLAHOMA
Aging Services Division
Department of Human Services
312 NE 28th Street
Oklahoma City, OK 73125
(405) 521-2327

OREGON
Department of Human Resources
   Senior and Disabled Services
   Division
500 Summer St., NE, 2nd Floor
Salem, OR 97310-1015
(503) 945-5811
(800) 232-3020

PALAU
State Agency on Aging
Department of Social Services
Republic of Palau
P.O. Box 100
Koror, Palau 96940

PENNSYLVANIA
Department of Aging
555 Walnut Street, 5th Floor
Harrisburg, PA 17101-1919
(717) 783-1550

PUERTO RICO
Governor's Office of Elderly Affairs
P.O. Box 50063
Old San Juan Station
San Juan, PR 00902
(787) 721-5710

**REPUBLIC OF THE MAR-
SHALL ISLANDS**
State Agency on Aging
Department of Social Services
Republic of the Marshall Islands
Marjuro, Marshall Islands 96960

RHODE ISLAND
Department of Elderly Affairs
160 Pine Street
Providence, RI 02903-3708
(401) 222-2858

SOUTH CAROLINA
Office on Aging
Department of Health and Human
   Services
P.O. Box 8206
Columbia, SC 29202-8206
(803) 253-6177

SOUTH DAKOTA
Office of Adult Services and Aging
700 Governors Drive
Pierre, SD 57501
(605) 773-3656

TENNESSEE
Commission on Aging
Andrew Jackson Building
9th Floor
500 Deaderick Street
Nashville, TN 37243-0860
(615) 741-2056

TEXAS
Department on Aging
4900 North Lamar, 4th Floor
Austin, TX 78751-2316
(512) 424-6840

UTAH
Division of Aging and Adult
   Services
120 North 200 West

Salt Lake City, UT 84145-0500
(801) 538-3910

VERMONT
Department of Aging and
    Disabilities
Waterbury Complex
103 S. Main Street
Waterbury, VT 05671-2301
(802) 241-2400

VIRGINIA
Department for the Aging
1600 Forest Avenue
Preston Building, Suite 102
Richmond, VA 23229
(804) 662-9333

VIRGIN ISLANDS
Senior Citizen Affairs Division
Department of Human Services
19 Estate Diamond Fredericksted
St. Croix, VI 00840
(809) 692-5950

WASHINGTON
Aging and Adult Services
    Administration
Dept. of Social and Health Services
P.O. Box 45050
Olympia, WA 98504-5050
(360) 586-8753

WEST VIRGINIA
Bureau of Senior Services
State Capitol Complex
Holly Grove - Building 10
1900 Kanawha Blvd., East
Charleston, WV 25305-0160
(304) 558-3317

WISCONSIN
Bureau of Aging and LTC Resources
217 S. Hamilton St., Suite 300
Madison, WI 53703
(608) 266-2536

WYOMING
Division on Aging
139 Hathaway Building
Cheyenne, WY 82002-0710
(307) 777-7986

APPENDIX B · STATES WITH HIGH-RISK HEALTH INSURANCE POOLS

ALABAMA
Alabama Department of Insurance
135 Union Street
P.O. Box 30551
Montgomery, AL 36130
(334) 269-3550

ALASKA
Alaska Division of Insurance
3601 C Street, Suite 1324
Anchorage, AK 99503-5948
(907) 269-7900
(800) 467-8725

ARKANSAS
Life & Health Divsion
Arkansas Insurance Department
1200 West Third Street
Little Rock, AR 72201-1904
(501) 378-2979

CALIFORNIA
Executive Director
Managed Risk Medical Insurance
    Program
818 K Street, Room 200
Sacramento, CA 95814
(916) 324-4695

COLORADO
Colorado Uninsurable Health
    Insurance Plan (CUHIP)
Division of Insurance
1600 Broadway, Suite 420
Denver, CO 80202
(303) 863-1960

CONNECTICUT
United Healthcare
450 Columbus Blvd. 9NB
P.O. Box 150450
Hartford, CT 06115-0450
(800) 842-0004

FLORIDA
Executive Director
Florida Comprehensive Association
175 Salem Court
Tallahassee, FL 32301
(850) 309-1200

ILLINOIS
Illinois Comprehensive Health
    Insurance Program
400 West Monroe Street
Suite 202
Springfield, IL 62704
(217) 782-6333

INDIANA
Indiana Comprehensive Health
    Insurance Association
Healthcare Solutions, Inc.
5543 West 74th Street
Indianapolis, IN 46268
(800) 552-7921

IOWA
Iowa Comprehensive Health
    Insurance Association
636 Grand Avenue
Des Moines, IA 50309
(800) 877-5156

KANSAS
Kansas Insurance Department
420 S.W. 9th Street
Topeka, KS 66612
(913) 296-3071

LOUISIANA
Louisiana Health Insurance
    Association
7907 Wrenwood Blvd., Suite B
Baton Rouge, LA 70809
(504) 926-6245

MINNESOTA
Minnesota Comprehensive Health
    Association
P.O. Box 64566
St. Paul, MN 55164
(612) 456-5290

MISSISSIPPI
Comprehensive Health Insurance
    Risk Pool Association
P.O. Box 13748
Jackson, MS 39236
(601) 362-0799

MISSOURI
Missouri Health Insurance Plan
Missouri Health Insurance Pool
4444 Forest Park Blvd.,
Suite 642
St. Louis, MO 63108
(314) 923-4444

MONTANA
Montana Comprehensive Health
    Association

Blue Cross/Blue Shield of Montana
560 N. Park Avenue
P.O. Box 4309
Helena, MT 59604
(406) 444-8200

NEBRASKA
Nebraska Comprehensive Health
    Insurance Pool
Blue Cross/Blue Shield of Nebraska
P.O. Box 3248
Omaha, NE 68180-0001
(402) 390-1814

NEW MEXICO
Vice President, Member Services
Blue Cross/Blue Shield of New
    Mexico
P.O. Box 27630
Albuquerque, NM 87125-7630
(502) 291-4398

NORTH DAKOTA
Blue Cross/Blue Shield of North
    Dakota
4510 13th Avenue, S.W.
Fargo, ND 58121-0001
(701) 282-1100
(800) 737-0016

OKLAHOMA
Oklahoma Insurance Department
3814 N. Santa Fe
Oklahoma City, OK 73152-3408
(405) 521-2930

OREGON

Regence Blue Cross/Blue Shield of
  Oregon
P.O. Box 1271
Portland, OR 97207-1271
(503) 225-5221
(800) 452-7278

SOUTH CAROLINA

Blue Cross/Blue Shield of South
  Carolina
P.O. Box 61173
Columbia, SC 29260-1173
(803) 736-0043
(800) 868-2503

TENNESSEE

Bureau of Tenn Care
729 Church Street
Nashville, TN 37247-6501
(615) 741-0213

TEXAS

Texas Health Insurance Risk Pool
301 Congress Avenue, Suite 500
Austin, TX 78701
(512) 499-0775

UTAH

Utah Comprehensive Health
  Insurance Pool
36 South State Street, 21st Flr.
Salt Lake City, UT 84111-1418
(801) 442-3782

WASHINGTON

Washington State Health Insurance
  Pool
Compliance Manager: Life &
  Disability
Insurance Building
P.O. Box 40256
Olympia, WA
  98504-0256
(360) 407-0380

WISCONSIN

Wisconsin Health Insurance Risk
  Sharing Plan
Office of the Commissioner of
  Insurance
121 East Wilson Street
P.O. Box 787a3
Madison, WI 53707
(608) 267-4395

WYOMING

Wyoming Insurance Department
Herschler Building
122 West 25th Street
Cheyenne, WY 82002
(307) 777-7401

APPENDIX C •	STATE INSURANCE COUNSELING PROGRAMS

ALABAMA
Insurance Information Counseling
  and Assistance Program
Alabama Commission on Aging
770 Washington Avenue
Montgomery, AL 36130
(334) 242-5743

ALASKA
Insurance Counseling & Assistance
  Program
Division of Senior Services
3601 C St., Ste 310
Anchorage, AK 99503-5209
(907) 269-3666

ARIZONA
Arizona Medicare Information and
  Referral
Aging & Adult Administration
Dept. of Economic Security
1789 W Jefferson #950A
Phoenix, AZ 85007
(602) 542-6439

ARKANSAS
Seniors Insurance Network
Arkansas State Insurance
  Department
1200 W 3rd Street
Little Rock, AR 72201
(501) 371-2785

CALIFORNIA
Health Insurance Counseling and
  Advocacy Program
CA Dept. of Aging

1600 K Street
Sacramento, CA 95814
(916) 323-6525

COLORADO
Senior Health Insurance Assistance
  Program
CO Division of Insurance
1560 Broadway, Suite 850
Denver, CO 80202
(303) 894-7499, x355

CONNECTICUT
Connecticut Programs for Health
  Insurance Assistance
Outreach Information and Referral
  Counseling Eligibility and
  Screening (CHOICES)
Department of Social Services
Elderly Services Division
25 Sigourney St. 10th Fl.
Hartford, CT 06106-5033 (860)
424-5244

DISTRICT OF COLUMBIA
Health Insurance Counseling Project
Building A-B, lst Floor
2136 Pennsylvania Avenue NW
Washington, DC 20052
(202) 676-3900

DELAWARE
Elder Info
Delaware Insurance Dept.
841 Silver Lake Blvd.
Dover, DE 19903
(302) 739-6266

Division of Aging
1901 N. DuPont Highway
New Castle, DE 19720
(302) 577-4791

FLORIDA
Serving Health Insurance
Needs of Elders (SHINE)
Dept of Elder Affairs
4040 Esplanade Way, #280 S
Tallahassee, FL 32399-7000
(850) 414-2060

GEORGIA
Health Insurance Counseling
    Asisstance and Referral for the
    Elderly
Division of Aging Services
#2 Peachtree St., N.E., 36th Fl
Atlanta, GA 30303
(404) 657-5347

HAWAII
SAGE PLUS
Executive Office on Aging
250 S. Hotel St., #107
Honolulu, HI 96813-2831(808)
586-7299

IDAHO
Senior Health Insurance Benefits
    Advisors
Department of Insurance
700 W. State, 3rd Floor
Boise, ID 83720-0043
(208) 334-4350

ILLINOIS
Senior Health Insurance Program
Department of Insurance
320 W. Washington Street
Springfield, IL 62767-0001
(217) 782-0004

INDIANA
SHIIP - Senior Health Insurance
    Information Program
Indiana Department of Insurance
311 West Washington Street
Suite 300
Indianapolis, IN 46204-2787
(317) 233-3551

IOWA
SHIIP - Senior Health Insurance
    Information Program
Iowa Insurance Division
330 Maple Street
Des Moines, IA 50319-0065
(515) 242-5190

KANSAS
Senior Health Insurance Counseling
    for Kansas (SHICK)
Kansas Insurance Department
130 S. Market St., Suite 4030
PO Box 3850
Wichita, KS 67201-3850
(316) 337-6010

KENTUCKY
Kentucky Benefits Counseling
Division of Aging
Cabinet for Human Resources
5th Fl. West - CCF

275 East Main Street
Frankfort, KY 40621
(502) 564-7372

LOUISIANA
Senior Health Insurance Information
   Program
Louisiana Dept. of Insurance
P.O. Box 94214
Baton Rouge, LA 70804-9214
(504) 342-0825

MAINE
Maine Health Insurannce
   Counseling Program
Bureau of Elder & Adult Services
35 Anthony Avenue
State House - Station #11
Augusta, ME 04333-0011 (207)
624-5335

MARYLAND
Senior Health Insurance Counseling
   and Advocacy Program (HICAP)
Office on Aging
State Office Bldg, Room 1007
301 West Preston Street
Baltimore, MD 21201
(410) 767-1074

MASSACHUSETTS
Serving Health Information Needs
   of Elders (SHINE)
Executive Officer of Elder Affairs
1 Ashburton Place, 5th Floor
Boston, MA 02108
(617) 222-7435

MICHIGAN
Medicare/Medicaid Assistance
   Program
Michigan Office of Services to the
   Aging
P.O. Box 30676
Lansing, MI 48909-8176 (517)
373-4071

MINNESOTA
Minnesota Health Insurance
   Counseling Program
Board on Aging
444 Lafayette Road
St. Paul, MN 55155-3843 (612)
296-3839

MISSISSIPPI
MS. Insurance Counseling and
   Assistance Program
Dept. of Human Services
Div. of Aging & Adult Svs.
750 N. State Street
Jackson, MS 39202
(601) 359-4956

MISSOURI
Community Leaders Assisting the
   Insured of MO (CLAIM)
MPCRF, CLAIM Program
505 Hobbs Road, Suite 100
Jefferson City, MO 65109 (573)
893-7900 x 137

MONTANA
Montana Partnership for Health
   Insurance Information Counseling
   and Assistance Program

212 Ridge Trail
Bozman, MT 59715
(406) 585-0773

NEBRASKA
Nebraska Health Insurance
    Information Counseling and
    Assistance Program
Department of Insurance
941 O Street, Suite 400
Lincoln, NE 68508
(402) 471-4506

NEVADA
Nevada Medicare Information
    Counseling and Assistance (ICA)
Nevada Department of Insurance
2501 E. Sahara #302
Las Vegas, NV 89104
(702) 964-1033

NEW HAMPSHIRE
HICEA - Health Insurance
    Counseling, Education and
    Assistance Service
Division of Elderly and Adult
    Service
State Office Park South
115 Pleasant St., Annex Bldg. #1
Concord, NH 03301-7325
(603) 271-3944

HICEAS - Health Insurance
    Counseling Education Assistance
    Service
110 B Pette Hall
55 College Road

Durham, NH 03824
(603) 862-0092

NEW JERSEY
Counseling on Health Insurance for
    Medicare Enrollees
Division of Senior Affairs
Box 807
Trenton, NJ 08625
(609) 588-3385

NEW MEXICO
Health Insurance Benefits Assistance
    Corps
State Agency on Aging
La Villa Rivera Bldg.
228 E. Palace Avenue, Ground Fl
Santa Fe, NM 87501
(505) 827-7640

NEW YORK
Health Insurance Information
    Counseling and Assistance
    Program (HIICAP)
Office for the Aging
2 Empire State Plaza
Agency Building #2
Albany, NY 12223-1251   (518)
473-5108

NORTH CAROLINA
Senior Health Insurance Information
    Program
Department of Insurance
111 Seaboard Avenue
Raleigh, NC 27604
(919) 733-0111
(800) 443-9354

NORTH DAKOTA

Senior Health Insurance Counseling
   Insurance Department
600 E. Blvd. 5th Floor
Bismarck, ND 58505
(701) 328-2977

OHIO

Ohio Senior Health Insurance
   Information Program
Office of Consumer Advocate
Department of Insurance
2100 Stella Court
Columbus, OH 43215-1067
(614) 644-3399

OKLAHOMA

Senior Health Insurance Counseling
   Program
Department of Insurance
P.O. Box 53408
1901 North Walnut
Oklahoma City, OK 73152-3408
(405) 521-6628

OREGON

SHIBA
Division of Insurance
350 Winter Street NE, #440
Salem, OR 97310
(503) 947-7250

PENNSYLVANIA

APPRISE
Department of Aging
Forum Place
555 Walnut St., 5th Fl.

Harrisburg, PA 17101-1919
(717) 783-8975

PUERTO RICO

ICA Program
Governor's Office for Elderly Affairs
P.O. Box 50063
Old San Juan Station
San Juan, PR 00902
(787) 721-8590

RHODE ISLAND

Senior Health Insurance Program
Department of Elderly Affairs
160 Pine Street
Providence, RI 02903-3708
(401) 222-2880 x220
(401) 222-2858 x116

SOUTH CAROLINA

Office of the Governor
Division on Aging
1801 Main Street
Columbia, SC 29209
(803) 253-6177

SOUTH DAKOTA

SHINE Program
Office of Adult Services & Aging
700 Governors Drive
Pierre, SD 57501-2291
(605) 773-3656

SHINE East River Legal Services
335 N Main Avenue, Suite 300
Sioux Falls, SD 57102-0305
(605) 336-2475

SHINE
2638 West Main, Suite #2
Rapid City, SD 57702
(605) 342-3494

TENNESSEE
TN Association of Legal Services
211 Union, #833
Nashville, TN 37201
(615) 242-0438

TEXAS
Texas Health Information,
    Counseling and Advocacy
    Program
Department on Aging
4900 North Lamar, 4th Floor
Austin, TX 78751
(512) 424-6840

Texas Department of Insurance
P.O. Box 149091
Austin, TX 78714
(512) 463-6461

UTAH
Health Insurance Information
Div of Aging & Adult Services
Department of Social Services
Box 45500
120 North - 200 West
Salt Lake City, UT 84103
(801) 538-3910

VERMONT
Health Insurance Counseling and
    Assistance Program
Northeastern Vermont AAA

180 Portland Street
St. Johnsburg, VT 05819   (802)
748-5182

VIRGINIA
Virginia Insurance Counseling
    Assistance Project (VICAP)
Department of the Aging
1600 Forest Avenue
Preston Building, Suite 102
Richmond, VA 23229
(804) 662-9333

VIRGIN ISLANDS
Virgin Islands ICA Program
Governor Juan F. Louis
Hospital and Medical Center
Estate Diamond Ruby/Box 18
St. Croix, VI 00820-4421 (809)
778-6311 x2338

WASHINGTON
Senior Health Insurance Benefits
    Advisors (SHIBA)
Department of Insurance Building
Olympia, WA 98504
(206) 654-1833

WEST VIRGINIA
West Virginia Senior Health
    Insurance Network
WV Bureau of Senior Service
1900 Kanawha Blvd. E
Charleston, WV 25305-0160
(304) 558-3317

WISCONSIN
Bureau of Aging and LTC Resources
Department of Health and Family
Services
217 S. Hamilton Street #300
Madison, WI 53703
(608) 267-3201

WYOMING
Wyoming Senior Health Insurance
    Information Program
Wyoming Insurance Department
122 W. 25th Street
Herschler Bldg., 3-East
Cheyenne, WY 82002
(307) 777-7401

Wyoming Senior Citizens
1130 Major Ave.
P.O. Box BD
Riverton, WY 82501
(307) 856-6880

| **APPENDIX D** • | STATE INSURANCE REGULATORS |

ALABAMA
Alabama Department of Insurance
201 Monroe Street, Suite 1700
Montgomery, AL 36104
(334) 269-3550

ALASKA
Alaska Division of Insurance
Dept. of Commerce & Economic
  Dev.
P.O. Box 110805
Juneau, AK 99811-0805
(907) 465-2515

Federal Express packages:
333 Willoughby Avenue, 9th Floor
Juneau, AK 99801

3601 C Street
Suite 1324
Anchorage, AK 99503-5948
(907) 269-7900

AMERICAN SAMOA
Office of the Governor
American Samoa Government
Pago Pago, American Samoa 96799
011-684-633-4116

ARIZONA
Arizona Department of Insurance
2910 North 44th Street, Suite 210
Phoenix, AZ 85018-7256
(602) 912-8400

ARKANSAS
Arkansas Department of Insurance
1200 West 3rd Street
Little Rock, AK 72201-1904
(501) 371-2600

CALIFORNIA
California Department of Insurance
300 Capitol Mall, Suite 1500
Sacramento, CA 95814
(916) 492-3500

State of California
45 Fremont Street, 23rd Floor
San Francisco, CA 94102
(415) 538-4040

300 South Spring Street
Los Angles, CA 90013
(213) 346-6400

COLORADO
Colorado Division of Insurance
1560 Broadway, Suite 850
Denver, CO 80202
(303) 894-7499

CONNECTICUT
Connecticut Department of
  Insurance
P.O. Box 816
Hartford, Connecticut 06142-0816

Federal Express packages:
153 Market Street, 11th Floor
Hartford, CT 06103
(860) 297-3802

DELAWARE
Delaware Department of Insurance
Rodney Building
841 Silver Lake Boulevard
Dover, DE 19904
(302) 739-4251

DISTRICT OF COLUMBIA
Dept. of Insurance & Securities
    Regulations
Government of the District of
    Columbia
441 Fourth Street NW
8th Floor North
Washington, DC 20001
(202) 727-8000 3018

FLORIDA
Florida Department of Insurance
State Capitol
Plaza Level Eleven
Tallahassee, FL 32399-0300
(850) 922-3101

GEORGIA
Georgia Department of Insurance
2 Martin L. King, Jr. Dr.
Floyd Memorial Bldg., 704 West
    Tower
Atlanta, GA 30334
(404) 656-2056

GUAM
Dept. of Revenue & Taxation
Government of Guam
Building 13-1, 2nd Floor
Mariner Avenue

Tiyan, Barrigada, Guam 96913
(671) 475-1817

HAWAII
Hawaii Insurance Division
Dept. of Commerce & Consumer
    Affairs
P.O. Box 3614
Honolulu, HI 96811-3614
(808) 586-2790

IDAHO
Idaho Department of Insurance
700 West State Street, 3rd Floor
Boise, ID 83720-0043
(208) 334-4250

ILLINOIS
Illinois Department of Insurance
320 West Washington St.,
    4th Floor
Springfield, IL 62767-0001
(217) 785-0116

100 West Randolph Street
Suite 15-100
Chicago, IL 60601-3251
(312) 814-2420

INDIANA
Indiana Department of Insurance
311 W. Washington Street,
    Suite 300
Indianapolis, IN 46204-2787
(317) 232-2385

IOWA
Iowa Division of Insurance
330 E. Maple Street
Des Moines, IA 50319
(515) 281-5705

KANSAS
Kansas Department of Insurance
420 S.W. 9th Street
Topeka, KS 66612-1678
(785) 296-7801

KENTUCKY
Kentucky Department of Insurance
P.O. Box 517
215 West Main Street
Frankfort, KY 40602-0517
(502) 564-6027

LOUISIANA
Louisiana Department of Insurance
Attn: Patrick Frantz
P.O. Box 94214
Baton Rouge, LA
    70804-9214
(504) 342-5423

MAINE
Maine Bureau of Insurance
Dept. of Professional &
    Financial Reg.
State Office Building, Station 34
Augusta, ME 04333-0034
(207) 624-8475

MARYLAND
Maryland Insurance Administration
525 St. Paul Place

Baltimore, MD 21202-2272
(410) 468-2090

MASSACHUSETTS
Division of Insurance
Commonwealth of Massachusetts
470 Atlantic Avenue, 6th Floor
Boston, MA 02210-2223
(617) 521-7794

MICHIGAN
Michigan Insurance Bureau
Department of Commerce
611 W. Ottawa Street,
    2nd Floor North
Lansing, MI 48933-1020`
(517) 373-9273

MINNESOTA
Minnesota Department
    of Commerce
133 East 7th Street
St. Paul, MN 55101
(612) 296-6848

MISSISSIPPI
Mississippi Insurance Department
1804 Walter Sillers
State Office Building
550 High Street
Jackson, MS 39201
(601) 359-3569

MISSOURI
Missouri Department of Insurance
301 West High Street, 6 North
Jefferson City, MO
    65102-690
(573) 751-4126

MONTANA
Montana Department of Insurance
126 North Sanders
270 Mitchell Building
Helena, MT 59601
(406) 444-2040

NEBRASKA
Nebraska Department of Insurance
Terminal Building, Suite 400
941 'O' Street
Lincoln, NE 68508
(402) 471-2201

NEVADA
Nevada Division of Insurance
1665 Hot Springs Road, Suite 152
Carson City, NV 89706-0661
(702) 687-4270

NEW HAMPSHIRE
New Hampshire Dept.
   of Insurance
169 Manchester Street
Concord, NH 03301
(603) 271-2261

NEW JERSEY
New Jersey Department
   of Insurance
20 West State Street CN325
Trenton, NJ 08625
(609) 292-5363

NEW MEXICO
New Mexico Department
   of Insurance
P.O. Drawer 1269

Santa Fe, NM 87504-1269
(505) 827-4601

NEW YORK
New York Department
   of Insurance
25 Beaver Street
New York, NY
   10004-2319
(212) 480-2289

Agency Building One
Empire State Plaza
Albany, NY 12257
(518) 474-6600

NORTH CAROLINA
North Carolina Department of
   Insurance
P.O. Box 26387
Raleigh, NC 27611
(919) 733-7349

Federal Express packages:
Dobbs Building
430 N. Sahsburg Street
Raleigh, NC 27603

NORTH DAKOTA
North Dakota Department of
   Insurance
600 E. Boulevard
Bismarck, ND
   58505-0320
(701) 328-2440

OHIO
Ohio Department of Insurance
2100 Stella Court
Columbus, OH 43215-1067
(614) 644-2658

OKLAHOMA
Oklahoma Department
    of Insurance
3814 N. Santa Fe
Oklahoma City, OK 73118
(405) 521-2686

OREGON
Oregon Division of Insurance
Dept. of Consumer & Business
    Services
350 Winter Street NE, Room 200
Salem, OR 97310-0700
(503) 378-4271

PENNSYLVANIA
Pennsylvania Insurance Department
1326 Strawberry Square,
    13th Floor
Harrisburg, PA 17120
(717) 783-0442

PUERTO RICO
Puerto Rico Dept. of Insurance
Cobian's Plaza Building
P.O. Box 8330
Fernandez Juncos Station
Santurce, PR 00910-8330
(787) 722-8686

RHODE ISLAND
Rhode Island Insurance Division

Dept. of Business Regulation
233 Richmond Street, Suite 233
Providence, RI 02903-4233
(401) 222-2223

SOUTH CAROLINA
South Carolina Department
    of Insurance
P.O. Box 100105
Columbia, SC 29202-3105
(803) 737-6160

SOUTH DAKOTA
South Dakota Division
    of Insurance
Dept. of Commerce & Regulation
118 West Capitol Avenue
Pierre, SD 57501-2000
(605) 773-3563

TENNESSEE
Tennessee Department
    of Commerce & Insurance
Volunteer Plaza
500 James Robertson Parkway
Nashville, TN 37243-0565
(615) 741-2241

TEXAS
Texas Department of Insurance
333 Guadalupe Street
Austin, TX 78701

Post Office Box Address:
P.O. Box 149104
Austin, TX 78714-9104
(512) 463-6464

UTAH
Utah Department of Insurance
3110 State Office Building
Salt Lake City, UT 84114-1201
(801) 538-3800

VERMONT
Vermont Division of Insurance
Dept. of Banking, Insurance &
    Securities
89 Main Street, Drawer 20
Montpelier, VT 05620-3101
(802) 828-3301

VIRGINIA
State Corporation Commission
Bureau of Insurance
Commonwealth of Virginia
P.O. Box 1157
Richmond, VA 23218
(804) 371-9694

VIRGIN ISLANDS
Division of Banking & Insurance
1131 King Street, Suite 101
Christiansted
St. Croix, VI 00820
(809) 773-6449
#18 Kongens Gade, Charlotte
    Amalie
St. Thomas, VI 00802
(304) 774-7166

WASHINGTON
Washington Office of the Insurance
    Commissioner
14th Avenue & Water Streets
P.O. Box 40255
Olympia, WA 98504-0255
(360) 753-7301

WEST VIRGINIA
West Virginia Department of
    Insurance
P.O. Box 50540
Charleston, WV 25305-0540
(304) 558-3354

WISCONSIN
Office of the Commissioner of
    Insurance
State of Wisconsin
P.O. Box 7873
Madison, WI 53707-7873
(608) 266-0102

WYOMING
Wyoming Department of Insurance
Herschler Building
122 West 25th Street, 3rd East
Cheyenne, WY
    82002-0440
(307) 777-7401

APPENDIX E · ORGAN DONOR ORGANIZATIONS

Eye Bank for Sight Restoration, Inc.
120 Wall Street
New York, NY 10005
(212) 742-9000

Kidney Foundation of New York, Inc.
1250 Broadway, Suite 2001
New York, NY 10001
(212) 629-9770

Living Bank
P.O. Box 6725
Houston, TX 77027
(713) 528-2971

Massachusetts Eye & Ear Infirmary
243 Charles Street
Boston, MA 02114
(617) 573-3700

National Kidney Foundation
30 E. 33 Street
New York, NY 10016
(212) 889-2210

National Temporal Bone Bank Center
University of Minnesota Medical Center
Harvard Street at E. River Road
Minneapolis, MN 55455
(612) 625-8437

APPENDIX F ·   DEPARTMENT OF HOUSING AND URBAN
DEVELOPMENT REGIONAL OFFICES

ALABAMA
Birmingham Field Office
Beacon Ridge Tower
Suite 300
600 Beacon Parkway, West
Birmingham, AL 35209-3144
(205) 290-7630

ALASKA
Anchorage Field Office
949 E. 36th Avenue
Suite 401
Anchorage, AK
(907) 271-4663

ARIZONA
Phoenix/Tucson Field Office
2 Arizona Center
Suite 1600
400 N. Fifth Street
Phoenix, AZ 85004-2361
(602) 379-4434

ARKANSAS
Little Rock Field Office
523 Louisiana Street
Lafayette Building
Suite 200
Little Rock, AR 72201-3707
(501) 378-5931

CALIFORNIA
San Francisco Regional Office
California State Office
Phillip Burton Federal Building and

U.S. Courthouse
450 Golden Gate Avenue
San Francisco, CA 94102-3448
(415) 436-3448

Fresno Field Office
Suite 138
1630 E. Shaw Avenue
Fresno, CA 93710-8193
(209) 487-5033

Los Angeles Field Office
5140 Crenshaw
Los Angeles, CA
90015-3801
(213) 894-296-0467

Santa Ana Field Office
34 Civic Center Plaza
Santa Ana, CA
92712-2850
(714) 569-0827

San Diego Field Office
2365 Northside Dr.
Suite 30
San Diego, CA 92108
(619) 557-5305

COLORADO
Denver Regional Office
633 17th Street
Denver, CO 80202-3607
(303) 672-5440

CONNECTICUT
Hartford Field Office
330 Main Street - First Floor
Hartford, CT 06106-1860
(860) 240-4800

DELAWARE
Wilmington Field Office
824 Market Street
Suite 850
Wilmington, DE 19801-3016
(302) 573-6300

DISTRICT OF COLUMBIA
Washington, D.C., Field Office
451 7th Street, S.W.
Washington, DC 20002-4205
(202) 708-1422

FLORIDA
Coral Gables Field Office
Gables 1 Tower
Suite 500
1320 S. Dixie Highway
Coral Gables, FL 33146-2926
(305) 662-4500

Jacksonville Field Office
Southern Bell Tower
301 W. Bay Street
Suite 2200
Jacksonville, FL 32202-5121
(904) 232-2627

Orlando Field Office
Langley Building
Suite 270
3751 Maguire Boulevard

Orlando, FL 32803-3032
(407) 648-6441

Tampa Field Office
Timberlake Federal Building Annex,
    Suite 700
501 E. Polk Street
Tampa, FL 33602-3945
(813) 228-2501

GEORGIA
Georgia State Regional Office
Richard B. Russell Federal Building
75 Spring Street, SW
Atlanta, GA 30303-3388
(404) 331-4576

HAWAII
Honolulu Field Office
Prince Jona Federal Building
300 Ala Moana Boulevard
P.O. Box 50007
Honolulu, HI 96850-4991
(808) 541-1323

IDAHO
Boise Field Office
Plaza IV Suite 220
800 Park Boulevard
Boise, ID 83712-7743
(208) 334-1990

ILLINOIS
Chicago Regional Office
Illinois State Office
Ralph H. Metcalfe Federal Building
77 West Jackson Boulevard

Chicago, IL 60604-3507
(312) 353-6236

INDIANA
Indianapolis Field Office
151 N. Delaware Street
Indianapolis, IN 46204-2526
(317) 226-6303

IOWA
Des Moines Field Office
Federal Building - Room 239
210 Walnut Street
Des Moines, IA 50309-2155
(515) 284-4512

KANSAS
Kansas/Missouri State Office
Gateway Tower II
400 State Avenue
Kansas City, KS 66101-2406
(913) 551-5462

KENTUCKY
Louisville Field Office
601 West Broadway
Louisville, KY 40201-1044
(502) 582-5251

LOUISIANA
New Orleans Field Office
Fisk Federal Building
1661 Canal Street
New Orleans, LA 70112-2887
(504) 589-7200

MAINE
FIELD OFFICES
Bangor Field Office
202 Harlow Street
Suite 101
Bangor, ME 04402-1384
(800) 767-7468

MARYLAND
Baltimore Field Office
The Equitable Building
10 N. Calvert Street - 3rd Floor
Baltimore, MD 21202-1865
(410) 962-2520

MASSACHUSETTS
Boston Regional Office
Massachusetts State Office
Thomas P. O'Neill, Jr. Federal
  Building
10 Causeway Street, Room 375
Boston, MA 02222-1092
(617) 565-5234

MICHIGAN
Detroit Field Office
Patrick V. McNamara
Federal Building
477 Michigan Avenue
Detroit, MI 48226-2592
(313) 226-7900

MINNESOTA
Minneapolis-St. Paul Field Office
220 Second Street, South
Minneapolis, MN 55401-2195
(612) 370-3000

MISSISSIPPI
Jackson Field Office
Doctor A.H. McCoy Federal
  Bulding
100 W. Capitol Street
Suite 910
Jackson, MS 39269-1096
(601) 965-4757

MISSOURI
St. Louis Field Office
Robert A. Young Federal Building
Third Floor
1222 Spruce Street
St. Louis, MO 63103-2836
(314) 539-6583

MONTANA
Helena Field Office
Federal Office Building, Room 340
Drawer 10095
301 S. Park
Helena, MT 59626-0095
(406) 449-5205

NEBRASKA
Omaha Field Office
10909 Mill Valley Road
Omaha, NE 68154
(402) 492-3100

NEVADA
Las Vegas Field Office
Suite 205
1500 E. Tropicana Avenue
Las Vegas, NV 89119-6516
(702) 388-6500

Reno Field Office
1565 Delucchi Lane
Suite 114
Reno, NV 89505-4700
(702) 784-5383

NEW HAMPSHIRE
Manchester Field Office
Norris Cotton Federal Building
275 Chestnut Street
Manchester, NH 03101-2487
(603) 666-7643

NEW JERSEY
Camden Field Office
800 Hudson Square
Camden, NJ 08102
(609) 757-5081

Newark Field Office
1 Newark Center
13th Floor
Newark, NJ 07102-5260
(973) 622-7900

NEW MEXICO
Albuquerque Field Office
625 Truman Street, N.E.
Albuquerque, New Mexico 87110-
  6443
(505) 262-6463

NEW YORK
New York Regional Office
26 Federal Plaza
New York, NY 10278-0068
(212) 264-6500

Albany Field Office
Leo W. O'Brien Federal Building
N. Pearl Street and Clinton Avenue
Albany, NY 12207-2395
(518) 464-4203

Buffalo Field Office
Lafayette Court
Fifth Floor
465 Main Street
Buffalo, NY 14203-1780
(716) 551-5755

NORTH CAROLINA
Greensboro Field Office
Koger Building
2306 West Meadowview Road
Greensboro, NC 27401-3707
(910) 547-4000

NORTH DAKOTA
Fargo Field Office
Federal Building
653 Second Avenue North
Fargo, ND 58108-2483
(701) 239-5136

OHIO
Cincinnati Field Office
525 Vine Street, 7th Floor
Cincinnati, OH 45202-3188
(513) 684-2884

Cleveland Field Office
Renaissance Building
Suite 500
1350 Euclid Avenue

Cleveland, OH 44115-1815
(216) 522-4058

Columbus Field Office
200 N. High Street
Columbus, OH 43215-2499
(614) 469-5737

OKLAHOMA
Oklahoma City Field Office
500 West Main Street
Suite 400
Oklahoma City, OK 73102-3202
(405) 553-7401

Tulsa Field Office
50 East 15th Street
Tulsa, OK 74119-4032
(918) 581-7434S

OREGON
Portland Field Office
520 Southwest Sixth Avenue
Portland, OR 97204-1596
(503) 326-2561

PENNSYLVANIA
Philadelphia Regional Office
The Wanamaker Building
100 Penn Square East
Philadelphia, PA 19107-3380
(215) 656-0603

Pittsburgh Field Office
339 6th Avenue
Pittsburgh, PA 15222-2515
(412) 644-6428

PUERTO RICO
Caribbean Field Office
New San Juan Office Building
159 Carlos Chardon Avenue
San Juan, PR 00918-1804
(787) 766-5201

RHODE ISLAND
Providence Field Office
Federal Building
10 Weybosset Street 6th Floor
Providence, RI 02903-1785
(401) 528-5351

SOUTH CAROLINA
Columbia Field Office
Strom Thurmond Federal Building
1835-45 Assembly Street
Columbia, SC 29201-2480
(803) 765-5592

SOUTH DAKOTA
Sioux Falls Field Office
Suite 116
300 N. Dakota Avenue
Sioux, Falls, SD 57102-0311
(605) 330-4223

TENNESSEE
Knoxville Field Office
John J. Duncan Federal Building
Third Floor
710 Locust Stret
Knoxville, TN 37902-2526
(423) 545-4384

Memphis Field Office
One Memphis Place
Suite 1200
200 Jefferson Avenue
Memphis, TN 38103-2335
(901) 544-3367

Nashville Field Office
251 Cumberland Bend Drive
Suite 200
Nashville, TN 37228-1803
(615) 736-5213

TEXAS
Fort Worth Regional Office
1600 Throckmorton Street
Ft. Worth, TX 76113-2905
(800) 568-2893

Dallas Field Office
525 Griffin Street, Room 860
Dallas, TX 75202-5007
(214) 767-8300

Houston Field Office
Norfolk Tower, Suite 200
2211 Norfolk
Houston, TX 77098-4096
(713) 653-3274

Lubbock Field Office
Federal Office Building
1205 Texas Avenue
Lubbock, TX 79401-4093
(806) 743-7265

San Antonio Field Office
Washington Square
800 Dolorosa
San Antonio, TX 78207
(210) 475-6800

UTAH
Salt Lake City Field Office
324 S. State Street, Suite 220
Salt Lake City, UT 84111-2321
(801) 524-5379

VERMONT
Burlington Field Office
Room B-28, Federal Building
11 Elmwood Avenue
P.O. Box 879
Burlington, VT 05401-0879
(802) 951-6290

VIRGINIA
Richmond Field Office
3600 W. Broad Street
Richmond, VA 23230-4920
(804) 278-4500

WASHINGTON
Seattle Regional Office
909 First Avenue, Suite 200
Seattle, WA 98104-1000
(206) 220-5101

Spokane Field Office
Farm Credit Bank Building
West 601 First Avenue
8th Floor East
Spokane, WA 99204-0317
(509) 353-2510

WISCONSIN
Milwaukee Field Office
Henry S. Reuss Federal Plaza
Suite 1380
310 W. Wisconsin Avenue
Milwaukee, WI 53203-2289
(414) 297-3214

WYOMING
Casper Field Office
100 East B Street
Room 4229
Casper, WY 82601
(307) 261-5252
1-888-245-2994

APPENDIX G • STATES WITH PROPERTY TAX RELIEF
PROGRAMS: 1996

State	Homestead Exemption or Credit	Deferral Program
Alabama	✔	–
Alaska	✔	–
Arizona	✔	–
Arkansas	–	–
California	✔	✔
Colorado	✔	✔
Connecticut	✔	–
Delaware	✔	–
District of Columbia	✔	✔
Florida	✔	✔
Georgia	✔	✔
Hawaii	✔	–
Idaho	✔	–
Illinois	✔	✔
Indiana	✔	–
Iowa	✔	✔
Kansas	–	–
Kentucky	✔	–
Louisiana	✔	–
Maine	✔	✔
Maryland	✔	✔
Massachusetts	✔	✔
Michigan	–	✔
Minnesota	✔	✔
Mississippi	✔	–
Missouri	–	–
Montana	–	–
Nebraska	–	–
Nevada	–	–
New Hampshire	✔	✔
New Jersey	✔	–
New Mexico	✔	–
New York	✔	–
North Carolina	✔	–

State	Homestead Exemption or Credit	Deferral Program
North Dakota	–	✔
Ohio	✔	–
Oklahoma	✔	
Oregon	–	✔
Pennsylvania	–	–
Rhode Island	–	–
South Carolina	✔	–
South Dakota	–	✔
Tennessee	✔	–
Texas	✔	✔
Utah	–	✔
Vermont	–	–
Virginia	✔	✔
Washington	–	✔
West Virginia	✔	–
Wisconsin	–	✔
Wyoming	–	✔

Soure: American Association of Retired Persons

| **APPENDIX H** • SENIOR CITIZENS ORGANIZATIONS |

A number of organizations represent senior citizens' interests in state legislatures and in Congress. Some of them also sell insurance and prescription drugs and offer discounts on a variety of services. If you consider buying insurance from any, be sure to compare their policies with those offered by other insurance companies.

> American Association of Retired Persons (AARP)
> 601 E Street, N.W.
> Washington, DC 20049
> (202) 434-2277

The AARP is a nonprofit membership organization dedicated to addressing the needs and interests of persons 50 and over. The organization aims to enhance the quality of life for all by promoting independence, dignity, and purpose. It sponsors seminars and offers publications on a variety of topics of interest to seniors. The AARP also sells insurance, investments, and prescription drugs through the mail and through its walk-in pharmacy in Washington.

> Gray Panthers
> 711 8th Street, N.W.
> Washington, DC 20001-3747
> (202) 347-9541

The Gray Panthers is an activist organization involved in issues such as health care, age discrimination, and problems of the disabled. Local chapters conduct letter-writing campaigns, collect signatures for petitions, and contact elected representatives to discuss issues of concern to the organization. Members receive a quarterly journal.

> National Council of Senior Citizens
> 8403 Colesville Rd. Suite 1200
> Silver Spring, MD 20910
> (301) 578-8800

The National Council of Senior Citizens is a nonprofit membership group that lobbies on behalf of senior citizens. It also offers a benefit package that includes various health-insurance policies, prescription drugs, and discounts from hotels, motels, and car-rental agencies. The organization also has a job-assistance program that helps seniors find jobs and offers training. Members receive a newspaper.

> National Committee to Preserve Social Security and Medicare
> 10 G Street NE, Suite 600
> Washington, DC 20002-4215
> 800-966-1935

The National Committee to Preserve Social Security and Medicare is a nonprofit, grassroots organization of 5.5 million members that advocates for seniors in Congress. The group maintains a political action committee and solicits contributions through direct mail. Its primary focus is keeping its membership informed about proposals that might positively or negatively affect Social Security and Medicare. It offers a number of publications, including a bi-monthly magazine, *Secure Retirement*, and a newsletter called Update on Congress, both aimed at keeping senior organizations abreast of legislative developments in Washington. Members and activists interested in legislative activities can also call Senior Flash, its toll-free hotline (800) 998-0180.

> Older Women's League
> 666 11th Street, N.W., Suite 700
> Washington, DC 20001
> (202) 783-6686

The Older Women's League is an advocacy organization that works on behalf of middle-age and older women. It is concerned with such issues as health care, Social Security, housing, and workplace discrimination. Local chapters write letters, pay visits to elected officials, and sponsor workshops on topics of interest to older women. Members receive a monthly newsletter.

APPENDIX I • HOMESTEAD EXEMPTION CREDIT PROGRAMS FOR STATES WITHOUT INCOME ELIGIBILITY GUIDELINES IN 1996

AV= Assessed value
L = Local option program

STATE	ELIGIBLE HOMEOWNERS	MAXIMUM HOMESTEAD EXEMPTION OR CREDIT
Alabama	All ages	$4,000 AV (state taxes) $2,000 AV (county taxes)*
	Age 65-plus	Full exemption (state taxes)
Alaska	Age 65-plus, disabled veterans or surviving spouses aged 60-plus	$150,000 AV
		$10,000 AV, L
	All ages	
Arizona	All ages	*
California	All ages	$7,000 AV
Connecticut	Age 65-plus or disabled	*
District of Columbia	All ages	$30,000 AV
Florida	All ages	$25,000 AV
Georgia	All ages	$2,000 AV
Hawaii	All ages	$40,000 AV
	Age 55-plus	*
Idaho	All ages	*
Illinois	All ages	$3,500 or $4,500 (Cook County) AV
	Age 65-plus	$5,500 or $7,000 (Cook County) AV
Indiana	All ages	*
Iowa	All ages	$4,850 AV
Kentucky	Age 65-plus or disabled	$23,100 AV
Louisiana	All ages	$7,500 AV*
Maryland	All ages	*
Minnesota	All ages	*
Mississippi	Under age 65	$240 tax credit
	Age 65-plus or disabled	$6,000 AV*
New Mexico	All ages	$2,000 AV
Ohio	All ages	12.5% of property taxes
Oklahoma	All ages	$1,000 AV

State	Eligible Homeowners	Maximum Homestead Exemption or Credit
South Carolina		$100,000 AV* $20,000 fair market value
Texas		$5,000 AV (school taxes) $3,000 AV (other local taxes) $15,000 AV (school taxes) $3,000 AV (other local taxes)*
West Virginia		$20,000 AV

Source: American Association of Retired Persons .

Alabama— optional $2,000 exemption for local taxing units. **Arizona** — 35 percent of school taxes for operating and maintenance costs with a $500 cap on tax reduction. **Connecticut** — Up to 10 percent of the total property taxes in the preceding year. It is a local option program. **Hawaii** — Exemptions increase with age ranging from $60,000 assessed value (ages 55 to 59) to $120,000 assessed value (aged 70 and over). **Idaho** — $50,000 assessed value or 50 percent of assessed value, whichever is less, for residential improvements. **Indiana** — Eight percent of tax plus a homestead deduction of $2,000 assessed value or one-half of the total assessed value (whichever is less). **Louisiana**—Does not apply to municipal taxes except in Orleans Parish. **Maryland** — State benefit equals the excess over the annual 10 percent increase in assessed value; local benefit is set by local government. **Minnesota**—60 percent of the tax on first $72,000 of assessed/market value. **Mississippi**—Do not pay tax on the first $6,000 AV. **South Carolina**—Applies to school operating taxes only. **Texas**—Additional local option of up to 20 percent of assessed value.

APPENDIX J • CIRCUIT BREAKER FOR RENTERS

Programs as of 1996

SSDI= Social Security
Disability Income

STATE	ELIGIBLE RENTERS	MAXIMUM HOUSEHOLD INCOME	MAXIMUM BENEFIT
Arizona	Age 65-plus	$3,750 (single) $5,500 (joint)	$502
California	Age 62-plus, blind or disabled	$13,200	$240
Colorado	Age 65-plus, disabled, or surviving spouse age 58-plus	$7,500 (single) $11,200 (joint)	$500
Connecticut	Age 65-plus, disabled, or surviving spouse age 50-plus	$21,800 (single) $26,800 (joint)	$700 (single) $900 (joint)
District of Columbia	All ages	$20,000	$750
Illinois	Age 65-plus or disabled	$14,000	*
Iowa	Age 65-plus or disabled	$14,000	$1,000
Kansas	Age 55-plus, disabled, or with dependent children	$17,200	$600
Maine*	Age 62-plus, or disabled age 55-plus	$10,000 (single) $12,400 (2 or more)	$400
	All ages	$25,700 (single) $36,000 (2 or more)	$700
Maryland	Age 60-plus, disabled, or with dependents	None	$600
Michigan	All ages	$82,650	$1,200
Minnesota	All ages	$38,170	$1,090
Missouri	Age 65-plus or disabled	$15,000 (single) $17,000 (joint)	$750
Montana	Age 62-plus	None	$1,000
Nevada	Age 62-plus	$19,100	*
New Jersey	Age 65-plus, blind, or disabled	$100,000	$500
New Mexico	Age 65-plus	$16,000	$250

STATE	ELIGIBLE RENTERS	MAXIMUM HOUSEHOLD INCOME	MAXIMUM BENEFIT
New York	All ages	$18,000	$375 (aged 65 and over) $75 (under age 65)
North Dakota	Age 65-plus or disabled	$13,500	$240
Oregon*	Age 58-plus	$10,000	$2,100
Pennsylvania	Age 65-plus disabled, or surviving spouses age 50-plus	$15,000	$500
Rhode Island	Age 65-plus or SSDI recipients	$12,500	$200
South Dakota	Age 65-plus or disabled	$9,000 (single) $12,000 (2 or more)	*
Utah	Age 65-plus	$19,425	$400
Vermont	All ages	$47,000	$1,500
West Virginia	Age 65-plus	$5,000	$125
Wisconsin	All ages	$19,154	$1,160

Source: American Association of Retired Persons

Illinois—Amount exceeding 3.5 percent of income, but not to exceed $700 less 4.5 percent of such income. Additional local option benefits available. **Maine**—Renters aged 62 and over will receive the maximum tax credit available from the program offered to all ages or only to ages 62 and over. The application is the same for both programs. **Nevada**—90 percent of tax owed up to $500. **Oregon**—Recipients ages 58 to 64 cannot own household assets that exceed $25,000 to qualify for the program. **South Dakota**—35 percent of taxes due (single) and 55 percent of taxes due (joint). **Alaska**—Features a local option program for older renters. Benefits and income guidelines vary depending on the local millage rate. It does not depend on household income; therefore it is not a circuit breaker program.

APPENDIX K · CIRCUIT BREAKER FOR HOMEOWNERS

AV = Asessed values
SSDI = Social Security Disability Income

STATE	ELIGIBLE HOMEOWNERS	MAXIMUM HOUSEHOLD INCOME	MAXIMUM BENEFIT
Arizona	Age 65-plus	$3,750 (single) $5,500 (joint)	$502
Arkansas	Age 62-plus	$15,000*	$250
California	Age 62-plus, blind or disabled	$13,200	*
Colorado	Age 65-plus, disabled, or surviving spouse age 58-plus	$7,500 (single) $11,200 (joint)	$500
Connecticut	Age 65-plus, disabled, or surviving spouse age 50-plus	$21,800 (single) $26,800 (joint)	$1,000 (single) $1,250 (joint)
District of Columbia	All ages	$20,000	$750
Hawaii	Age 55-plus	$20,000	$500
Idaho	Age 65-plus, veterans, disabled, blind, or surviving spouses	$17,430	$800
Illinois	Age 65-plus or disabled	$14,000	*
Iowa	Age 65-plus or disabled	$14,000	$1,000
Kansas	Age 55-plus, disabled, or with dependent children	$17,200	$600
Maine*	Age 62-plus, or disabled age 55-plus	$10,000 (single) $12,400 (2 or more)	$400
	All ages	$25,700 (single) $36,000 (2 or more)	$700
Maryland	Age 60-plus, disabled, or with dependents	None	*
Michigan	All ages	$82,650	$1,200
Minnesota	All ages	$65,450	$470
Missouri	Age 65-plus or disabled	$15,000 (single) $17,000 (joint)	$750

Continued on next page

State	Eligible Homeowners	Maximum Household Income	Maximum Benefit
Montana	Age 62-plus All ages	None $15,307 (single) $20,410 (joint)	$1,000 *
Nebraska	Age 65-plus Disabled	$19,501 (single) $23,001 (joint) $21,501 (single) $25,001 (joint)	* *
Nevada	Age 62-plus	$19,100	*
New Jersey	Age 65-plus, blind, or disabled	$100,000	$500
New Mexico	Age 65-plus	$16,000	$250
New York	All ages	$18,000*	$375 (aged 65 and over) $75 (under age 65)
North Dakota	Age 65-plus or disabled	$13,500*	$2,000 taxable value
Ohio	Age 65-plus or disabled	$20,800	$5,000 AV
Oklahoma	Age 65-plus or disabled	$10,000	$200
Pennsylvania	Age 65-plus disabled, or surviving spouses age 50-plus	$15,000	$500
Rhode Island	Age 65-plus or SSDI recipients	$12,500	$200
South Dakota	Age 65-plus or disabled	$9,000 (single) $12,000 (2 or more)	*
Utah	Age 65-plus	$19,425	$500
Vermont	All ages	$47,000	$1,500
Washington	Age 61-plus	$28,000	*
West Virginia	Age 65-plus	$5,000	$125
Wisconsin	All ages	$19,154	$1,160

Source: American Association of Retired Persons

Arkansas—*WWI veterans and their widows exclude Social Security and retirement income.*
California—*96 percent of tax on first $34,000 assessed value.*
Illinois—*Amount exceeding 3.5 percent of income, but not to exceed $700, less 4.5 percent of such income. Additional local option benefits available.*

Maine—*Homeowners aged 62 and over will receive the maximum tax credit available from the program offered to all ages or only to ages 62 and over. The application is the same for both programs.*

Maryland—*the net work of homeowners cannot exceed $200,000 (not including the homestead itself). the maximum benefit is up to taxes paid on the first $60,000 AV.*

Montana—*The tax credit applies only to the first $100,000 of the homestead's fair market value.*

Nebraska—*The homestead value cannot exceed $115,000 or 150 percent of the county's average assessed value plus $20,000 (whichever is greater). The maximum homestead exemption cannot exceed $40,000 assessed value or 80 percent of the county's average assessed value of single family homes (whichever is greater) for homeowners aged 65 and over. The maximum homestead exemption cannot exceed $50,000 assessed value or 80 percent of the county's average assessed value of single family homes (whichever is greater) for disabled homeowners.*

Nevada—*90 percent of tax owed up to $500.*

New York—*The fair market value for all real property cannot exceed $85,000.*

North Dakota—*Assets may not exceed $50,000 (excluding the first $80,000 of the homestead's market value).*

South Dakota—*35 percent of taxes due (single) and 55 percent of taxes due (joint).35*

Washington—*Up to 50 percent of total assessed value or $34,000 assessed value (whichever is greater).*

APPENDIX L • PROPERTY-TAX DEFERRAL PROGRAMS

L=Local option program AV= Assessed value
AGI=adjusted gross income SSI=Supplemental security income

STATE	ELIGIBLE HOMEOWNERS	DEFERRAL AMOUNT	INCOME CAPS
California	Age 62 and over, blind, or disabled	All property taxes	$24,000
Colorado*	Age 65 and over	All property taxes	None
District of Columbia	All ages	Taxes above 110% of prior tax liability	None
Florida*	All ages	Taxes exceeding 5% of income	None
	Age 65 and over	Taxes exceeding 3% of income	None
Georgia	Age 62 and over	Taxes on the first $50,000 AV	$15,000
Illinois*	Age 65 and over	All taxes up to 80% of the equity value	$25,000
Iowa	SSI recipients	All property taxes	None
	Age 65 and over	*	None
Maine*	Age 65 and over	All property taxes	$32,000
Maryland*	Age 65 and over or disabled	All property taxes, L	*
Massachusetts*	Age 65 and over	Up to 50% of AV	$40,000
Michigan*	Age 65 and over or disabled	Special assessments over $300	$15,400
Minnesota	Age 65 and over or disabled	Special assessments, L	None
New Hampshire	Age 65 and over	Up to 85% of the tax, L	None
North Dakota*	Age 65 and over or disabled	All special assessments	$13,500
Oregon*	Age 62 and over	All property taxes Special assessments	$24,500 $17,500
South Dakota*	Age 70 and over	All property taxes	None
Tennessee*	All ages	Taxes can be deferred up to $60,000 of the property's market value, L	$12,000
Texas	Age 65 and over	All property taxes	None
Utah	Age 65 and over	50% of tax, up to $300, L	None

STATE	ELIGIBLE HOMEOWNERS	MAXIMUM HOUSEHOLD INCOME	MAXIMUM BENEFIT
Virginia	Age 65 and over or disabled	Taxes that exceed 105% (or more) of prior year's tax, L	$30,000
Washington	Age 60 and over	Taxes on 80% of the equity value	$34,000
Wisconsin	Age 65 and over or disabled	Up to $2,500 of taxes	$20,000
Wyoming	Age 62 and over	50% of taxes, L	150% of the poverty level

Source: American Association of Retired Persons

Colorado—Additional local option program if tax is 130 percent or greater than prior year's tax owed. Additional local option program to work to pay off tax liability. **Florida**—Homeowners can receive a full tax deferral if income is below $10,000 (all ages) or $12,000 (age 70 and over). **Illinois**—Recipients must have lived in their homes for at least three years. **Iowa**—Local option tax relief is available for homeowners age 65 and over. **Maine**—Only homeowners that first applied to the deferral program in 1990 qualify. **Maryland**—A local option program available to homeowners age 65 and over who are disabled and have lived in their home at least five years and have met local income guidelines. **Massachusetts**—Recipients must have lived in their homes for at least five years and resided in Massachusetts for at least 10 years. **Michigan**—Recipients must have lived in their homes for at least five years. **North Dakota**—Assets may not exceed $50,000 excluding the first $80,000 of the homestead's market value. **Oregon**—After entering the deferral program for all property taxes, recipients must have federal AGI of $29,000 or less to continue qualifying for the program. Once recipients enter the deferral of special assessments program, they can continue qualifying for the program with any income. **South Dakota**—Homeowners must have owned their home for at least three years and have lived in the state for at least five years. **Tennessee**—For homesteads under $50,000 in market value, homeowners can defer all taxes above 1979 levels.

INDEX

Doctors. *See* Physicians
Dollar-cost averaging, 11
Dollars per year of service (pension plans), 52
Dread-disease policies, 169-170
Drug benefits
  employer-offered plans, 154
  HMOs, 152, 166-167, 181-185, 186
  Medicare, 136
  Medicare-supplement policies, 165
Durable power of attorney, 124, 125, 289

· E ·

Early retirement, 24-26
  employer-offered health insurance, 144-149
  health insurance, 24, 25, 144-149
  life insurance, 25
  pension plans, 56-57
  Social Security, 26, 33-34
Early-withdrawal penalty
  annuities, 96-97, 98
  IRAs, 71-72
  Roth IRA, 72
Earnings test, 38
Efficient market hypothesis, 13
Emergency care in foreign countries, 166
Employee Retirement Income Security Act (ERISA), 53, 56, 58, 61
Employment. *See* Working (after retirement)
Equities. *See* Stocks
Estate planning. *See also* Estate taxes; Trusts; Wills
  community property, 282
  costs, 268-269
  keeping current, 283
  lawyers, 267, 268-269, 288, 291
  liquidity, 268
  spouses, rights, 282
Estate taxes
  audits, 283
  charity, 282-283
  family-owned business, 277, 280-281
  federal, 274
  generation-skipping, 275
  income taxes, 275
  life insurance, 272-273, 279-280
  marital deduction, 276, 277
  pension plans, 273, 275
  state death taxes, 274-275
  trusts, 289, 293, 298, 299
  unified credit, 275-276, 277-278, 296
Excess charges (Medicare), 130, 134, 164
Executor, 273-274, 287

· F ·

Family benefits, maximum, 37, 43, 47-48
Family-owned business, estate taxes, 277, 280-281
Fannie Mae program, 232-233
Federal Housing Administration (FHA), 229-234
Final-average salary plan, 52
Financial planning tools, 4-6
Five-percent owner, 57-58, 72, 73
Five-year averaging, 66
Fixed-income investments, 10-11
401(k) plans, 3, 24, 53
  and delayed retirement, 27
  taxes, 67

· G ·

Gifts
  and Medicaid, 212
  to minors, 295-296
Gift taxes, 275, 276-277, 279, 281, 292, 293, 298
Goals
  budgeting, 5
  investing, 7
Government workers, 39
GRAT (grantor retained annuity trust), 292-293
GRUT (grantor retained unitrust), 292-293
Guaranty associations, 100
Guardians
  for children, 274
  estate management, 125-126, 289

· H ·

Health Care Financing Administration (HCFA), 186-187
Health-care proxies, 218-219, 220-221
Health insurance, 18. *See also* Medicare; Medicare +; Medicare-supplement policies
  conversion policies, 146-147
  and early retirement, 24, 25, 144-149
  employer-offered, 143-149, 150-154
  employers' caps, 152
  exclusion riders, 148
  high-risk pools, 149, 168
  insurer of last resort, 148, 149
  preexisting-conditions requirement, 149, 163, 167, 171
  renewability clause, 148, 167

• I •

• J •

• K •

• L •

·M·